赵一鼎 著

Chinese and English Cultural
Connotations via Idiom Vignettes
A Comparative Study

英汉成语
文化内涵
比较研究例解

中央编译出版社
Central Compilation & Translation Press

图书在版编目（CIP）数据

英汉成语文化内涵比较研究例解／赵一鼎著. —北京：中央编译出版社，2024.7
ISBN 978-7-5117-4602-3

Ⅰ. ①英… Ⅱ. ①赵… Ⅲ. ①英语–成语–对比研究–汉语–成语 Ⅳ. ①H313.3

中国国家版本馆 CIP 数据核字（2024）第 040158 号

英汉成语文化内涵比较研究例解

责任编辑	苗永姝
责任印制	李　颖
出版发行	中央编译出版社
网　　址	www.cctpcm.com
地　　址	北京市海淀区北四环西路 69 号（100080）
电　　话	（010）55627391（总编室）　（010）55625179（编辑室）
	（010）55627320（发行部）　（010）55627377（新技术部）
经　　销	全国新华书店
印　　刷	山东韵杰文化科技有限公司
开　　本	880 毫米 ×1230 毫米　1/32
字　　数	259 千字
印　　张	12.5
版　　次	2024 年 7 月第 1 版
印　　次	2024 年 7 月第 1 次印刷
定　　价	95.00 元

新浪微博：@中央编译出版社　微　信：中央编译出版社（ID: cctphome）
淘宝店铺：中央编译出版社直销店(http://shop108367160.taobao.com)
　　　　　(010)55627331

本社常年法律顾问：北京市吴栾赵阎律师事务所律师　闫军　梁勤
凡有印装质量问题，本社负责调换，电话：(010) 55627320

前 言

人类社会已进入多元化的时代,文化交流更呈现广泛、深入、双向的状态,比较文化的研究已经进入各个领域。本书属于比较语言学和跨文化交际学范畴。

本书要研究的内容正如书名《英汉成语文化内涵比较研究例解》所示,是非常具体、明确的,而且范围也比较狭窄。

英语成语和汉语成语,既是这两种语言的精华,又是这两种语言中不易掌握的部分。鉴于成语的这种特点,本书专门就英汉成语的文化内涵、来龙去脉,以例解的形式进行类同平行比较研究,也对其异同作一定的评述。

近年来,中国学习、使用、研究英语、英美文学、英美文化的人越来越多。同样,在以英语为母语的人中学习、使用、研究汉语、中国文学、中国文化的人也越来越多。鉴于此种情况,笔者以这两种语言中最富文化内涵、最能显示其文化传统的元素——成语为突破口,对这两种世界上使用人口最多、历史也最悠久的语言进行广泛的对比研究,并举出大量例子予以解释,以期达到学以致用的实际效果。

本书的读者对象主要有两类：

一是学习、使用和研究英语、英美文学和英美文化的中国人；

二是以英语为母语，学习、使用和研究汉语、中国文学和中国文化的外国人。

目 录
Contents

	总　论	001
1	"in for a penny, in for a pound" 与 "一不做，二不休"	028
2	"a hair to make a tether of" 与 "小题大做"	032
3	"seek a knot in a bulrush" 与 "吹毛求疵"	041
4	"six of one and half a dozen of the other" 与 "半斤八两"	045
5	"money makes the mare go" 与 "有钱能使鬼推磨"	050
6	"put all one's eggs in one basket" 与 "孤注一掷"	054
7	"hang by a hair" 与 "千钧一发"	067
8	"carry water to the river" 与 "画蛇添足"	074
9	"a misfortune and a friar seldom go alone" 与 "福无双至，祸不单行"	081
10	"teach one's grandmother to suck egg" 与 "班门弄斧"	085
11	"poor as a church mouse" 与 "一贫如洗"	088
12	"ambitious as Phaethon" 与 "自命不凡"	105
13	"Dame Partington and her mop" 与 "螳臂当车"	114
14	"talk nineteen to the dozen" 与 "喋喋不休"	120

15	"shut the stable-door when the steed is stolen" 与 "亡羊补牢"	**127**
16	"Spilled water is not picked up again" 与 "覆水难收"	**130**
17	"in the altogether" 与 "一丝不挂"	**134**
18	"In the country of the blind, the one-eyed man is king." 与 "山中无老虎，猴子称大王"	**139**
19	"Castor and Polydeuces" 与 "刎颈之交"	**143**
20	"the pot calling the kettle black" 与 "老鸹嫌猪黑"	**148**
21	"Talk of the devil, and he is bound to appear." 与 "说到曹操，曹操就到"	**152**
22	"Walls have ears." 与 "隔墙有耳"	**155**
23	"Love me, love my dog." 与 "爱屋及乌"	**158**
24	"a flash in the pan" 与 "昙花一现"	**161**
25	"all my eye" 与 "胡言乱语"	**165**
26	"Hair by hair you will pull out the horse's tail." 与 "只要功夫深，铁杵磨成针"	**172**
27	"look for a needle in a haystack" 与 "海底捞针"	**176**
28	"do in Rome as the Romans do" 与 "入乡随俗"	**191**
29	"an eye for an eye and a tooth for a tooth" 与 "以眼还眼，以牙还牙"	**195**
30	"ants in one's pants" 与 "如坐针毡"	**206**
31	"kick when he is down" 与 "落井下石"	**212**
32	"between the devil and the deep sea" 与 "进退维谷"	**216**

33	"hammer and tongs" 与 "全力以赴"	228
34	"at sixes and sevens" 与 "乱七八糟"	245
35	"all one's geese are swans" 与 "敝帚千金"	251
36	"kill two birds with one stone" 与 "一箭双雕"	255
37	"Alexander and the Robber" 与 "一丘之貉"	258
38	"pinch penny" 与 "一毛不拔"	264
39	"hoist with one's own petard" 与 "作法自毙"	269
40	"The mills of the God grind slowly, but they grind exceeding small." 与 "善有善报, 恶有恶报"	288
41	"give him an inch and he will take a yard" 与 "得寸进尺"	298
42	"hit the ceiling" 与 "怒发冲冠"	302
43	"all mops and brooms" 与 "酩酊大醉"	323
44	"go west" 与 "与世长辞"	340

总 论

　　成语，是一个概念上存在于多种语言之中，但含义上并未被明确界定的词。在汉语成语的学术研究中，关于如何界定成语的讨论从未停歇。例如，马国凡（1978年）把成语描述成一类有历史性和民族性的，人们习用的定型词组。而史式（1979年）认为一些定型的谚语也可以归到成语的范畴。无独有偶，在英语语言学研究中，一些知名研究者（如：Chomsky，1980）把成语认定为在句法和语义上表现为词汇的"长单词"。而随着英语语言学研究角度和研究方法不断细化，有关成语的属性被持续发掘，英语中关于成语的概念，也由于词频、构成、语境等研究的加入，而被定义为："由多个单词组成的固定表达形式"（Hubers et al.，2020；Senaldi & Titone，2020）。要问什么是成语，实乃言人人殊。

　　但毕竟理论是理论，实践是实践，成语的定义不易准确给出，并不妨碍人们对成语的准确认识。真正学习、使用和研究成语的人，丝毫都不受到成语定义的影响。

　　在语言中，成语是一种特殊词汇的总和，它是一个大的范畴，但并不是一个总的范畴。

人类的语言尽管可能因为民族、地域等原因，呈现不同类型，在语音和文字上差异很大，但它们的形成和发展规律却有很多相同之处，几乎每种语言都有自己的成语。所以各种语言之间的成语比较研究带有相当大的普遍性。只是这种研究的历史还不长，充其量也不过半个多世纪。

本书不是泛泛研究成语，而是专门对英语和汉语中的成语进行对比研究，并且着重于其文化内涵研究。

首先说英语，英语的成语同样也是一个难以准确定义的概念。若是细分，其种类也不少。为了研究和叙述的方便，我们不妨把成语看成是一个广义的概念，即英语习惯用语的总和，其中包括成语、典故、习语、俚语、俗语、谚语、格言等，或者用英语语汇称为 idiom。它是英语中定型的词组或句子，即在使用英语的民族中长期运用、广泛流传而形成的相对比较固定的习惯表达方式。如用汉语表达，可称为习语或熟语。

但这种叫法有相当大的不严密之处，英文的 idiom 有时译为"成语"，有时译为"习语"，还有时译为"熟语"或"惯用语"等，而这些术语之间还是有一定差别的。Idiom 这个词在英语中所表达的意义，会在汉译时出现这么多的对应词，足以说明它在汉语中也确实难以找到一个恰如其分的对应词，这也说明了英语 idiom 的奇特性与复杂性。其实，英语的 idiom 和汉语的"成语"有许多不同之处。本书在原则上把 idiom 看成是成语，主要还是为了比较研究上的方便，并不是我们认为英语的 idiom 与汉语的"成语"完全等值。

英国语言学家史密斯曾对 idiom 一词的来源作过考究。他说，英语之中原本没有 idiom 这个词，它 16 世纪来源于希腊语，经过拉丁语进入法语，原形为 idiotisme，17 世纪进入英语后，其拼写形式为 idiotism，因为其词形使人一下子联想到 idiot（白痴）一词，使用起来令人不大舒服，因此后来改为 idiom，并一直沿用至今。

正是由于 idiom 这个词不是"土生土长"的，因此它在英语中概念不清，更使得它在翻译中难以找到对等的词。这种情况进一步反映出，idiom 的来历曲折和背景复杂。

那么在汉语中"土生土长"的词汇"成语"的定义就非常准确吗？恰恰不然。在汉语中，对"成语"一词的解释也是多种多样的，几乎各种主要的辞书和专业教科书都不一样。这种情况同我们开篇说的"成语，是一个非常明确的词汇，但语言学界对它的含义的界定却是相当模糊的"之说法是完全吻合的。

即使分歧再大，也得有一个相对公认的定义，在这种前提下，综合各种见解，《汉语成语研究》（史式，1979）对汉语中的成语的含义，给出如下的描述：

"凡在语言中长期沿用，约定俗成，一般具有固定的结构形式与组成成分，有其特定含义，不能望文生义，在句子中的功能相当于一个词的定型词组或短句，谓之成语。"

虽说如此，所谓"在语言中""长期沿用""具有固定的结构形式与组成成分""有其特定含义，不能望文生义""在句子中的功能相当于一个词""定型词组或短句"等说法，在系统性定义成语的同时，又成倍扩大了成语界定的范围，并模糊了成语和其他熟语类型的界限。

再者，成语在英语中可以当作习语总体概而论之。但在汉语中，如不作特别说明，就不宜将成语概之以习惯用语的总体而论。因为在古有成语一说之后，近代又引进了"熟语"一说，"熟语"并不是中国传统语言学中的术语，是从西方语言中借过来的，是经过翻译而沿用下来的术语。"熟语"一词虽然是被引进的，但在汉语中也是一个不明确、不清晰的概念，其范畴也很广泛，诸如成语、古语、常言、谣谚、格言、俗语、俚语、歇后语、俏皮话等，都可列入熟语之中。

成语是熟语的一种，可以说也是主要的一种，它除了具有熟语的共性，还有自己的特点。成语的特点构成了成语的本质属性。

汉语成语在形式上的最大特点是四个字为一个单位，这也体现了其形式上的骈体性，即汉语成语的民族性标志之一。汉民族在长期的社会生活中形成了对于对偶形式的特殊爱好，在语言的运用上，也有这种习惯，从先秦诸子散文，到汉代的赋、魏晋以后的骈体文，以至到唐代以后的律诗，都喜欢使用四字的对偶词句。汉语成语的骈体性，既是汉语形式的特点，又是汉语形式美的突出体现。

汉语成语绝大多数为四字格，非四字格成语虽然有，但不多。还有很多成语，原先并非四字格，但由于多数成语的影响，在语言类推规律作用之下，也都逐渐压缩或增加成四字格了。

四字格是构成汉语成语骈体性的基础，它使汉语成语无论在结构形式上，语法关系上，还是语义的配合上，都有利于形成有规律的对偶性排列组合。

从语音结构上看，四字格成语节奏整齐匀称，两字一顿成为一个基本音步，两两相配，互相衬托，节奏感鲜明。

从语法结构上看，四字格成语中双体结构的占相当大的比例。语音结构和语法结构的整齐性，保证了成语在结构形式上的骈体性，加上语义配合上的对偶性，就构成了成语整体的骈体性。

凝聚性是汉语成语在语义方面的特点，言简意赅是汉语成语在语义方面的突出特点。形式上简短，表意深远丰富，这就是汉语成语的凝聚性。

汉语成语的另一大特点，就是习用性。这表现在它世代相传，年代久远。有很多成语来源于先秦的文献典籍，使用至今，已有两千多年的历史了。习用性的另一表现就是通行范围广泛，地方变体极少。

汉语成语显著的特征之一就是使用频率很高。成语由于言简意赅、表意功能强，很多人都乐于使用，而且适用于口语和书面语。文化素养越高，成语的使用频率也就越高，一个文化素养高的人，在他的著作中成语的出现率要高于一般人。

汉语成语的特点是比较突出的，尤其是构造的规律性极强。

与其相比，英语成语在结构特征和语义特征上，虽与汉语成语有许多相似之处，但差异也是很大的。这种差异主要还是由于它们不属于相同类型的语言。

论其结构特征，英语成语主要反映在结构的严密及固定方面，组成成语的词序比较固定，不得随意分隔或拆开。成语的组成词也不得随意更换。在这方面，几乎是与汉语成语完全相同的。

英语成语中的组成词稍有变化，就可能发生意义的巨大变化。例如，before long（不久之后），若改成 long before，意思就变成了"很久以前"。Rain cats and dogs（下倾盆大雨），若将其中 cats 和 dogs 的位置对调一下，写成或说成 rain dogs and cats，意思就只能是"下雨下了狗和猫"，意思完全变了样。甚至一个冠词，一个语素或是看来微不足道的一词之差，都可能使原有的成语发生巨大的变化。例如，in a state（乱七八糟）去掉不定冠词 a，说成或写成 in state，意思就变成"隆重地"了。这样的例子不胜枚举：

out of question（毫无疑问）⟷ out of the question（绝不可能）

hard line（强硬路线）⟷ hard lines（倒霉、厄运）

in a mood（心情不好）⟷ in the mood（有兴趣）

go to a show（去看演出）⟷ go to show（证明……）

甚至英语成语中名词的数都受到严格的限制，单复数不可随意调换。例如，John kicked the bucket last week（约翰上周死了），若改成"John kicked the buckets last week"，就只能表示"约翰上周踢了几只木桶"之意。同样，成语原形中的复数名词也不能随意变成单数。例如，Mary spilled the beans（玛丽泄露了秘密），若是说成或写成"Mary spilled the bean"，意思就变成"玛丽泼出了那个豆",其意义可能不知所云。此类例子,不一而足。

有些英语成语的构成违反了正常的语法规则,尽管这种成语为数不多。

英语由于属于屈折语,在句子中有些词的形态要根据不同时间和语态发生变化。但一些英语成语在使用时,它的动词则不可随意进行语态上的转换。

意义对于成语来说是首要的,成语的意义要作为一个整体来对待,这也是成语最重要的特征。但有一些英语成语在意义上具有两重性,既具有字面意义又具有成语意义,而其字面意义往往又与成语意义风马牛不相及,如果没有上下文作参照,难以确定一个表达形式是字面意义还是成语意义。例如,a rainy day 的字面意义是"雨天",其成语意义是"艰难时刻"。又如,miss the boat 的字面意义是"误船",其成语意义是"失去机会"。如此为数不少的具有两重性意义的成语,常常给理解带来困难,解决这种困难在很大程度上依赖于语境信息。英语成语的这种特征,是与汉语成语有很大差异的。

英语成语有一个奇异的特征,这几乎是汉语成语所没有的,那就是有些成语的字面意义明显违反思维逻辑或生活逻辑,比如,face the music(勇敢面对),不仅词的搭配不符合逻辑,成语的意义与原意也截然不同,看不出两者之间有任何内在的联系。又如,think on one's feet(思维敏捷)的字面意义是"在脚上想",这种联系不符合生活逻辑。另外还有一些成语,其字面意义看起来怪里怪气,令人费解。例如,go the whole hog

(一干到底),the world and his wife(多数人),等等。

成语的形成与语言所属的民族文化是紧密相连的,从某种意义上说,文化是产生成语的温床。每个民族都有其自身的民族文化,每个民族都有自己语言的独特风格与传统。

成语是经过人们长期使用,千锤百炼而成的语言形式,它在很大程度上依赖于特定的社会文化背景,因此成语比词汇更富有文化内涵。成语产生于文化,反过来,成语又反映文化。通过研究一个民族语言中的成语,人们可以了解这一民族文化的某些特征。语言学家兼翻译理论研究学者奈达于1993年说过:"文化对词语、成语的意义的影响是非常深远的,如果不去认真研究背景,就难以透彻理解成语的深刻含义。成语不仅带有浓厚的民族色彩,而且是一种语言与另一种语言差别最为显著的部分之一。"因此可以说,了解成语形成的文化背景是透彻理解成语的关键。可以想象,一个不知道汉语成语"叶公好龙"典故的人,是无论如何也不可能恰如其分地运用这个成语的。同样,如果不知道美元纸币的底色是绿色以及它的指代意义,也就不可能明白 green power 为什么意为"金钱的力量"。

成语是人类思想的结晶,是语言中的精华,它们需要漫长的时间才能提炼出来,而且具有鲜明的时代特征和民族色彩。居住在不同地域的民族,会产生不同地域的文化,在这一文化下形成的成语还会带有地域文化的特色。成语的形成与发展,与一个民族的地理环境、宗教信仰、文学作品、历史事件、民间传说、风俗习惯、饮食作息、娱乐游戏等都有千丝万缕的联系,而且还与和其他民族的文化交流交融有关系。

汉语是历史极其悠久的语言，而且使用汉语的人口数量也是世界上首屈一指的。中国灿烂的文化形成了庞大的成语体系。成语是数千年积淀的成果，其文化内涵极为丰富多彩。

成语的文化内涵与它们千奇百怪的出处密不可分，若想发掘成语的文化内涵，就需找出成语形成的源头，即要找出成语最初出现的年代和所载成语文献典籍。一个成语如果既见于前书（年代早的书籍），又见于后书（年代晚的书籍），则前书是源，后书是流，引证语源应引前书，而不应引后书。例如，成语"水落石出"出自宋代欧阳修的《醉翁亭记》，成文在1045年至1046年。而《辞海》在注释这条成语时，却把语源算在苏轼身上，认为出自苏轼的《后赤壁赋》。他写赤壁赋应该是在欧阳修写《醉翁亭记》近40年以后的事。再如，成语"破釜沉舟"，《辞海》注为出自《史记·项羽本纪》。这仍然是流而不是源。这一成语真正出自《孙子兵法·九地篇》："帅与之期，如登高而去其梯；帅与之深入诸侯之地，而发其机，焚舟破釜。"其实项羽的做法本身就是按《孙子兵法》的教导。

汉语成语的来源，总的来看共有两个，一个是书面语，另一个是口语。来源于书面语的成语，从年代来看，大都起源较早，流传时间较长，稳固性较强。源于口语的成语，多数是无直接语源可考察。它在人们的口语中形成，在口语中流传，待到它见于书面时，可能是早已定型，流传很久了。有的虽然在文献或著作中可以找到出处，但很难断定它的真实出处。

对成语语源的探求是一件有意义、有价值的工作，它对掌握成语的意义，了解成语形成、发展乃至变化的过程，以及考察民族语言发展的历史都有重要意义。

来自书面语的汉语成语大致来源于以下五个方面。

1. 出自古代神话传说

例如，"夸父追日"出自《山海经·海外北经》，通过夸父逐日的神话反映了中华民族祖先希望征服自然的愿望。

又如，"精卫填海"出自《山海经·北山经》，通过一段神话反映了中华民族祖先坚持不懈的顽强斗争精神。

2. 出自历代寓言

与源自古代人民对人与自然生存关系想象的神话不同，寓言是一种暗含更多智慧和思考的文学形式。在百家争鸣的先秦时期，各个学派经常通过一则小故事，表达哲理和观点，借以抒发主张。随着这些哲理小故事的流传，存于其间的表达不断凝练成为成语而流传至今。例如：

"唇亡齿寒"来自《韩非子·十过第十》

"智子疑邻"来自《韩非子·说难第十二》

"虚与委蛇"来自《庄子·应帝王》

"大相径庭"来自《庄子·逍遥游》

"天府之国"来自《战国策·秦策一》

"同日而语"来自《战国策·赵策二》

"亡羊补牢"来自《战国策·楚策》

3. 出自历史典故

如果说神话反映的是人与自然的故事，寓言体现的是思想和哲理的表达,那么历史典故指代的则是大家耳熟能详的人物和事件,其中也不乏教育意义。这些历史典故在被反复引用、传诵的过程中精练为成语。例如:

"负荆请罪"出自《史记·廉颇蔺相如列传》将相和的故事。

"完璧归赵"出自《史记·廉颇蔺相如列传》蔺相如凭借自己的大智大勇,把宝玉完好带回赵国的故事。

"三顾茅庐"出自三国时刘备访求诸葛亮出山相辅的历史故事。

"乐不思蜀"出自三国时刘禅在魏国的洛阳贪图享乐不愿回蜀国的故事。

"草木皆兵"出自淝水之战东晋大败前秦的历史故事。

4. 出自文学作品

与神话、寓言、历史典故类似,一些传诵度很高的文学作品也能最终沉淀为成语。例如,"世外桃源"一词源于陶渊明的作品《桃花源记》,其中描述了在混乱的现实社会中幻想找到的一块安静的、过自由生活的栖息之地。虽然《桃花源记》通篇并没有提到"世外桃源",但这四个字所代表的思想却几经传承,变成成语。再如,成语"破镜重圆"一词,来自唐代孟棨《本事诗·情感》,讲述的是南北朝末年徐德言和乐昌公主夫妻历尽辛苦,终得团圆的故事。

5. 出自有书面文字记载的名句或常用表达

值得注意的是,不是所有的成语都要依托于一段叙事,还有相当数量的成语是由史书、传记、小说、诗歌、戏曲等作品中的名句转换而来的。这些名句有些是作者原创，有些则是引自民间口头熟语，而书面化的记录让这些表达形式逐步固定，最后以成语的形式被人们所熟知。例如《桃花源记》的"豁然开朗"是作者陶渊明直接创造而生成的表达，而源自唐代房玄龄《晋书·赵王伦传》中的"狗尾续貂"，则是从当时人们讽刺晋朝时期赵王司马伦大肆封官晋爵以至貂尾供应不足的民谣而来。

进一步来看，这些转化自名句的成语还可以分为直接转化和间接转化两类：像"人面桃花"这种由唐代诗人崔护的诗句"人面桃花相映红"简单缩略而来的成语就属于直接转化。类似的还有从宋代诗人苏轼的"事如春梦了无痕"转化来的成语"春梦无痕"，从清代文人龚自珍的"不拘一格降人才"而来的成语"不拘一格"；而像"豆蔻年华"这类由唐代诗人杜牧原句"娉娉袅袅十三余，豆蔻梢头二月初"引申而来的成语"豆蔻年华"则属于间接转化。类似的有，源于宋朝诗人张耒"荒林春雨足，新笋进龙雏"的成语"雨后春笋"，源于唐朝诗人孟郊"春风得意马蹄疾，一日看尽长安花"中的成语"走马观花"。

除了上述五类主要来源，有些汉语成语的产生和使用，也受到了舶来文化的影响。例如，来自国外神话体系的成语"三位一体"，来自国外寓言故事的成语"火中取栗"。来自文人名句的成语"以眼还眼，以牙还牙"和来自国外民间口头熟语的成语"条条大路通罗马"等。

总结起来说，英语成语的来源亦与汉语成语的来源大致相同，只是各民族文化色彩不同。英语成语通常来自如下几个方面。

1. 源自《圣经》记载的故事和传说

《圣经》里有许多故事和比喻，给人们留下了深刻的印象，致使英语的许多成语来自《圣经》。例如，make bricks without straw 这一成语就出自《圣经·出埃及记》第 5 章中的一个故事。据说埃及法老担心以色列人口剧增，威胁到埃及的安全，因此强迫他们做苦役——烧砖，以折磨他们。上帝看到以色列人在埃及受压迫，便派摩西去把他们从苦难中拯救出来。摩西去埃及请求法老准许以色列人到远处拜神，他想借此把以色列人带离埃及，法老不但不肯，反而变本加厉。他吩咐监工不给以色列人造砖用的稻草，但烧砖的数量却不能少。这句成语的意思就是强人所难，相当于汉语成语的"巧妇难为无米之炊"。

2. 引自《圣经》英译本原文

《圣经》是英国人需要反复诵读的书，所以有许多经文已深入人心，更由于其语言浅显易懂，许多人在说话或写文章时直接引用一些经文，久而久之便成了成语。例如：still small voice 便是引自《圣经·列王纪上》第 19 章，据说，先知以利亚为了逃避杀身之祸，躲进山洞，但是神叫他到山上去，并显示神力。顿时，狂风、地震、火焰相继而起，然而神始终没有显现，只有一个微小的声音在叫以利亚，这就是神的声音。直接引自经文的 still small voice 就用来表示"理智的声音"，成为成语。

3. 源自各种文学作品

文学巨匠们笔下精彩的故事情节、富有教益的哲理和含义深刻的词句，往往进入人们的生活而经常被引用，久而久之亦成为成语而沉淀下来。英国的文学大师莎士比亚、弥尔顿、狄更斯等的大作，希腊、罗马神话以及其他名家的著作，如《伊索寓言》等，对丰富英语语言作出了难以估量的贡献，都已成为现代英语成语的重要源泉。

文学作品对成语的贡献主要表现为四种形式：

（1）文学作品中的精彩词句进入社会语言，经过反复使用，脍炙人口，逐渐成为成语；

（2）文学作品中的故事情节给人以深刻的印象，经过读者的广泛传颂，久而久之成为成语；

（3）文学作品中的一些人物，由于性格特征鲜明，其名字具有象征意义，流传广泛，也逐渐成为成语；

（4）原有的一些成语，起初使用范围小，后来经文学作品的引用，扩大了影响力，得以广泛流传。

莎士比亚的作品语言丰富，生动优美，其剧作中许多词句广为人们引用，逐渐成为成语。其中有些成语来自剧作的故事情节。例如，one's pound of flesh 来自《威尼斯商人》。剧中的威尼斯商人安东尼奥为了帮助友人求婚，向高利贷者夏洛克借钱，并立了契约，如不能如期还债，夏洛克将从他身上割下一磅肉。安东尼奥的船队不幸遇难，因此未能如期还债，夏洛克便要求依约从安东尼奥身上割下一磅肉。后来，one's pound of flesh 被用来比喻"合法而不合理的要求"。

莎士比亚的作品语言丰富广博，文字简洁优美，寓意深刻，便于引用，因而有不少的英语成语是直接引用莎士比亚作品的词句而形成的。诸如：

引自《第十二夜》中的 cakes and ale 成为成语"吃喝玩乐"。

引自《约翰王》中的 paint the lily 成为成语"多此一举"。

除了莎士比亚，还有许多英国著名作家的作品也成为英语成语的源泉。例如，成语 albatross round someone's neck 便是从柯勒律治的长诗《老水手之歌》摘取出来的。信天翁（albatross）是非洲南部好望角一带的海鸟，相传它不必拍动翅膀就能浮在空中睡觉，谁杀死了它就会遭殃。柯勒律治的诗歌里说有个水手射杀了一只信天翁，结果他所在的船差点儿遇难。上岸后他把那只死鸟挂在脖子上，以示忏悔。后来，人们使用 an albatross round one's neck 一语来表示"因某人曾经的过失而造成的沉重负担"从而成为成语。这样的例子，还有许多。

4. 来自神话和寓言

世界文化相通而且互相影响，英语中有相当一部分成语来自其他民族的文学作品，其中要数神话和寓言对其影响最大。

希腊和罗马两个民族的语言同属印欧语系，英语的形成虽然比它们晚，但发展得快，因此，作为印欧语系的重要成员之一，英语受到希腊和罗马文化的影响很深。

达摩克勒斯（Damocles）是意大利叙拉古暴君狄奥尼修斯二世的朝臣，常常羡慕帝王的福分。狄奥尼修斯为让他明白帝王无久福，随时都有杀身之祸，决定召见他赐宴，让他坐黄金宝座,但在他头顶上方用一根头发悬挂一把利剑。达摩克利斯见状惊恐万分,几乎不能终席。后人把 sword of Damocles(达摩克利斯之剑)喻为"随时可能发生的危险",遂成了成语。

又如,斯库拉(Scylla)是海上女妖,住在意大利半岛和西西里岛之间的岩洞里,她有六头十三腿,以鱼虾为生,如有过往船只,她一口可吞六个人。卡律布狄斯(Charybdis)是住在斯库拉对面的怪物,它每天吞吐海水三次,形成巨大的漩涡。一边是女妖,一边是怪物,谁想从他们之间通过,那是极其危险的,因此 between Scylla and Charybdis 就成了"进退两难"的意思,因常被人引用,便成为表示"进退维谷"的成语。

类似的源自希腊和罗马神话的成语还有许多。

另外,寓言常在流传过程中被浓缩并升华为成语。世界上许多民族的寓言都为英语成语作出了贡献,其中功绩最大的是《伊索寓言》。

例如,count one's chickens before they are hatched 说的是有个挤奶的姑娘,头上顶着一桶刚挤的牛奶,边走边盘算:我要用卖牛奶的钱买些鸡蛋,然后孵小鸡,小鸡长大后下蛋,以后就靠卖蛋赚钱。当她想到有钱后要骄傲地向求婚者说"不"时,高兴地头一摇,头上的牛奶桶掉了下来,牛奶洒在地上,她的白日梦就此破灭。后来人们便用此语表示"鸡蛋未孵先数鸡"的人或事,久而久之成为成语。

除来自《伊索寓言》的成语外,还有一些来自其他民族寓言的成语,例如,pull someone's chestnuts out of the fire 就是出自法国寓言诗人拉封丹的寓言诗《猴子和猫》。故事说,有只猴子发现火堆里有些栗子,很想吃,但又怕烧伤不敢去抓,于是它骗来一只猫,答应分享,让猫从火堆里取出栗子,结果猫非但没有吃到栗子,反而把脚上的毛给烧了。后来人们便用这句话来形容"受人利用,替人冒险",使之成为成语。

5. 来自历史事件及民间传说

英国有文字记载的历史虽不长,但从《贝奥武夫》的残稿被发现算起距今也有千余年了,大大小小给人们留下深刻印象的事件不少,有些已经逐渐成为成语。同样,有些民间传记或者趣闻逸事,尽管不一定都真实,但还是活跃在人们的语言中,久而久之,有些也成为成语。例如,传说18世纪爱尔兰起义期间,驻守在基尔肯尼(Kilkenny)这个地方的士兵将两只猫的尾巴绑在一起,看它们互相厮咬取乐。当军官来时,一士兵匆忙拔剑砍断两只猫的尾巴,让猫跑掉。当军官问地上为何有两根血淋淋的猫尾巴时,一个士兵回答道:两猫相斗,互相吞噬,只剩下了尾巴。于是 fight like Kilkenny cats 一语便成了"拼死相斗"的替代语,最后成为成语。

除上述一些来源外,尚有许多英语成语来自民族的风俗习惯、宗教信仰、饮食文化、职业行当以及其他方方面面,乃至直接借用外民族的成语。

两个不同民族的成语比较研究本是一个多角度的课题,可以从成语的结构、语义、功能和风格色彩等方面入手研究。但本书只限于对英汉成语的文化内涵的民族色彩加以研究。

从英汉成语文化内涵的民族性方面加以考虑,经过大量的分析对比，我们发现英汉成语之间有三种关系：一致关系、相应关系、不相应关系。

1. 一致关系，或基本对应

这就是说英语成语和汉语成语，在结构成分和结构关系上、表层意义和深层意义上，各方面都是相同的。这样的成语可以直译，即可以按照成语表面的意义直接翻译，二者的语义完全相同。例如，英语成语 to strike while the iron is hot 与汉语成语"趁热打铁"一致，英语成语 to burn one's boats 与汉语成语"济河焚舟"一致。

所谓基本对应，是指英语成语与其对应的汉语成语在意义和用法上都基本一致，可以互译。基本对应不是对等，两者仍有差别。例如：An eye for an eye, a tooth for a tooth 可以与汉语成语"以眼还眼，以牙还牙"互译。同样，Pour oil on the flame 可以与汉语成语"火上浇油"互译。Kill two birds with one stone 可以与汉语成语"一箭双雕"或"一举两得"互译。Kill the goose that lays the golden eggs 可以与汉语成语"杀鸡取卵"互译。Give somebody an inch and he'll take an ell 可以与汉语成语"得寸进尺"互译。Build castles in the air 可以与汉语成语"空中楼阁"互译。

这种基本对应的成语，是由于生活实践和思维完全一致而形成的，在两种语言中是少数的。

2. 相应关系，或部分对应

一个英语成语和一个汉语成语，其结构成分、表层意义均不相同，看起来两者毫不相干，但是分析起来就可以发现，它们的深层意义极为相近。这类成语不能按其表层结构来进行直译，必须透过表层结构弄清它的深层结构的真正含义，然后根据其深层意义到汉语中去寻找与其语义相近的成语。所找到的成语，从表层构造与含义上看，可能没有什么一致的地方，但实际的含义却是相近的。例如，英语成语 after meat mustard（饭后芥末）就可以用汉语成语"雨后送伞"来翻译，用以比喻不及时的帮助。又如，英语成语 nothing is stolen without hands（没有贼不会失盗）可译成汉语成语"无风不起浪"，用以比喻事情不会无缘无故地发生。

两种语言成语之间的这种关系，我们称为相应关系，或部分对应。

类似的部分对应的成语还有：Even the walls have ears. 其相应的汉语成语是"隔墙有耳"；Six of one and half a dozen of the other 其相应的汉语成语是"半斤八两"；Diamond cut diamond 其相应的汉语成语是"棋逢对手"或"强中自有强中手"；Hang by a thread 其相应的汉语成语是"千钧一发"或"岌岌可危"；New brooms sweep clean. 其相应的汉语成语是"新官上任三把火"；Plain sailing 相应的汉语成语是"一帆风顺"；At sixes and sevens 相应的汉语成语是"乱七八糟"；Kick somebody when he is down. 相应的汉语成语是"落井下石"；Apple of somebody's eye 相应的汉语成语是"掌上明珠"；Gild the lily 相应的汉语成语是"画蛇添足"。

3. 不相应关系，即不对应或基本不对应

此类关系指英语的一个成语在汉语中找不到一个同它对应的成语。这类成语都是民族语言所特有的，对译时要作具体分析，视具体成语而定。原成语意义比较明确，从表层结构的分析即可掌握了解的，则可进行直译。直译成汉语后，虽不是汉语的成语，但人们都能明白它的寓意，丝毫不影响对原文的理解。有的时候直译后还可能成为汉语的新成语，这可是一举两得、令人皆大欢喜的事。例如英语的 crocodile tears 直译成汉语为"鳄鱼的眼泪"，现在已成为汉语的成语了，拿过来就可以使用。

有些英语成语不能直译为汉语，因为直译后人们无法了解其真正的含义，其表面意义与上下文不合，妨碍交际，所以在这种情况下必须使用意译的方法。例如，英语成语 to show the white feather 如译成"露出白色的羽毛"，就会造成不知所云的情况，如按意译译成"显示出怯懦"，就谁都明白了。又如，英语成语 a sheet in the wind，如译成"风中的一片帆"，人们就难以理解说话人或写作人想表达的意思，如意译成"有些醉了"，那谁都不会不明白。

这种不对应、不可直译又不可互译的英语成语为数不少。如果望文生义就会出大笑话。例如：

For a time I actually believed that his wife had royal blood. Then I realized he was pulling my leg.

这个句子中的 pull somebody's leg 就不是拉后腿或扯后腿的意思。上面这句话译为汉语是"我一度真的相信他太太有皇族

血统。后来我明白原来他是在愚弄我。"如果译成"后来我明白原来他是拉我的腿"那就大错特错了。

反之亦然。例如,在王汶石的《新结识的伙伴》中,有这样一句话:"以前,他们都说女人拉男人后腿;现在,倒过来了,有些男人,拉起女人的后腿啦。"

将这个句子翻译成英语是"Before, they used to say it was the wives who held the husbands back; now, it's the other way round some husbands hinder their wives."

如果真的逐字逐句地译成英文,就会出现 pull somebody's leg 的形式,那么就会产生差之毫厘,谬以千里的后果。

之所以会出现这种字面意思与寓意不同的情况,多半是由于成语有其来源,可能与一个事件或故事有关,与当时的情景有关。即是说典故成语与各自的民族渊源有关,所以在理解和翻译上,都要考虑它的特殊性。

通过英汉两种语言成语的比较,可以明显地看出,一致关系的成语只是极少数。多数成语是一种相应关系和不相应关系。成语的民族性和文化色彩集中地表现在这两种语言成语对比的相应关系和不相应关系中。

英语和汉语由于语言系统各不相同,使其成语的结构形式也各自表现出一定的民族特征。汉语是有声调的语言,声调高低升降的变化致使汉语成语构成平仄搭配的格律。英语是没有声调的语言,它的成语便不可能有平仄的结构形式,但英语的词汇是有重音的,它的一些成语便利用词的重音构成轻重律或重轻律的结构形式。

从结构形式而论，由于汉语的语素是方块字，一个字是一个音节。音节由于声调的作用，长度大致相等，因此容易形成节拍整齐、和谐、匀称的结构。汉语成语大多为偶数的四字格式，这一特点是英语成语所不可能具备的。

词的重叠也是汉语成语构成方面的一个特点，如：熙熙攘攘、林林总总、千千万万、花花绿绿等。英语成语虽没有这种结构形式，但有利用词的重复作为构成成语的手段，同时中间经常插入 and、by 等虚词，如 again and again, horse and horse, more and more, one by one, step by step 等。

汉语又由于骈体性特别强，所以经常利用对偶的形式构成成语。例如：男女老少、风花雪月、欢天喜地、天翻地覆、丰功伟绩等。英语成语也有利用对仗形式的，但多注意内容上的对称，音节形式上无法像汉语成语那样整齐匀称。例如：Like father, like son. Like master, like man. Easy come, easy go. No and never. Penny wise, pound foolish. 等。

一个民族语言中的成语，它的构成自然要使用民族语言的材料。这些材料不仅从形式上反映了民族语言的特点，构成成语的民族性的风格色彩，而且在表层结构的内容上也具有强烈的民族性，反映了民族的生活、风俗习惯、历史，以及民族的文化传统，从而形成一个民族语言所特有的成语体系。

成语所使用的语言材料，有许多是同本民族人民的生活紧密相连的。有的与本民族所生活的自然环境有关，用自然环境做比喻构成成语的表层结构。英语成语中有大量是用海或航海生活为材料的。这是因为英国是个岛国，人们对海非常熟悉，国内外的联系通常都要渡海。

例如：

  half seas over（超过海的一半，喻饮酒无度）
  be all at sea（在茫茫的大海上，喻不知所措）
  between the devil and the deep sea（置身于魔鬼和大海之间，喻腹背受敌、进退两难）
  at full sea（在高潮上，喻登峰造极）

  中华民族千百年来的生活与泰山结下了不解之缘，所以泰山进入了许多汉语成语之中，例如：泰山压顶、泰山北斗、泰山鸿毛、泰山压卵、安如泰山、有眼不识泰山等。

  中国有很多人信奉佛教，因此用反映佛教内容的语言材料构成的成语也较多。例如：放下屠刀，立地成佛；一佛出世，二佛涅槃；不二法门；大吹法螺；半路出家等。在英语中就找不到以佛教内容为语言材料构成的成语，但可以找到许多与基督教有关的语言材料构成的成语。例如：be on the anxious bench（忏悔者的座位，喻坐立不安，或如坐针毡）即是如此。

  汉语作为中华民族文化的载体，成语作为汉语的精华，其中所浸润的思想意识主要体现在具有中华民族特征的世界观和价值观上。

  道教是中国本土的宗教，其核心观念是自然无为。汉语成语中留有道家思想的痕迹，例如："天网恢恢，疏而不漏""车到山前必有路""福无双至，祸不单行""塞翁失马，焉知非福"等成语都浸透着道家思想。

儒家思想在中国古代历史上始终占据统治地位，是中华文化的思想基础，其影响远远超过佛教和道教。儒家思想在汉语成语中得到大量体现，可以说是俯拾即是。例如："己所不欲，勿施于人""言必行，行必果""名不正，言不顺""国家兴亡，匹夫有责""学而不厌，诲人不倦"等成语都反映了儒家思想的观点。

英语成语中蕴含大量反映基督教义，涉及基督教传说、典故、人物、事件的内容，体现出英国人的思想意识。例如，成语 If anyone strikes you on the right cheek, turn to him the other also. 意为"如果有人打你的右脸，就把左脸也转过来由他打"。这句成语充分体现了基督教爱一切人甚至包括仇敌的宗教思想。其本义并非姑息迁就恶人恶行，而是要用爱心去感化对方令其弃恶从善，喻指待人要宽容忍让。诸如此类的成语还有：They that live by the sword shall perish by the sword. (凡动刀者必死于刀下)、You cannot serve God and Mammon. (你们不能既做基督徒，又一心想发财)等。

英美人的个人主义价值观强调个人利益，崇尚个人奋斗，追求个人自由，这种观点渗入一定数量的英语成语之中，例如：God gives every bird its food but they must fly for it. (上帝给每只鸟都准备了食物，但它们得自己飞出去寻找)。诸如此类的成语还有：God helps these who help themselves. (天助自助者)、God gives the cow, but by the horn. (机会上帝给，成功靠自己)等。

中国人历来看重集体利益，重视集体力量，强调集体作用。

汉语成语"众志成城""众人拾柴火焰高""独木不成林"等都是这种观念的反映。

英汉两种语言的成语的文化内涵都是极其丰富的。有些成语的民族色彩和内涵，并不表现在成语的字面上，这样的成语往往会被误译或译得不够理想。

例如："说到曹操，曹操就到"和 talk of the devil and he will appear 比较起来，汉语的民族色彩就显得更浓一些，请看下面几个句子：

1. There you are. I told you George would come in; you've only to talk of the devil to hear the flutter of his wings.

你看，我不是说乔治要到吗？你只要一提到某人，某人准到。

2. Johnny: Speak of the devil. We was just talking about you.

姜尼：我们正谈到你。真是说到就到。

3. "嘴说曹操，曹操就到！"熟悉戏文的安兆丰接着说。（吴强，《红日》第四十五节）

"Talk of Tsao Tsao and he's sure to appear!" added An Chao-feng, who knew all the operas. （A. C. Barnes 译）

4. "说着曹操，曹操就到。好，到厂长室找他去！"（周而复，《上海的早晨》第一部第七章）

"Talk of the devil! Well, let's go and see him in his office！" （A. C. Barnes 译）

例1和例2两个英语句子，都不宜用"说到曹操，曹操就到"来译。例3用替代的办法，在英译译文中用 Tsao Tsao 代替

devil,既利用了英语成语的结构,又保留了汉语成语的特色,例4直接就译成了英语成语。

又如:汉语成语"一个和尚挑水吃,两个和尚抬水吃,三个和尚没水吃"。

作家艾芜在《百炼成钢》第三章中引用了这个成语,外文出版社1961年的英译本是这样译的:

A lone monk brings his own bucket of water to drink, two monks carry their bucket of water jointly, but when three monks are together, there is no water at all.

《英语成语与汉语成语》一书作者陈文伯先生认为这个译文令人费解。他说:"为什么三个和尚就不能carry their bucket of water jointly? 为什么就一定是no water at all? 关键是译者没有把'挑'和'抬'精确地译出来,也就是说没有把内含的民族色彩表达出来。这里面隐含着汉语人民生活中常用的工具——扁担。一个人用扁担则挑,两个人则抬,三个人便不好办了。如果让一个人挑另两个人抬,挑的人必不满意,于是就争吵,解决不了,便大家都不干,结果便是'没水吃'。"

此成语的中心意思在于第三部分"三个和尚没水吃",比喻互相推卸责任便干不成事,相当于英语成语 Everybody's business is nobody's business.。范存忠先生提到英文报刊上出现过这样的句子:One boy is a boy, two boys half a boy, three boys no boy.。他认为这话译成汉语便是"一个和尚挑水吃,两个和尚抬水吃,三个和尚没水吃"。

这是英语谚语,同样的谚语还有:

He that has one servant has two, he that has two has but half a one, and he that has three has none at all. (一个仆人顶两个用，两个仆人顶半个用，三个仆人不顶用。)

One cook's a cook, two cooks are half a cook, and three cooks are no cook at all. (一个厨子是一个厨子，两个厨子是半个厨子，三个厨子就等于没有厨子。)

One girl is a girl, two girls are half a girl, and three girls are no girl at all. (一个姑娘是一个姑娘，两个姑娘就是半个姑娘，三个姑娘就是没了姑娘。)

如果译成谚语 In the house where there are two girls, the cats die of thirst. (房中有两女，猫儿准渴死。) 也很相当。

总之，英汉成语比较是一项十分复杂而艰巨的工作，涉及方方面面，贯穿两个民族几千年的历史和文化，是一个非常有意义而又有发掘深度的工作。本书选择了千余条成语为例进行平行比较，并以具体实例和来源加以诠释。这种比较仅是英汉成语比较的一个方面，也是比较文化类同研究在语言领域里的推广，希望能对英汉成语的理解和使用有所帮助。这种帮助是双向的，它是指对学习和使用英语的中国人和学习，以及使用汉语并以英语为母语的外国人都有帮助。

1 "in for a penny, in for a pound" 与 "一不做，二不休"

英语成语：

1. in for a penny, in for a pound

2. send the helve after the hatchet

3. over shoes, over boots

4. go the whole hog

5. one may as well be hanged for a sheep as for a lamb

6. either win the horse or lose the saddle

7. he that would go to sea for pleasure, would go to hell for pastime

汉语成语：

一不做，二不休

英语成语例解：

（1）成语 in for a penny, in for a pound 的原意是"既然花了一便士，就干脆花一个英镑吧"。英国使用旧币时，按旧币制，一便士为十二分之一先令，一先令为二十分之一英镑。这样一便士就是小钱，一英镑就是大钱。这句成语的喻义是既然已经卷入了一件事件，即使卷入不深，也只得不顾障碍和困难，把它干到底。相当于汉语成语"一不做，二不休"。

例：Being in for a penny, I am ready, as the saying is, to be in for a pound. (Charles Dickens, *The Old Curiosity Shop*)

我既然已经开始做了，就准备像俗话所说的那样，一不做，二不休。（查尔斯·狄更斯，《老古玩店》）

（2）英语成语 send（或 throw）the helve after the hatchet 出自一则寓言，说一个樵夫在山上砍柴，一下用力过猛，将斧头甩出落到山谷下面的溪流里，他一气之下把手中的斧柄也扔下山谷。约翰·海伍德（John Heywood）的《谚语集》（*Proverbs*, 1546）中收进了这一成语，这句成语的意思也近于汉语的"一不做，二不休"。

例：Rather throw the helve after the hatchet, and leave your ruins to be repaired by your prince.

你干脆一不做，二不休，让你的王子去收拾残局。

（3）英语成语 over shoes, over boots 意为"既然鞋子陷进去了，索性让靴子也陷进去"。喻指硬着头皮不顾一切地把已经开始做的事坚持做下去，而且不计后果，其义与汉语"一不做，二不休"几乎没什么两样。

例：Considering how far he had gone, and now he would be laughed at if he backed out, he determined to let it be "over shoes, over boots".

他考虑到自己已经走得这样远了，如果停止不干将会遭到别人的嘲笑，就决定来一个一不做，二不休。

（4）关于 go the whole hog 这句成语的起源，有人认为 hog 在句中指的是尚未剪毛的羔羊。由于羔羊的毛不易剪，所以牧羊人通常会分次修剪，而有些牧羊人没有耐性，索性一次将羊毛通通剪光。后来，这句话便用来表示"一不做，二不休"，什么事不干则已，要干就干到底。

关于这句成语还有另外一种说法，认为这里的 hog 是指猪，一个人本来是想去买些猪肉，后来他索性把整个猪都买下来了。作这种解释仍然是"一不做，二不休"的意思。

例：Since we have painted the living room, why don't we go the whole hog and paint the kitchen?

既然我们已经将客厅粉刷，何不一鼓作气，把厨房也刷一刷呢？

（5）One may as well be hanged for a sheep as for a lamb 是一句谚语，意为"偷小羊、偷大羊都会被绞死"（旧时英国法律条文），即偷大、偷小都是贼，喻指"一不做，二不休"，干就索性干到底。

例：If you're wise, George, you'll go to your office and write me your check for three hundred thousand dollars… You can't be hung any more for a sheep than you can for a lamb. (Theodore

Dreiser, *The Financier*)

倘若你聪明一些,乔治,你就应该到办公室去,开一张三十万块钱的支票给我……索性干到底,一不做,二不休。(西奥多·德莱塞,《金融家》)

(6) Either win the horse or lose the saddle. 这是一句谚语,意思是"不是赢马,就是输鞍",喻"一不做,二不休"。

(7) He that would go to sea for pleasure, would go to hell for pastime. 意为愿到海上娱乐的人,就会到地狱去消遣,是一句谚语,喻指"一不做,二不休"。

汉语成语例解:

"一不做,二不休"语出唐代赵元一撰《奉天录》卷四:"传语后人:第一莫做,第二莫休。"谓除非不去做,一旦做了,就干脆做到底。

例:一不做,二不休,掀转鼻孔,捺下云头。(宋·释惟白,《续传灯录》卷十八)

2 "a hair to make a tether of" 与 "小题大做"

英语成语：

1. a hair to make a tether of
2. kill cocks with clubs
3. to make a fuss about a trifle
4. to break a butterfly on the wheel
5. a storm in a tea-cup
6. make a mountain out of molehills
7. make a big deal out of
8. make a Federal case out of
9. make a long harvest of a little corn
10. make two bites of a cherry
11. make a time over
12. make heavy weather of
13. nineteen bites to a bilberry
14. die for want of lobster sauce

15. take a sledgehammer to crack a nut

16. kick up a stink

17. much ado about nothing

18. tea-pot tempest

19. shoot butterflies with rifles

20. a leaf slipped into a well and seven men fell in while looking for it

21. much matter of a wooden platter

22. he builds cages for oxen to bring up birds in

汉语成语：

> 1. 小题大做　2. 借题发挥　3. 杀鸡用牛刀　4. 大惊小怪

英语成语例解：

（1）成语 a hair to make a tether of 的意思是把一根头发弄成一根拴牲口的粗绳子，隐喻小题大做，尤其是指借别人偶尔失言等细微过错，兴起大风波。

例：Those who wish to undermine it want, but, according to our Scotch proverb, a hair to make a tether of.

照我们苏格兰谚语来说，那些想要搞破坏的人只需要一丁点儿小借口便可以兴风作浪。

（2）kill cocks with clubs 是一句民间俚语，其意思是杀鸡用牛刀，仍为小题大做之意。

（3）成语 to make a fuss about a trifle 的意思是为一点琐碎的小事就大吵大闹，比喻凡事小题大做。

例：She will never make a fuss about trifles.

她决不会在小事上大吵大闹。

（4）成语 to break a butterfly（或 fly）on the wheel 的字面意思是用大轮子碾死一只蝴蝶，比喻小题大做，枉费气力。Wheel 原是中世纪欧洲的一种大型刑具，将犯人四肢绷紧绑在轮架上，转动轮子，使肢体断裂，乃酷刑之一种。用这种大型刑具去碾死一只小蝴蝶，未免是小题大做，枉费气力。亚历山大·蒲柏（Alexander Pope）在《与阿布斯诺博士书》（Epistle to Dr. Arbuthnot）中使用过这一成语。

例：Why you should call a Director's meeting, just to reprimand a junior clerk. It passes my comprehension. It's simply breaking a butterfly on the wheel.

我不理解，为什么你们仅仅为了申斥一个低级职员而要召开一次董事会，这简直是小题大做。

（5）成语 a storm in a tea-cup 来源于拉丁语，意为"在茶杯里兴风作浪"，比喻小题大做。此成语亦作"tempest in a tea-pot"。

例：The people next door are continually quarrelling, but it is usually a storm in a tea-cup.

隔壁屋的住户老是争吵不休，常常是为了点鸡毛蒜皮的事破口大骂。

（6）成语 make a mountain out of molehills 原意为"在鼹鼠

窝里造大山"。虽然它一直到16世纪末才被广泛使用，但在几个世纪以前希腊作家卢西恩（Lucian）的 *Ode to a Fly* 一文中就出现过这个成语。此成语亦作 make mountains out of molehills。

例：I'm sure he'll give you the money back when he gets paid, so there's no need to start making mountains out of molehills. (*Longman Dictionary of English Idioms*)

我相信他拿到工资后会还你钱，所以没有必要这样小题大做。(《朗文英语成语辞典》)

（7）成语 make a big deal out of 意为对某事过分重视或过于庄重地处理，颇有小题大做或大惊小怪之意。

例：Don't make such a big deal out of it, please.

请别对此事如此小题大做。

（8）成语 make a Federal case out of 原意为把某事夸大成举国轰动的大案，喻指对某事夸大其词，小题大做。

例：I was only a little late, but she made a Federal case out of it.

我只迟到一小会儿，可她却小题大做。

（9）成语 make a long harvest of a little corn 的字面意思是对小小的一颗谷粒进行长时间收割，喻指小题大做。

例：But why...should I make a long harvest of so little corn?

可是我又何必小题大做呢？

（10）成语 make two bites of a cherry 原意为"一颗樱桃分作两口吃"，喻指小题大做，徒然浪费时间和精力。此成语始用于16世纪初，亦有变体 make three bites of a cherry。

例：Let us do this work at a stretch and not make two bites of a cherry.

我们把这项工作一口气做完吧，不要小题大做分为两次了。

（11）成语 make a time over（或 about）的原意是把时间花费在某事情上，喻指对某事小题大做。

例：Don't make a time about trifles.

不要为鸡毛蒜皮的小事争吵不休。

（12）成语 make heavy weather of 原指船遇到暴风雨难以驾驭，现在指一个人对某种简单易行的事情表现出过多的忧虑或付出不必要的劳动，把事情弄得复杂化，有小题大做之嫌。

例：You're making terribly heavy weather of a perfectly simple calculation.

你把一个十分简单的计算搞得复杂化了。

（13）成语 nineteen bites to a bilberry 原意为"一个越橘分作 19 口吃"，越橘（bilberry）是原产于北欧等地的一种浆果，果子的直径仅为四分之一英寸。在一个如此小的果子上咬 19 口，至少可以说是太作秀了。这一成语始于 19 世纪初，比喻在微不足道的事情上"小题大做"或"无事空忙"，有时亦作 nineteen bits to a bilberry。

（14）成语 die for want of lobster sauce 意为小题大做。其典出自法国波旁王朝的路易二世在尚蒂伊（Chantilly）为路易十四举行的一次盛宴。厨师长得知他打算用于筵席的龙虾未能及时运到，感到羞愤万分，竟拔剑自杀。后来就用这一成语喻指为一点不值得的小事大动干戈，小题大做。

（15）成语 take a sledgehammer to crack a nut 意为拿锻铁的大锤去砸一个核桃，这岂不是杀鸡用牛刀，小题大做吗？

例：Three men spent all day yesterday mending my telephone. One man could have done the job in an hour or so. It was like taking a sledgehammer to crack a nut.

昨天三个人花了一整天时间修我的电话，其实一个人用个把钟头就可以修好的，这真是杀鸡用牛刀。

（16）成语 kick up a stink 意为滋事大吵大闹，转义为借题发挥，小题大做。

例：If I lose my job, I'm certainly going to kick up a big stink.

如果我丢了饭碗，我肯定要借题发挥大闹一场的。

（17）成语 much ado about nothing 亦是"大惊小怪"或"小题大做"之意。这句成语原为莎士比亚一出喜剧的剧名，朱生豪译本根据剧情把它译成"无事生非"，以后一些英汉辞书收录此语时也作了如是释义，有的辞书把它解释为"无事空忙""无事自扰"，这似乎更接近它的本义。语中 ado 在中世纪英语作 at do，相当于 to do，即 fuss（忙乱、大惊小怪）之意。

例：The whole controversy is far too much ado about nothing.

这场争论完完全全是无事生非，小题大做。

（18）成语 tea-pot tempest（亦作 tempest in a tea-pot 或 tempest in a teapot）原意为"茶壶中的风波"，转义为小题大做，大惊小怪。

例：Her anger was unreasonable a tempest in a teapot!

她发脾气是没有道理的,小题大做!

(19)成语 shoot butterflies with rifles 的意思是用枪打蝴蝶,喻小题大做。

例:Don't shoot butterflies with rifles.

不要小题大做。

(20)A leaf slipped into a well and seven men fell in while looking for it 是英语谚语,意思是一片树叶掉进井里,为了找它跌进去七个人,喻小题大做。

(21)Much matter of a wooden platter 是英语谚语,意思是为一只浅盘闹得满城风雨,喻小题大做。

(22)He builds cages for oxen to bring up birds in 是英语谚语,意为盖起牛棚养鸟,谓小题大做。

汉语成语例解:

(1)"小题大做"是中国明、清时代科举考试的惯用语。当时,凡以"四书"文句命题的称"小题","五经"文句命题的称"大题"。以做"五经"文的章法做"四书"文的,便称为"小题大做"。后来用以比喻人不恰当地把小事情当作大事来处理。

例:"我道:'他用了多少本钱,费了多少手脚,只骗得七千银子,未免小题大做了。'"(清·吴趼人,《二十年目睹之怪现状》六三回)

(2)"借题发挥"谓借某事为题而发表自己对这个问题的真正看法,或指借做某事为理由而做别的事情。

例：我的习性不大好，每不肯相信表面上的事情，所以我疑心薛先生辞职的意思，想怕还在先，现在不过是借题发挥，自以为去得格外好看。(鲁迅，《两地书》)

(3)"杀鸡用牛刀"是从"杀鸡焉用牛刀"转化而来的。杀鸡何必用宰牛的刀，比喻做小事没有必要使用大的力量。如果说杀鸡用牛刀，那不就是小题大做了吗？"杀鸡焉用牛刀"亦作"割鸡焉用牛刀"。

"割鸡焉用牛刀"这句话，出自《论语·阳货》，原文是："子之武城，闻弦歌之声。夫子莞尔而笑，曰：'割鸡焉用牛刀？'……"

春秋时期，孔子的弟子子游，在一个小县城（武城）做县令。一次，孔子来到武城，听到琴音袅袅，读书声阵阵，知道子游在此兴师办学，便笑他道："割鸡焉用牛刀"。意在揶揄他治理个小县城还要大费周章。明明当地连基础的教学设施都难凑出来，还要推行礼乐教育。

但子游却回答："老师您以前说过：'上等人物接受了我们的教育就会有仁爱之心，寻常百姓接受了我们的教育也会听从政令，便于管理。'"

孔子听了立刻向随行的另外三名学生说，"大家注意！偃（子游）的话是对的，我刚才所说的不过是一句玩笑罢了。"

例：则这割鸡焉用牛刀乎，小将那消大帅收。(元·尚仲贤，《单鞭夺槊》二折)

(4)"大惊小怪"虽是指对于不足为奇的事情故作声势或过分惊讶，亦未尝没有小题大做之意。

例：要须把此事来做一平常事看，朴实头做将去，久之自然见效，不必如此大惊小怪，起模画样也。(宋·朱熹，《答林择之书》)

3 "seek a knot in a bulrush" 与 "吹毛求疵"

英语成语：

1. seek a knot in a bulrush
2. find quarrel in a straw
3. pick holes in something
4. look a gift horse in the mouth
5. correct Magnificent
6. shoot something full of holes
7. dump on somebody or something

汉语成语：

1. 吹毛求疵　2. 鸡蛋里挑骨头

英语成语例解：

（1）seek a knot in a bulrush 的字面意思是"在香蒲上找节疤"。众所周知，只有木本植物有节疤，在草本植物香蒲上找节疤自然是浪费时间，徒劳无益。此语转义为"故意找碴""吹毛求疵""无事生非"。

例：Those that sought knots in bulrushes are to obstruct the king's affairs in Parliament.

那些故意找碴的人是要阻止国王过问议会。

（2）成语 find quarrel in a straw 的字面意思是"为了一根草而争执不休"，喻指"吹毛求疵""故意找碴"。语出莎士比亚悲剧《哈姆莱特》第四幕第四场：挪威王子福丁布拉斯（Fortinbras）率领一支军队通过丹麦国境开往波兰，去夺取一块徒有虚名而毫无价值的土地。哈姆莱特为此大发感叹：一支勇猛的大军竟为一块不毛之地，拼着血肉之躯，去接受死亡的挑战。他说："Rightly to be great is not to stir without great argument, bat greatly to find quarrel in a straw when honour's at the stake."（真正的伟大不是轻举妄动，而是在荣誉遭遇危险的时候，即使为了一根稻秆之微，也要慷慨力争。）

例：He is not one to find quarrel in a straw.

他不是吹毛求疵的人。

（3）成语 pick holes（或 a hole）in something 的字面意思是"在什么东西上挑洞"，喻指"挑毛病""找漏洞""吹毛求疵"。

例：The Divine himself was ill-pleased at not being able to pick a hole in poor Miss Fortheringay's reputation.（William

Makepeace Thackeray, *Pendennis*）

对于可怜的福瑟林盖伊小姐，牧师本人也因为没法找到她名誉上的污点，心中怏怏不乐。（威廉·梅克比斯·萨克雷，《潘登尼斯》）

（4）成语 look a gift horse in the mouth 是"吹毛求疵""过分挑剔"的意思。有经验的人在买马时往往要仔细察看马的嘴和牙齿，从而断定马的年龄，估计马的价值。但如果对于朋友"赠送的马"也这样做，则未免欠妥。此成语通常用在否定句里，其用意是让人们不要重利轻义，过分计较礼物本身的价值。在西欧大多数语言里都有类似的成语，典出公元 4 世纪时的拉丁文之父圣杰罗姆（St. Jerome）的作品。1546 年约翰·海伍德在他的《谚语集》（*Proverbs*）里收进了这条成语："No man ought to look a gift horse in the mouth."（收到礼物切不可挑毛病。）自此，该成语开始在英国流行。

例：Who the hell am I, to look a gift horse in the mouth?

对收到的礼物还要挑剔，那我成了什么人？

（5）成语 correct Magnificent 的字面意思是"纠正圣歌"，喻指"吹毛求疵""鸡蛋里挑骨头"。

例：To try to find fault with such a man is like correcting Magnificent.

想找这种人的碴儿是不可能的。

（6）成语 shoot something full of holes 的意思是"把什么东西射得千疮百孔"，喻指"专挑毛病"或"吹毛求疵"。此成语有时亦作 crab something full of holes（把什么东西抓得千疮百孔）。

(7) 成语 dump on somebody or something 的字面意思是"往他人身上或别人的成就上倾倒垃圾",喻指诋毁他人或他人的成就,转喻"吹毛求疵""故意挑剔"。

例:Nobody likes those people who are always trying to dump on others.

没人喜欢那些对别人吹毛求疵的人。

汉语成语例解:

(1) 成语"吹毛求疵"是说吹开皮上的毛,细寻里面的小瑕疵,比喻苛刻挑剔,硬找缺点。此语最早见于《韩非子·大体》。所谓"大体",是说要目光远大,顾及整体全面,不要专注于局部小处。"古之全大体者,望天地,观江海,……不以智累心,不以私累己,……不吹毛而求小疵,不洗垢而察难知……"意思是说,古代全面把握事物的贤人,……不吹开毛皮,去寻求里面的瑕疵;也不把污垢洗掉,去细察隐藏在污垢下面的伤疤。

例:竟没有一处叫我满意,大概又是我太会吹毛求疵。(奥诺雷·德·巴尔扎克,《幻灭》,傅雷译)

(2) "鸡蛋里挑骨头"是一句俗语,比喻故意挑毛病,这句俗语多用来指责人过分挑剔,没有缺点硬要找出缺点。

例:张师傅专门鸡蛋里挑骨头,你的活儿干得再好,他也能挑出点儿毛病。

4 "six of one and half a dozen of the other" 与 "半斤八两"

英语成语：

1. six of one and half a dozen of the other
2. even Steven
3. nip and tuck
4. neck and neck
5. much of a muchness
6. horse and horse
7. There is very little difference between the one and the other

汉语成语：

1. 半斤八两 2. 势均力敌 3. 不相上下 4. 伯仲之间
5. 并驾齐驱 6. 棋逢对手

英语成语例解：

（1）成语 six of one and half a dozen of the other 的说法出自英国作家马里亚特（Frederick Marryat, 1792—1842）的小说《海盗》(*The Pirate*, 1836)。英国度量单位中的 dozen 表示十二个，六个就是半打。在日常生活中，当人们说六个的时候，有时说 six，有时则说 half a dozen（或 half-a-dozen）。六个与半打，虽说法不一样，但所表示的数量是相等的。当这种表示数量的说法引申到一般的两种事物时，便转义为彼此相当。

例：Not much of that, sir, though that HAS happened. Mostly they come for skill—or idleness. Six of one, and half a dozen of the other. (Charles Dickens, *Bleak House*, Chapter XXIV)

这种情形不多，先生，不过也确实发生过。人们主要是来学射击技巧——也有为了解闷的。这两种人各有一半。（查尔斯·狄更斯，《荒凉山庄》第 24 章）

（2）成语 even Steven 典出英国作家斯威夫特（Jonathan Swift, 1667—1745）的书信集《给斯特拉的信》(*Journal to Stella*)。斯特拉其实就是斯威夫特在爱尔兰的女友艾斯特·约翰逊（Esther Johnson）。在这些信中他对她描述了自己在伦敦的生活和见闻，其中讲了这样一个故事：有个名叫 Steven 的人，妻子每打他一下，他就要回敬她六下，说这是机会均等（even），谁也不欠谁的。Even Steven 一语即由此而来，在口语中，尤其是在美国口语中，常用它来表示"机会均等""比分相等""半斤八两"等义。此语有时亦作 even Stepen。用 Steven 还是 Stephen 本身并没有多少意义，可能只是因为它们都和

even 同韵的缘故。也正因如此,Steven 和 Stephen 的首字母往往大写。

例:Give me the hundred and fifty, and we'll call it even Steven.

给我这150元,我们就谁也不欠谁了。

(3) nip and tuck 系美国口语成语,意为"不相上下""势均力敌",一般用作 neck and neck 的同义语。但严格地说,两者之间还是有细微差别的。Neck and neck 着重表示"并驾齐驱",源自赛马,原指两匹马齐头并进,不分先后。而 nip and tuck 则暗含互有先后、时先时后之义,至于其来源,说法很多。一说 nip and tuck 是由 rip and tuck 演变而来。其中 rip 是受 let her (it) rip(让船或车开足马力全速前进)一语的影响而变为 nip 的,而 tuck 原是俚语,意为"活力",另一说认为 nip and tuck 源于旧时决斗。Nip 指造成对方轻伤的夹击,而 tuck 则指决斗用的双刃长剑。以 nip and tuck 的方式决斗,一般都不会有哪一方大败的情况出现。

例:The Republicans and Democrats are nip and tuck in the opinion polls.

在民意测验中,共和党人和民主党人难分高低。

(4) 成语 neck and neck 原来用于赛马,表示"并驾齐驱""不分上下"。喻义与原意都始于19世纪初,现在仍经常使用,表示"势均力敌""不分高低"。

例:The top two students were obviously neck and neck for the class prize.

领先的那两名学生显然势均力敌，可以同获年级奖。

（5）成语 much of a muchness 的意思是"大同小异""不相上下""半斤八两"，其来源不详，字面意思"大量中的大量"又与成语所表达的意思不完全一致。

例：It was difficult to know which players were experienced and which were completely new to the game—they all seemed much of a muchness.

很难看出哪些运动员久经沙场，哪些还是初出茅庐——他们的技术好像都差不多。

（6）成语 horse and horse 与成语 neck and neck 相似，亦是表示"并驾齐驱""旗鼓相当""不相上下"之义。

例：It was horse and horse between the teams.

两个球队旗鼓相当。

（7）There is very little difference between the one and the other. 是一句谚语，意思是两者之间差别极小，谓一个半斤、一个八两。

汉语成语例解：

（1）成语"半斤八两"（或八两半斤）最早出自宋代释惟白的著作《建中靖国续灯录》之卷二十四《法恭禅师》中："踏着秤锤硬似铁，八两原来是半斤。"中国度量旧制一斤为十六两，八两即是半斤。说法虽不同，但所指数目是完全一样的。当其用法引申为一般事物时，便表示彼此一样，不相上下。但较多用于贬义。

例：你两个八两半斤，好一对客人和主人。(无名氏，《张协状元》第二十四出)

(2) 成语"势均力敌"谓双方力量相等、相当。

例：群臣有所见不同，势均力敌，莫能相壹者，伏望陛下特留圣意，审察是非。(宋·司马光，《乞裁断政事札子》)

(3) 成语"不相上下"比喻高低、好坏等相等或相当。语出唐代陆龟蒙《蠹化》："翳叶仰啮，如饥蚕之速，不相上下。"

例："令郎，字忠华，年纪与你不相上下。"(清·曾朴，《孽海花》第二回)

(4) 成语"伯仲之间"谓兄弟之间，比喻不相上下。伯、仲为兄弟排行中的老大、老二。语出三国魏曹丕《典论·论文》："文人相轻，自古而然。傅毅之于班固，伯仲之间耳。"

例：大樽七古，较之同时李舒章《蓼斋集》，伯仲之间，才力差胜。(清·李慈铭，《越缦堂诗话》)

(5) 成语"并驾齐驱"原本指几匹马并排拉车一齐奔跑，后比喻彼此不分高下，齐头并进，也形容齐步前进，不分先后。语出南朝梁刘勰《文心雕龙·附会》："是以驷牡异力，而六辔如琴；并驾齐驱，而一毂统辐。"

例：不久也就赶上前去，骎骎乎与后者并驾齐驱了。(朱自清，《哪里走》)

(6) 成语"棋逢对手"谓下棋的双方水平相当，多比喻双方本领相当，可相匹敌。

例：他两个在半空中，这场好杀：棋逢对手，将遇良才。(明·吴承恩，《西游记》第三十四回)

5 "money makes the mare go" 与 "有钱能使鬼推磨"

英语成语：

1. money makes the mare go
2. money answereth all things
3. money can put even gods to work for you
4. money can buy devil himself
5. money talks
6. money makes dogs dance
7. money makes the old wife trot
8. abundance will make cotton pull a stone
9. money will make the pot boil

汉语成语：

1. 有钱能使鬼推磨 2. 钱能通神

英语成语例解：

（1）Money makes the mare go 这句谚语出自英国一首民谣。有一个人想向邻居借一匹马使用，马主人推说马腿有毛病不肯借。但当这个人说明自己是付租金的，马的主人便立即改口答应了。歌谣如下：

Will you lend me your mare to go a mile?

No, she is lame leaping over a stile.

But if you will her to me spare.

You shall have money for your mare.

Oh, Ho! Say you so?

Money will make the mare go.

你可否把马儿借我跑一遭？

不，这马腿瘸跑不了。

可要是你把马儿借给我，

我给你钱绝不少。

哎哟，既然你是这么说，

有钱马儿就能跑。

这谚语的意思是钱能通神，恰似汉语的"有钱能使鬼推磨"，讽刺金钱万能。

例：This comes of your reading your story-books. No, no, no! It is money makes the mare go. Keep your eye upon the main chance, Mary. (Royall Tyler, *The Contrast*)

这是从你读的故事书来的。不，不，不！孩子，只有钱才能使得鬼推磨，玛丽，你要盯住这个重要的机会。（罗亚多·

泰勒,《对比》)

(2) 成语 money answereth all things 之意为钱能让万事应心。典出《圣经·旧约·传道书》第10章：Through sloth the roof sinks in, and through indolence the house leaks. Bread is made for laughter, and wine gladdens life, and money answereth everything. (因人懒惰，房顶塌下；因人手懒，房屋漏水。设摆筵席，是为喜笑。酒能使人快活，钱能让人万事应心。)

(3) Money can put even gods to work for you 是一句谚语，意思是有钱甚至可以让神仙为你工作，亦即有钱能使鬼推磨。

(4) Money can buy devil himself 是一句谚语，意思是钱能把鬼买来，极言钱能通神之说。

(5) Money talks 是一句谚语，意为钱会说话，亦言金钱的威力。

(6) Money makes dogs dance 是一句谚语，意为有钱可使狗跳舞，喻有钱能使鬼推磨。

(7) Money makes the old wife trot 是一句谚语，意为金钱能使老妻奔跑，喻有钱能使鬼推磨。

(8) Abundance will make cotton pull a stone 是一句谚语，意为有钱能使棉生石，喻有钱能使鬼推磨。

(9) Money will make the pot boil 是英语谚语，意思是钱能烧开锅里水，意指有钱就有饭吃，相当于汉语成语钱能通神。

汉语成语例解：

(1) "有钱能使鬼推磨"的说法最早来自南朝刘义庆《幽

明录·新鬼》里的一个故事。说的是一个新鬼初到阴间,不得谋生之法,饿得瘦弱不堪。一天忽然偶遇一个死了二十多年的旧友,丰腴肥胖,显然过得不错。新鬼遂向其讨教生存心得。旧鬼见他可怜,便告诉了他一个生财的法子:去生人家里作祟。主人被闹得不得安宁,自然会烧纸钱遣神送鬼,这样一来便不愁衣食。新鬼习得此法,就找了一户人家,一番思索之后,开始推磨捣臼。主人出来见到自家石磨自己干起活来,感叹道:"佛怜吾家贫,乃令鬼推磨。"

例:有钱能使鬼推磨,一分钱钞一分货。若有说谎负心时,难免天灾与人祸。(明·沈璟,《义侠记·萌奸》)

(2)"钱能通神"语出唐代张固的《幽闭鼓吹》一书:"钱至十万贯,通神矣,无不可回之事。"来后演化为"钱能通神"而成为成语。

6 "put all one's eggs in one basket" 与 "孤注一掷"

英语成语：

1. put all one's eggs in one basket

2. venture all in one bottom

3. win the horse or lose the saddle

4. lay on the line

5. go for the gloves

6. put one's shirt on a horse

7. go for broke

8. neck or nothing

9. shoot the works

10. ball the jack

11 shoot the moon

12. scrape the bottom of barrel

13. shoot one's bolt

14. shoot one's wad

15. take a dare

16. take a flyer

17. throw the great cast

18. go nap on something

19. go the whole pile

20. sink or swim

21. bet one's bottom dollar

22. throw the handle after the blade

23. throw the helve after the hatchet

24. I will make either a shaft or a bolt of it.

25. Whosoever draws his sword against the prince must throw the scabbard away.

26. shoot Niagara

27. with a rope around one's neck

28. cross the Rubicon

29. go the vole

30. bet the ranch

31. load everything into one ship

汉语成语：

1. 孤注一掷 2. 铤而走险 3. 破釜沉舟

英语成语例解：

（1）成语 put all one's eggs in one basket 的字面意思是某人

把他自己所有的鸡蛋都放在了一个篮子里,喻指此人孤注一掷,把一切希望寄托在一件事情上。

例:In the organization of the Hyde Park Company Cowperwood, because he never cared to put all his eggs in one basket, decided to secure a second lawyer and a second dummy president. (Theodore Dreiser, *The Titan*)

在海德公园公司的组织中,柯柏乌由于绝不愿孤注一掷,便决定再请一个律师,再请一个傀儡总经理。(西奥多·德莱塞,《巨人》)

(2) 成语 venture all in one bottom 之意为孤注一掷,语出莎士比亚喜剧《威尼斯商人》(*The Merchant of Venice*) 第一幕第一场:威尼斯商人安东尼奥(Antonio)闷闷不乐,心头充塞着难以名状的忧愁。他的朋友萨莱里奥(Salerio)自作聪明地说安东尼奥是为满载货物、正在海上的商船担忧。安东尼奥答道:"I thank my fortune for it, my ventures are not in one bottom trusted, nor to one place." (感谢我的命运,我的买卖的成败并不完全寄托在一艘船上,更不是倚赖着一处地方。)安东尼奥的忧愁预示着不祥之兆,语中的 bottom 指船底,也指货船。

例:I wish Clara's venture had not been in such a bottom. (Walter Scott, *St. Ronan's Well*)

我真希望克莱拉当初并未孤注一掷。(沃尔特·司各特,《圣罗南之泉》)

(3) 成语 win the horse or lose the saddle 的字面意思是要么赢来马,要么输掉鞍,决心孤注一掷,义无反顾。亦作 win the

mare or lose the halter。

（4）成语 lay on the line 有几种不同的意思，其中之一便是冒着巨大危险而孤注一掷。

例：I've laid a year's wages on the line for you, and if you leave me now it will have been a year wasted.

我已将一年的工资孤注一掷押在你身上，如果你现在离我而去，那我这一年就白费了。

（5）成语 go for the gloves 的意思是空手下赌，也就是孤注一掷。

例①："I am going for the gloves," he thought. "If it doesn't come off, I'm done anyhow." (John Galsworthy, *The Country House*)

他想："我要孤注一掷，假使这一次失败，那我就完蛋了。"（约翰·高尔斯华绥，《别墅》）

例②：Sir James turned to Soames. "If there's no question of a settlement, we'd better go for the gloves." (John Galsworthy, *The Silver Spoon*)

詹姆士爵士转过头来对索米斯说："假使没有和解的可能，我们只好孤注一掷蛮干一场了。"（约翰·高尔斯华绥，《银匙》）

（6）成语 put one's shirt on a horse 的意思是把全部赌本都押在一匹马上，亦即孤注一掷。

例：This horse will win. I would put my shirt on it.

这匹马会赢，我孤注一掷，把全部钱都押上去。

（7）成语 go for broke 是近年出现在美国的一句成语，与赌博活动有关。Broke 是破产，赌徒们常常拿出所有的钱孤注一掷，这样做是要冒很大风险的，因为很可能顷刻间变得一贫如洗。

例：The biggest auto race of the year is ready to start. All the drivers are ready to go for broke and drive their cars until fall apart.

今年规模最大的一次汽车比赛快要开始了。所有参加比赛的驾驶员都准备竭尽全力争取获胜，哪怕担当一切风险，把汽车开得散了架也在所不惜。

(8) 成语 neck or nothing 的意思是孤注一掷，将生命和财产置之度外，脖子可不要，一无所有更不在话下。

例：For a bare living he would have to sell—why, three dozen big and four dozen small balloons a day…But it was neck or nothing now—he must try it, and in off hours go on looking for a job. (John Galsworthy, *The White Monkey*)

为了勉强维持生活，他就得去卖——喏，一天卖掉三打大气球和四打小气球，……但现在只有孤注一掷地拼——他一定要试试看，同时在有空的时候再去找找工作看。(约翰·高尔斯华绥,《白猿》)

(9) 成语 shoot the works 的意思是孤注一掷，最早是赌徒的用语，也有"不遗余力"和"铤而走险"的意思。有时也表示豁出去，花光所有钱的意思。

例：The motor of Tom's boat was dangerously hot, but he decided to shoot the works and try to win the race.

汤姆船上的马达已经热得很厉害，但他豁出去了，决心力争取胜。

（10）成语 ball the jack 原意为"全速前进"。在铁路术语中，ball 是 highball 的缩略形式，它指的是连接在信号杆上的一个金属球。在这个成语中它作动词用，表示发出信号，指示火车头（jack）快速前进。现在这句成语可指任何类型的"快速行动"。此外，这句成语还有"孤注一掷"的含义，这可能与开足马力以达到最高速度有关。

（11）成语 shoot the moon 通常有两种意思。一种意思是不付房租偷偷地趁着月夜携带家私逃走。另外一种意思就是铤而走险，因为成功的希望犹如"用箭或枪射月亮"那样渺茫。又指在一种称为"拿红桃"的纸牌游戏中，设法将所有的"红桃"牌及"黑桃皇后"赢到手，以置对方于死地的打法。因这种打法风险大，成功希望小，一旦失败就会使打牌人陷入无可挽回的败局。所以，此成语常用来表示"孤注一掷"或"铤而走险"之意。

（12）成语 scrape the bottom of barrel 的字面意思是刮桶底，转义为在别无选择的情况下，只能退而求其次，无奈采取下策，颇含孤注一掷、铤而走险之意。

例：The government are scraping the bottom of the barrel if they can only produce a man like that to speak for them.

政府但凡能推出那样一个人作为他们的代言人，他们也不会铤而走险。

（13）成语 shoot one's bolt 表示尽了最大的努力，使出最后一招，用尽全部手段，亦有孤注一掷之意，它原来是从一句谚语"a fool's bolt is soon shot"(傻瓜射箭,很快射完)演变而来的。

例:When the debate reached this point, the Prime Minister shot his bolt; but the bill was rejected all the same.

辩论进行到这个阶段时,首相孤注一掷讲出了他最后要讲的话,可法案还是被否决了。

(14)成语 shoot one's wad 的意思是把一笔数目不小的钱或所有的钱一下子花光,意即孤注一掷。

例:We've shot our wad for the summer and can't buy a new car.

一个夏天我们把钱都花光了,买不起新车了。

(15)成语 take a dare 的本意是接受挑战,但接受这样挑战,具有很大的冒险性,意即铤而走险或孤注一掷。

例:If he did not take that "dare", he was disgraced in Holly's eyes.(John Galsworthy, *In Chancery*).

他若不铤而走险接受那次挑战,他就会在霍丽面前丢尽了脸。(约翰·高尔斯华绥,《骑虎》)

(16)成语 take a flyer 之意为铤而走险、孤注一掷,尤其是在金钱方面。

例:I don't believe you, but what the hell, I'll take a flyer.

你的话我不信,管它呢,反正我豁出去了。

(17)成语 throw the great cast 的字面意思是掷一把最大的骰子,意即孤注一掷。

例:In a word George had thrown the great cast. He was going

to be married. (William Makepeace Thackeray, *Vanity Fair*)

总而言之,乔治豁出去孤注一掷,准备结婚。(萨克雷,《名利场》)

(18) 成语 go nap on something 的意思是在纳普牌戏中,冒险自报满贯,即孤注一掷,转义为把一切都押在某事情上。成语中的 nap 是牌戏 Napoleon 的缩写。

例:"Why ever doesn't he apply for that appointment? With all his qualifications and experience, I'd go nap on his getting it. No one else'd stand a chance."

"他为什么不去申请这个职位呢?凭他的资格和经历,我敢保证他能得到这个位置,其他的人可就未必有希望了。"

(19) 成语 go the whole pile 之意为孤注一掷做冒险的事情。

例:He is the right person for the task, because he won't go the whole pile.

他是完成这项任务的最佳人选,因为他不是那种孤注一掷冒险的人。

(20) 成语 sink or swim 的本义是要么沉下去,要么浮起来,转义为孤注一掷,成败在此一举。

例:He must sink or swim by his own effort now.

现在他必须孤注一掷凭自己的努力来决定成败,我再也无能为力了。

(21) 成语 bet one's bottom dollar 原为扑克牌戏用语。在赌博时人们通常不直接押钱而代之以圆形筹码,一般把筹码摞起来,下赌注时总是自上而下地拿。要是把最底下的筹码也押上,那就意味着倾囊下注。Bet one's bottom dollar 一语表示的就是这个意思，其中 bottom dollar 指的就是最底下的筹码。这句成语相当于汉语成语"孤注一掷"，但它常用于表示"拿一切打赌"或"确信"。

例：I bet my bottom dollar you can't swim across the pool.
我敢拿一切打赌，你游不到池塘对面。

（22）成语 throw the handle after the blade 的字面意思是"刀身丢失后连刀柄也扔掉"，转喻"破罐子破摔""孤注一掷"。

（23）Throw the helve after the hatchet 是一句谚语，意为斧头没了干脆把斧柄也扔掉，喻孤注一掷。

（24）I will make either a shaft or a bolt of it. 是一句谚语，意为不管发生什么事，也要冒险试一试，喻孤注一掷。

（25）Whosoever draws his sword against the prince must throw the scabbard away. 是一句谚语，意为拔剑刺杀王子的人需把剑鞘扔掉，喻孤注一掷。

（26）成语 shoot Niagara 的意思是迅速通过尼亚加拉大瀑布，转意为冒大险、孤注一掷。

（27）成语 with a rope around one's neck 的意思是孤注一掷、破釜沉舟。

（28）成语 cross（或 pass）the Rubicon 原意为渡过卢比肯河，转义为采取断然行动，破釜沉舟。卢比肯河是意大利境内的一个小河，古罗马时罗马共和国三执政官之一兼高卢总督盖乌斯·凯撒断然率部队跨越作为高卢与意大利一段疆界的卢比肯河。这一举动事实上等于公开宣布发动内战，因为当时罗马法律规定,任何将军未接到命令不得率领武装部队越过这条河,否则就要被当作谋反治罪。凯撒率领军队过河后就开始了与另一执政官庞培的战争。庞培失败后,凯撒成为罗马的独裁者,由这一历史事件产生了这条成语。

(29) 成语 go the vole 之意为孤注一掷。

(30) 成语 bet the ranch 的意思是敢以牧场打赌,喻不惜一切,孤注一掷。

例：Spielberg, Katzenberg and Geffen have their own stake in the company：$33.3 million each. That's bus fare to Spielberg and Geffen but a big wad to working stiff Katzenberg, who has mortgaged all he owns to prove he's serious. "I have not just figuratively bet the ranch." he says.

斯皮尔伯格、凯岑伯格和葛芬三人都在这家公司里下了赌注：每人3330万美元。对斯皮尔伯格和葛芬来说,这只等于他们的车资,可是对打工仔凯岑伯格来说,这的确是一大笔钱,为了表示决心,他把所有的财产全部抵押。他说："我可是孤注一掷,而不是打比方。"

(31) load everything into one ship 是英语成语,意为将所有东西都放到一只船上,喻孤注一掷,常用否定说法,构成谚语。

例：Do not load everything into one ship.

莫把全部东西都装在一艘船上。（莫孤注一掷）

汉语成语例解：

(1) 成语"孤注一掷"是由两个词汇"孤注"和"一掷"

合拼而成。"孤注"是指把所有的钱都作赌注。"一掷"是指掷最后一次骰子。

北宋真宗（赵恒）景德六年（1004年）九月，来自北方的契丹王耶律隆绪和太后萧氏率兵袭扰北宋。朝内一片恐慌，大臣王钦若、陈尧叟主张迁都避敌。新任宰相寇准（961—1023年）挺身而出，力排众议，坚持主张抗敌，并建议真宗亲征。宋真宗采纳了寇准的主张。当北宋大军到达澶州（河南开封北濮阳县）时，有人建议真宗不要渡黄河。高琼和寇准劝说真宗打消疑虑，并架起了渡河浮桥。前线将士望见了华盖，又听到皇帝和宰相过河，士气大振，打了胜仗。

随后契丹主将萧挞凛在一次出战中被宋将张瑰射死，契丹秘密使人求和。王钦若嫉妒寇准的功劳，在真宗面前巧进谗言，说寇准把皇帝当成了自己的赌注。他向真宗说道："赌徒每逢要输光的时候就会拿出所有赌资一决输赢，称为'孤注'。寇准百般要您亲征，真是把您当作他的'孤注'而至您的安危不顾啊。结果真宗的决心被王钦若所动摇，在宋军处于战略优势的情况下，订立了一个屈辱性合约，即，澶渊之盟。

明代文学家宋濂在《元史·伯颜传》中把"孤注"和"一致"连用，说"我宋天下，犹赌博孤注，输赢在此一掷耳。"后来便演化成"孤注一掷"。

例①："无如他被全台的公债，逼迫得没有回旋余地，只好挺身而出，作孤注一掷了。（清·曾朴，《孽海花》三三回）

例②："款子还没有汇来，可是我们要放手干一干！——哦，那么老赵也是孤注一掷了，半斤对八两！"（茅盾，《子

夜》)

（2）成语"铤而走险"，语出《左传·文公十七年》："铤而走险，急何能择。"铤，快跑的样子；走险，到危险的地方去。形容人因无路可走而采取冒险行动。

春秋时期，诸侯争霸，国与国之间争斗得异常激烈。大一些的诸侯国时而联合，时而对峙，而一些小的诸侯国如孤叶扁舟，在战争汪洋中依附于大国求得生存。对于小国国君来说，如何选择依附是一门生存艺术，稍有不慎就是国破家亡。

作为一个小国的君主，公元前610年的郑国国君也面临着艰难抉择。一方面，深陷晋楚争霸夹缝中的郑国不愿依附于任何一方，从而成为双方争霸的战争消耗品。另一方面，两个大国用出各种手段逼迫小国表态做出选择。彼时，晋国国君对郑国心生不满，怀疑郑国于楚国暗中往来，不肯与郑国国君相见。被恐惧和焦虑所笼罩的郑国国君与公子归生商议对策，决定由公子归生给晋国执政大臣赵盾致信一封，大意是：郑国国君一向尊敬晋国，不敢有冒犯。但是现在晋国对郑国仍然不大满意，这使得郑国非常为难，既不敢得罪晋国，又不敢得罪楚国。郑国像一只被猎人追赶的鹿，一旦被追得太急，走投无路，再危险的悬崖峭壁摆在面前，它也会一头扎下去。目前郑国的处境就如同这只鹿，希望晋国不要把他们逼得无路可走，倘若那样，郑国就只能寻求楚国的保护，虽然不想至此，但也别无选择。

赵盾读过信后，觉得有道理，就说服晋国国君改变了对郑国的态度。

例①：在官已无余积，必至苛敛军民，铤而走险，盗将复发。(《明史·西域三》)

例②：忍之无可忍，望之无可望，不得不思铤而走险也。(梁启超，《敬告当道者》)

(3) 成语"破釜沉舟"一语出自《史记·项羽本纪》："项羽乃悉引兵渡河，皆沉船，破釜甑，烧庐舍，持三日粮，以示士卒必死，无一还心。"釜是古时烧饭用的大锅。舟即船。成语由此概括而来，意思是打破饭锅，弄沉渡船，以示决一死战。喻孤注一掷，不惜牺牲一切。

7 "hang by a hair" 与 "千钧一发"

英语成语：

1. hang by a hair
2. by the skin of one's teeth
3. hang by eyelids
4. close call
5. close shave
6. tight squeeze
7. cop and heel
8. hang on one's eyebrows
9. hairbreadth escape
10. near go
11. near touch
12. near thing
13. on a razor's edge
14. Bataan Death March

15. within an inch of
16. a near touch

汉语成语：

1. 千钧一发　2. 危如累卵　3. 危在旦夕

英语成语例解：

（1）成语 hang by a hair（或 thread）的意思一目了然，但它的来历却与一则古希腊传说联系着。公元前4世纪时，西西里岛上的希腊城邦国家叙拉古（Syracuse）暴君狄奥尼修斯（Dionysius）手下有一佞臣名叫达摩克利斯（Damocles）。他对王室气派极为羡慕，常说君王多福。一日，国王请他赴宴，让他坐在自己的宝座上。他一时受宠若惊，待到心神稍定，猛一抬头，只见头顶上方悬挂着一把用一根细线（一说马鬃）系着的出鞘利剑，随时可能坠落下来。他吓得魂飞魄散，几乎不能终席。国王作此安排，有意让他明白，君王虽身在宝座，却惶惶不可终日，杀身之祸随时可能临头。古罗马政治家、演说家、哲学家西塞罗曾在其《图斯库卢姆谈话录》中记录了这一故事。后人称此剑为 the Sword of Damocles（达摩克利斯之剑），并用以喻指"临头大祸"。此形象比喻已进入多种语言，与汉语成语"千钧一发"形象意义差不多，也可译成"岌岌可危"或"摇摇欲坠"。

例：The mayor's political future has been hanging by a thread since the fraud scandal.

欺诈丑行被揭露后，市长的政治前途岌岌可危。

（2）成语 by（或 with）the skin of one's teeth 之意为"好不容易""侥幸""间不容发"或"千钧一发"。典出《圣经·旧约·约伯记》第 19 章第 20 节。上帝为了考验约伯（Job）使他备受危难，屡遭不幸，但约伯一直忍受着，对上帝始终笃信不渝。小孩藐视嘲笑他，亲友嫌弃反对他。他说："My bone cleaveth to my skin and to my flesh, and I am escaped with the skin of my teeth."（我的皮肉紧贴骨头，只剩牙皮逃脱了。）牙本无皮，约伯用 with the skin of one's teeth 一语意在说明他幸免于难，除保全住性命之外什么都丧失了。人们认为此语不失为一形象说法，以后介词 with 多被代之以 by，用于口语表示"侥幸"，亦有"千钧一发"之意。

例：Other letters recorded its perils in Committee of the whole, and by-and-by its victory, by just the skin of its teeth, on third reading and final passage. (Mark Twain and Charles Dudley Warner, *The Gilded Age*)

在其他的几封信里，他谈到这个议案怎么样在千均一发的时刻胜利地经过三读，终于得到最后的通过。（马克·吐温、查尔斯·沃纳，《镀金时代》)

（3）成语 hang by eyelids 的意思不言自明，却形象生动，它的出现时间可追溯到 17 世纪后半叶，现已很少使用。

例：A magic quarto…with one of the covers hanging by the

eyelids.

一个神秘的四开本……它的封面眼看着就要脱落了。

(4) 成语 close call 的意思是"千钧一发""死里逃生""幸免于难"。

例：Why, he mighty near starved…So he learnt the trade, and then he was all right—but it was a close call.

他当时险些饿死……因此他才学了这个行当，然后才活下去——但已经是命悬一线、死里逃生。

(5) 成语 close（或 narrow）shave 除当把胡子刮得很干净讲之外，还有"命悬一线""千钧一发""死里逃生"之义。

例：His life is no longer in any danger, but is was a close shave.

他的生命不再有危险了，却有过九死一生的经历。

(6) tight squeeze（或 narrow squeeze，或 close squeeze）除作"非常拥挤"和"穷困"解之外，还有"千钧一发""九死一生"之义。

(7) 成语 cop and heel 的意思是"千钧一发""九死一生""命悬一线"。原为黑社会用语，现已很少使用。

(8) 成语 hang on one's eyebrows 和 hang on the eyelids 都是说什么东西悬在某人的眉毛或眼睑上，极言情态之岌岌可危。

例：His affair hangs by the eyebrows.

他的那件事可太危险了。

(9) 成语 hairbreadth escape 的意思是"九死一生""幸免于难"。一根头发的宽度极其细微，因此 hairbreadth escape 喻指从一个极其狭窄的空隙中逃脱。古希腊人也用过同样形象的说法,莎士比亚在《奥赛罗》中也用过它。

例:Wherein I speak of most disastrous chances, Of moving accidents by flood and field, Of hair-breadth scapes i'th' imminent deadly breach, … (William Shakespeare, *Othello*)

我说起最可怕的灾祸,海上陆上惊人的奇遇,九死一生的脱险,……(威廉·莎士比亚,《奥赛罗》)

(10)成语 near go 之意为"侥幸逃脱""差点丢了命""九死一生"。

例:Some Christchurch men remember that go, and how a near go it was!

一些新西兰克赖斯特彻奇城的人都记得那次逃离的情景,真是九死一生啊!

(11)成语 near touch 的意思是与 near go 相同,也是"侥幸脱险""九死一生"之义,亦作 near teacher。

例:Heavens! That was a near touch.

天哪!那真是死里逃生。

(12)成语 near thing 的意思是"千钧一发""死里逃生""极其危险"。

例:That was a near thing—he almost caught us cheating!

真险——他差一点儿当场抓住我们作弊!

(13)成语 on a(或 the)razor's edge 的字面意思是"站在刀刃上",极言情态之危险,转喻"千钧一发""处在危急关头""命悬一线"。

例：Here am I back; we stand no more on the razor's edge.

我可回来了，我们真是虎口余生。

（14）成语 Bataan Death March 的字面意思是"巴丹死亡行军"，转喻"九死一生""命悬一线"。第二次世界大战期间，被日军俘虏的7万名美国和菲律宾战俘，在日军的驱赶下徒步从菲律宾巴丹半岛南端的马里韦莱斯出发，向奥唐奈集中营强行军。由于饥饿、恶劣的气候、非人的折磨和艰难的长途跋涉，约有1万人死于途中，6000人逃入丛林，到达目的地奥唐奈集中营时，只剩下5.4万人，现在人们用这个短语比喻"九死一生"。

（15）成语 within an inch of 意为间不容发，喻极其危险。

例：This had terrified the Home Secretary within an inch of his life, on several occasions. (Charles Dickens, *Hard Times*)

这样就不止一次地把内政大臣吓得半死。（查尔斯·狄更斯《艰难时世》）

（16）成语 a near touch 之意为差点儿完蛋，喻九死一生。

汉语成语例解：

（1）千钧一发"亦作"一发千钧"。钧为古代重量单位，一钧为30斤，一根头发吊着千钧的重物，比喻情况万分危急。

西汉景帝时，吴王刘濞企图反叛朝廷，进行积极准备，枚乘不赞成，曾上书劝谏。枚乘的《谏吴王书》在《汉书·枚乘传》中有记载，其中有一句话说："夫以一缕之任，系千钧之重，上悬之无极之高，下垂之不测之渊，虽甚愚之人犹知哀其将绝也。"这句话用现代汉语来说就是：拿一根细线来派用场，一头缚着三万斤的重物，上面挂在不知有多高的高处，往下吊在不知有多深的深渊里，这样的做法，虽是最愚蠢的人也一定知道其危险的结果将多么可悲可怕！

从这句话，后来演化出成语"一发千钧"。唐代韩愈《与孟尚书》文中"其危如一发引千钧"大概要算是"一发千钧"这句成语之较早见于文字者。

例：际兹一发千钧，全国国民宜各立所志，各尽所能，各抒所见。（鲁迅，《二心集·沉滓的泛起》）

（2）成语"危如累卵"出自《韩非子·十过》："故曹小国也，而迫于晋楚之间，其君之危，犹累卵也。"成语由此演化而来，后用以形容危险的程度十分严重。

（3）成语"危在旦夕"出自《太平御览·鲁连子》："今楚军南阳，赵伐高唐，燕人十万之众，在聊城而不去，国亡在旦暮耳，先生将奈何？"又见《三国志·吴书·太史慈传》："今管亥暴乱，北海被围，孤穷无援，危在旦夕。"此成语的意思是危险就在早上和晚上之间，形容形势危急。

8 "carry water to the river" 与 "画蛇添足"

英语成语：

1. carry water to the river

2. carry coals to Newcastle

3. send owls to Athens

4. gild refined gold

5. dig a well at a river

6. put butter on bacon

7. paint the lily

8. hold a candle to the sun

9. knock at an open door

10. give apples to orchards

11. reinvent the wheel

12. to carry water into the sea

13. pepper to Hindustan

14. carry salt to Dysart and puddings to Tranent

汉语成语：

1. 画蛇添足 2. 多此一举

英语成语例解：

（1）成语 carry water to the river（往河里担水）显然是毫无道理、多此一举的事。所以从字面上的意思，人们立刻就能领会说话或写文章人的用意。

（2）成语 carry coals to Newcastle 的意思是向纽卡斯尔运煤。纽卡斯尔是位于英格兰东北部的一个城市，全称为 Newcastle-upon-Tyne，Newcastle 是其简称，自亨利三世时代该城获得开采煤矿的权利以后，便成为英国的煤炭中心。16 世纪以后，它成为英国主要的煤港，每年大量向外输送煤炭。所以说，如果要从外地往纽卡斯尔运送煤炭，这就好像卖冰箱给爱斯基摩人一样（to sell refrigerators to the Eskimos），多此一举。成语中的动词 carry 可用 bring 或 take 代替。

例①：You are carrying coals to Newcastle when talking about horoscope to us. We write them for the newspaper.

你和我们谈论星座真是多此一举，我们为报社撰写星座专栏呢。

例②：Telling the doctor how to cure a cold is carrying coals to Newcastle.

告诉医生如何治疗感冒真是多此一举。

（3）成语 send owls to Athens 的意思是往雅典送猫头鹰。雅典本是盛产猫头鹰的地方，雅典守护神雅典娜（Athena）的标志就是猫头鹰，因此 send owls to Athens 实属多余之举。有时亦作 carry owls to Athens。

例：I may be thought to pour water into the sea, to carry owls to Athens, and to trouble the reader with a matter altogether needless and superfluous.

人们也许会认为我是用完全多余的废话来打扰读者，好比往大海里倒水，往雅典送猫头鹰，多此一举。

（4）成语 gild refined gold 典出莎士比亚历史剧《约翰王》（*King John*）第四幕第二场：约翰决心再度举行加冕仪式。贵族们认为国王已经加冕过，他的至高权威从来不曾失落，国泰民安，没有必要重新加冕。他们力劝约翰王放弃这一想法。萨立斯伯雷（Salisbary）伯爵说道：Therefore, to be possess'd with double pomp, to guard a title that was rich before, to gild refined gold, to paint the lily, …is wasteful a little and ridiculous excess.（所以，炫耀着双得的豪华，在尊贵的爵号上添加饰美的谀辞，把纯金镀上金箔，替洁白的百合花涂抹粉彩，……实在是浪费而可笑的多余事。）莎士比亚在剧中用了一连串的比喻，集中表达一个概念——做徒劳的、可笑的多余之事，与汉语成语"画蛇添足"同义。

例："I ask only this: don't send for the jewel, and don't crown me with roses; you might as well put a border of gold lace round that plain pocket handkerchief you have there. " "I might as well 'gild refined gold.' I know it: your request is granted then—for the time. " (Charlotte Brontë. *Jane Eyre*)

"我只请求:别叫人送珠宝来,别给我头上戴玫瑰花,要是那样做,你还不如把黄金的花边钉在你那普通的手帕上。""我还不如'在纯金上镀金'。这我知道;那么,我就同意你的请求——暂时同意。"(夏洛蒂·勃朗特,《简·爱》)

(5) dig a well at a river

这句成语同上句成语几乎是使用了同样的指喻方法,河中有现成的水,有什么必要在河边掘井取水呢,显然也是在说某事多此一举。

(6) 成语 put butter on bacon(往咸肉上加奶油)更是说明某事大可不必,企图改进已经很完善的事情,只能是适得其反、画蛇添足。

(7) 成语 paint the lily 的意思是替百合花涂彩。在基督教的艺术中,百合花被视为"贞洁""清白"和"纯正"的象征。天使加百列总是带着百合花前来报喜,摆在正在祈祷的圣母玛丽亚的面前的花瓶里也插着百合花。她的丈夫圣约瑟手里也拿着一枝百合花。这表示他们都是圣洁的。百合花已成为高洁、纯洁和美丽的象征。如果说"替百合花涂彩",就显得多此一举了,更有画蛇添足之意。

例:While it may seem to be painting the lily, I should like to add somewhat to Mr. Alistair Cook's excellent article.

我想往阿利斯泰尔·库克先生的杰作上加几笔,尽管这也许是为百合花涂彩，费力不讨好。

（8）成语 hold a candle to the sun 的字面意思是"太阳底下持蜡烛"，谓其行为之徒劳无益，即多此一举。

例：Some future strain, in which the muse shall tell How science dwindles, and how volumes swell. How commentaries each dark passage shun, And hold their farthing candle to the sun. (Edward Young, *Love of Fame*)

将来总有人在诗句中揭发，

今天学识萎缩而卷帙增加，

注释家们回避艰深的章句，

所做的无用功只能是白搭。

（爱德华·杨格，《名声之爱》）

此成语有时亦作 light not a candle to the sun 不要多此一举。

（9）成语 knock at（或 force）an open door 本义为"敲一扇开着的门"，喻指多此一举，此成语是法语成语 enfoncer des portes ouvertes 的仿造句。

例：To do so is to knock at an open door.

如此行事是多此一举。

（10）成语 give apples to orchards 的本义是往苹果园送苹果，这岂不是多此一举，徒劳无益？

例：To tell the dancer how to dance is to give apples to orchards.

告诉舞蹈演员如何跳舞是多此一举。

（11）成语 reinvent the wheel 中的 invent 意为发明，wheel

意为轮子，合在一起的意思是再发明一遍车轮子，喻指重复劳动，浪费时间，多此一举。

例：Don't waste time to reinvent the wheel. This kind of cheap product we can buy on any market.

别再浪费时间多此一举了，这种便宜的产品我们在任何市场都能买到。

（12）To carry water into the sea. 是英语谚语，意思是往海里运水，喻多此一举。

（13）Pepper to Hindustan 是英语谚语，意思是往印度运胡椒，喻多此一举。

（14）Carry salt to Dysart and puddings to Tranent 是英语谚语，意思是运盐到戴萨特，运腊肠到特拉嫩特。戴萨特出盐，特拉嫩特产香肠，意指多此一举。

汉语成语例解：

（1）"画蛇添足"典出《战国策·齐策二》。

战国时期，楚怀王有一次派邵阳为大将，率军征伐魏国。邵阳英勇善战，一连攻破魏国八座城池，大胜而归。接着邵阳又转而要攻打齐国，齐王听到消息，十分着急。恰逢陈轸要以秦国使者的身份访问齐国。齐王便请求陈轸去楚国，替齐国求情，让邵阳放弃进攻齐国的打算。陈轸见到邵阳以后，便向他讲述了一个故事：

从前楚国有一个贵族，祭祀先祖之后，就把祭祀用的酒给了为他办事的几个人。几个人觉得酒有点儿少，平分下来就不够喝了,于是其中有人提议大家比赛在地上画蛇,大家把酒让给画得最好的人。大家纷纷赞同。

其中有一个人很快就完成了。当他正要拿起酒壶享用美酒时,看到其他人还在手忙脚乱地画蛇,便洋洋得意地一边端着酒壶,一边给蛇画起脚来。可是正当他画脚的时候,另一个人已经画好了蛇,那人马上把酒抢过来,毫不客气地说:"蛇本来就是没有脚的,你怎么可以给它添上脚呢?我才是第一个画完的,这酒应该归我。"说完就仰起头,咕咚咕咚地把酒喝掉了。那个本来第一个画出蛇的人,反而没喝到酒。

陈轸讲完故事,又对邵阳说:"现在您为楚国打败魏国,夺取了八座城池,又要去讨伐齐国。万一失利,岂不是前功尽弃?楚王也不会高兴的。这种做法就跟那个画蛇添足的人一样了。"邵阳听了以后,觉得有道理,便不再讨伐齐国了。

后来,"画蛇添足"就被用来表达"多此一举""弄巧成拙"的意思。

例:但知市菜求增,是之谓"画蛇添足",又文人之通弊也。(清·章学诚,《文史通义·古文十弊》)

(2)"多此一举"是一句口头和书面都常用到的、人人皆知的成语,没有什么典故。最早出于何种典籍亦不易确定,但历代文献使用频仍。

例:以愚意论之,奇士固断断乎出贿赂之外,真才亦未必不在人情之中,昔人所谓非亲非故,何由习知之也?此二者已当不同视,而况于避影匿形,惟恐多此一举,为身累者乎?(明·侯方域,《南省策·二》)

9 "a misfortune and a friar seldom go alone" 与 "福无双至，祸不单行"

英语成语：

1. a misfortune and a friar seldom go alone
2. add insult to injury
3. one woe doth tread upon another's heel
4. of one evil comes many
5. an evil chance seldom comes alone
6. one misfortune comes on the neck of another
7. misfortune binds together
8. misfortunes never come singly
9. one misfortune brings on another
10. one misfortune shakes hands with another
11. bad luck always comes in threes
12. ill comes often on the back of worse

汉语成语：

1. 福无双至，祸不单行 2. 雪上加霜

英语成语例解：

（1）A misfortune and a friar seldom go alone 是一句谚语，意为灾祸和修道士不单行，喻祸不单行。

（2）Add insult to injury 是英语最古老的成语之一，源出古罗马寓言作家菲得洛斯（Phaedrus）根据《伊索寓言》改写的一则故事，一只苍蝇老叮在某人的秃头上，此人气极，往自己头上狠狠地打了一巴掌。结果没有打着苍蝇，反而把自己的头打疼了。苍蝇讥笑他说："You wanted to kill me for a mere touch. What will you do to yourself, now that you have added insult to injury?"（你想一下子把我打死，结果除了羞恼和疼痛之外，还能得到什么？）此成语字面意思虽是"伤害之外又加侮辱"，却常喻"雪上加霜""祸不单行""赔了夫人又折兵"之意。

例：First, the basement flooded, and then, to add insult to injury, a pipe burst in the kitchen.

先是地下室被水淹了，接着厨房里面的水管爆裂了，这真是雪上加霜。

（3）成语 one woe doth tread upon another's heel（祸不单行）语出莎士比亚悲剧《哈姆莱特》（*Hamlet*）第四幕第七场：御

前大臣波洛涅斯（Polonius，奥菲利娅之父）被哈姆莱特误杀身亡之后不久，精神失常的奥菲利娅（Ophelia）也掉进水塘淹死。奥菲利娅的哥哥雷欧提斯正与国王密谋杀害哈姆莱特，王后进来告诉他们："一桩祸事刚刚过去，又一桩接踵而至。雷欧提斯，你的妹妹掉到水里淹死了。"（One woe doth tread upon another's heel, so fast they follow. Your sister's drown'd, Laertes.）

（4）Of one evil comes many 是一句谚语，意为一害生百害，喻一事不顺，事事倒运，祸不单行。

（5）An evil chance seldom comes alone 是一句谚语，意为祸不单行。

（6）One misfortune comes on the neck of another 与 One misfortune rides upon another's back 是二则谚语，前者意为一个不幸搂着另一个不幸的脖子而来。后者意为一个不幸骑在另一个不幸的后背上而来，皆喻祸不单行，屋漏偏遭连夜雨。

（7）Misfortune binds together 是一句谚语，意为不幸都是捆在一起的，喻祸不单行。

（8）Misfortunes never come singly 是一句谚语，意为灾祸从来不单行。

（9）One misfortune brings on another 是一句谚语，意为一祸招致另一祸，喻祸不单行。

（10）One misfortune shakes hands with another 亦是一句谚语。意为灾难手拉手，一个接一个，喻祸不单行。

（11）Bad luck always comes in threes 是一句谚语，意思是恶运总是接踵而至，喻祸不单行。

(12) Ill comes often on the back of worse 是一句谚语，意思是恶运常接祸事来，喻祸不单行。

汉语成语例解：

（1）"福无双至，祸不单行"谓幸运的事不会连续到来，灾祸一来却不止一种。语出汉代刘向《说苑·权谋》："此所谓福不重至，祸必重来者也。"也单作"祸不单行"。

例：福无双至犹难信，祸不单行却是真。（元·高则诚，《琵琶记》）

（2）成语"雪上加霜"比喻灾难、祸患接连到来，使受害程度加重。语出宋代释道原《景德传灯录》："师云：'汝只解瞻前，不解顾后。'伊云：'雪上更加霜！'"

例：一连断餐两日，并未遇着一船。正在惊慌，偏又转了迎面大风，真是雪上加霜。（清·李汝珍，《镜花缘》五十一回）

10 "teach one's grandmother to suck egg" 与 "班门弄斧"

英语成语：

1. teach one's grandmother to suck egg
2. don't teach fishes to swim
3. teach a dog to bark
4. learn your grandame to make milk-kail
5. teach your grandame to grope her ducks
6. teach your grandame to spin
7. teach your grandame to sup sour milk
8. Jack Sprat would teach his grandame

汉语成语：

班门弄斧

英语成语例解：

（1）Teach one's grandmother to suck egg 这句成语始见于 19 世纪初流传的一个故事。故事中说在鸡蛋的两端各扎一个孔，可以把鸡蛋里的蛋清和蛋黄吸空，而不至散一地。这本来是一种很平常的技能，但有人却要教老人做这件事。由此引申出该句成语，意思是在比自己有经验和高明的人面前卖弄本领，也可转义为教训老前辈，意近汉语成语"班门弄斧"或俗语"关公面前耍大刀"。

例①：He is always telling the director how to run the business, that's like teaching his grandmother to suck eggs.

他总在告诉主任要如何经营管理，这好像是在给比自己更有经验的人出主意。

例②：I don't want to teach my grandmother to suck eggs, but may I make a suggestion?

我不想班门弄斧，但我可以提个建议吗？

（2）Don't teach fishes to swim 是一句谚语，意为不要教鱼游泳，喻班门弄斧。

（3）Teach a dog to bark 是一句谚语，意为教狗学叫，喻班门弄斧。

（4）Learn your grandma to make milk-kail 是一句谚语，意思是教你的祖母做牛奶青菜汤，喻班门弄斧。

（5）Teach your grandame to grope her ducks 是英语谚语，意思是教你的祖母摸鸭蛋，喻班门弄斧。

（6）Teach your grandame to spin 是英语谚语，意思是教你

的祖母纺线，喻班门弄斧。

（7） Teach your grandame to sup sour milk 是英语谚语，意思是教你的祖母喝酸奶，喻班门弄斧。

（8） Jack Sprat would teach his grandame 是英语谚语，意思是三尺童子也要教祖母，喻班门弄斧。

汉语成语例解：

"班门弄斧"最早见于唐代文学家柳宗元的著作《柳河东集·王氏伯仲唱和诗序》："操斧于班、郢之门，斯强颜耳。"鲁班原名叫公输般，是我国古代著名的能工巧匠，因为他是鲁国人，所以人们都称他鲁班。鲁班使用斧头能出神入化地制造出许多精美的器具。成语"班门弄斧"广泛应用在后来的书面语和口语之中。

例①：昨在真定，有诗七八首，今录去，班门弄斧，可笑可笑。(宋·欧阳修，《与梅圣俞书》)

例②：兄弟对着哥哥跟前，怎敢提笔，正是班门弄斧，徒遗笑耳！(元·关汉卿，《金线池》楔子)

英汉这两句成语都采用了类比的方法，其概念也基本相同，但也有用法不一样的地方。英语的成语在基本用法之外，还有教训长者之意。但从比喻形象上看，两者有明显的不同，这就充分显示出民族文化色彩的差异。

11 "poor as a church mouse" 与 "一贫如洗"

英语成语：

1. poor as a church mouse

2. poor as Job

3. poor as Lazarus

4. carry off meat from the graves

5. not have a red cent

6. not have two halfpennies to rub together

7. in Queer Street

8. not have a shot in one's locker

9. not have a pot to piss in

10. not have a sou

11. not have a sausage

12. on one's uppers

13. on the hog

14. not have a bean

15. not have a penny to one's name

16. bare as the back of one's hand

17. on the beach

18. out at elbows

19. have not a shirt to one's back

20. shatting on one's uppers

21. go broke

22. clean broke

23. dead broke

24. stone broke

25. flat broke

26. Tap City

27. tapped out

28. be cleaned out

29. broke to the world

30. flat on one's ass

31. down and out

32. down on the knuckle-bone

33. hard up

34. in low water

35. in the barrel

36. soldier's thigh

37. on the breadline

38. out of pocket

39. be poorly off

40. abject poverty

41. poor as a rat

42. on the rocks

43. walk on one's shoe strings

44. not a stiver

汉语成语：

1. 不名一钱　2. 一寒如此　3. 家徒四壁　4. 阮囊羞涩
5. 一贫如洗　6. 囊空如洗　7. 一无所有　8. 室如悬磬
9. 捉襟见肘

英语成语例解：

（1）Poor as a church mouse 字面的意思是"穷得像一只教堂的老鼠"，形容人非常穷，穷到了极点。有一个故事讲到，有一只老鼠饿急了，到处寻找东西吃，它来到一座教堂。东找西找，始终没有找到任何可以吃的东西，因为教堂一般是不设厨房的，所以不存放吃的东西。老鼠很难在那里生存下去，这句成语从17世纪就开始流行。

例：She is going to marry a perfect hog of a millionaire for the sake of her father, who is as poor as a church mouse.

为一贫如洗的父亲着想，她就要嫁给一个贪得无厌的百万富翁了。

（2）Poor as Job 字面的意思是"穷得像约伯一样"。这句成语典出《圣经·旧约·约伯记》：富人约伯善良正直、敬畏上帝，是个好人，受到上帝称赞，魔鬼撒旦却不相信他对上帝的虔诚，怂恿上帝允许他考验约伯。撒旦得到上帝默许后便降下天灾人祸，使约伯转眼之间失去了全部财富：示巴人抢去了他的牛，雷电击死了他的羊群，迦勒底人抢去了骆驼。约伯的儿女们被刮倒的房屋压死。面对灾难的约伯撕裂外袍，剃光头发，伏地敬拜上帝说："我赤身而来，也要赤身而去，上帝的赐予，当由上帝收回。"上帝让撒旦进一步考验约伯，使他从头到脚长满毒疮，约伯仍不埋怨上帝。上帝见约伯历尽种种磨难，信奉上帝之心不变，就使他从苦难中解脱出来，并且双倍地赐福于他。后来，约伯被看作是贫穷和忍耐的化身，poor as Job 表示"一贫如洗""家徒四壁"的意思。

例①：I am as poor as Job, my lord, but not so patient. (William Shakespeare, *Henry IV*)

我是像约伯一样穷，大人，可不像他那样有耐性。（威廉·莎士比亚，《亨利四世》）

例②：Having entered his first ministry under Louis Philippe poor as Job, he left it a millionaire. (Karl Marx, *The Civil War in France*)

梯也尔刚当上路易·菲力普王朝的大臣时，穷得家徒四壁，而到离职时已经成了百万富翁。（马克思，《法兰西内战》）

（3）Poor as Lazarus 的意思与 poor as Job 的意思相差无几，都表示贫困交加到了极点。这一成语典出《圣经·马可福音》第 16 章。

例：He spent all his parent's money within two years, and now he's as poor as Lazarus.

父母留下的钱，他两年就给花光了，现在已经身无分文。

（4）成语 carry off meat from the graves 的字面意思是"穷到要去坟墓偷祭品吃"。昔日希腊人和罗马人习惯在某些时节到已故亲人墓前去设宴祭祀，祭祀完毕将部分食物留在墓碑前，给鬼魂享用。这些食物自然成了饥饿的穷人的美餐。后来这一成语喻人贫穷已极。

（5）成语 not have a red cent 是形容人穷得连一分的硬币都没有。Red cent 是旧时的紫铜硬币，因呈暗红色，故有此称。

例：I'm sorry, I can't lend you anything—I haven't got a red cent.

真对不起，我拿不出什么借给你——我自己一个子儿都没有。

（6）成语 not have two halfpennies to rub together 的字面意思是"连两个半便士的硬币在一起摩擦一下的可能都没有"，形容人囊空如洗、不名一文的贫困程度。此成语亦作 not have one penny to rub against another。

例：I don't know how that family get enough to eat—they never seem to have two halfpennies to rub together.

我不知道那户人家是如何设法糊口的，他们手头似乎总是非常拮据。

（7）成语 in Queer Street 自 19 世纪初一直沿用至今，来源不详。一说它和画于账簿上的疑问号（query）有关。商人往往在拖欠债务的人名字后面标上这样一个疑问号。欠人钱还不起，自然是穷到家了。又根据《朗文英语成语词典》(Longman Dictionary of English Idioms)，Queer Street 是由 Carey Street（凯里街）演变来的。凯里街是伦敦市中心的一条街道，街上有处理破产欠债事宜的破产法院。这句成语现在专指经济状况严重困窘，即落到一贫如洗、不名一文的境地。

例：I fully expect these commitments will put us in Queer Street next year. (John Galsworthy, *The White Monkey*)

我完全相信这些债务明年会使我们一贫如洗。（约翰·高尔斯华绥，《白猿》）

（8）成语 not have a shot in one's locker 亦作 without a shot in one's locker，原指旧时战舰的弹药仓里没有弹药了，现转义为口袋里没有钱了，即不名一文之义。

例：He went to the bar every night, and at the end of the week he didn't have a shot in his locker.

他每晚上酒吧去，到周末口袋里就一个钱也没有了。

（9）成语 not have a pot to piss in 的字面意思是说人穷得连往里撒尿的一个便壶都没有，形容穷困潦倒之极，不名一文。

例：My family didn't have a pot to piss in, but we were proud as devils.

当时我全家不名一文，却个个自视甚高。

（10）成语 not have a sou 是说人穷得分文皆无，连一个大字也没有。Sou 是法国旧辅币，面值很小，20 个 sou 才合一法郎，所以说人到了连一个 sou 都没有的时候，说他一贫如洗绝不为过。

例：He hasn't a sou.

他身无分文。

(11) 成语 not have a sausage 也是说人穷到了分文皆无的程度。这里的 sausage 是俚语一分钱的意思。

例：I haven't a sausage.

我是一个子也没有。

(12) 成语 on one's uppers 也是形容人穷困潦倒至极的一种说法。此处 uppers 的词义是鞋帮，这是说人穿的鞋鞋底已经被磨光了，只剩鞋帮了，人如果不是太穷，何能如此。相当于汉语"穷掉底了"。此成语源出美国，见于1891年出版的《世纪词典》(*The Century Dictionary*)。

例："Dad, the miners there are awfully on their uppers."

"爸爸，那里的矿工们贫困极了。"

(13) 成语 on the hog 是说人过得像猪一样生活，也是形容穷得要命。

例："Railroader," say I again, "On the hog." (O. Henry, *Cabbages and Kings*)

"他是个铁路职工，"我又说，"现在穷得要命。"（欧·亨利，《白菜与国王》）

(14) 成语 not have a bean 也是说人的经济状况到了一分钱都没有的地步。此句中的 bean 并非是通常意义上的"豆"，而是俚语"一分钱"之义。所以，该成语的意思还是形容人穷得厉害。

例：I'd love to go to the cinema but I haven't a bean until I get paid.

我很想去看看电影，但是身上分文皆无，要等到发工资才有钱呢。

（15）成语 not have a penny to one's name 是说在某人的名下没有一分钱，可见贫穷到了何种地步。此成语有时亦作 without a penny to one's name。

例：When I first arrived in this town I didn't have a penny to my name.

我刚到本城时，身上一点钱都没有。

（16）成语 bare as the back of one's hand 也常用来形容人穷得厉害，一无所有，就像人的手背那样光秃秃的。

（17）成语 on the beach 原意为"离船上岸"，指被解雇或退休后离船上岸的船员。最早见于1903年出版的杰克·伦敦的小说《深渊里的人们》(*The People of the Abyss*)。转义为因失业而造成穷困潦倒，一贫如洗。

例：He's been on the beach for weeks and he's flat broke. (*The World Book Dictionary*)

他已经失业几个星期了，弄得一贫如洗。（《世界图书辞典》）

（18）成语 out at elbows 原意为"衣服袖子磨破了，穿着时露出肘部"。无独有偶，汉语中也有"捉襟见肘"一句成语，意象完全一样。这句成语自古以来就是贫穷的象征，早在莎士比亚时代就已见诸文字。

例：But for being a little out at elbows, I should have had it put to rights. (Charles Dickens, *Dombey and Son*)

要不是我穷得捉襟见肘的话，这地方我早就给修理了。（查尔斯·狄更斯，《董贝父子》）

（19）成语 have not a shirt to one's back 是说人衣不蔽体，形容极为贫穷。

例：When he came to work for us, he hadn't a shirt to his back.

他刚来给我们工作时，穷得衣不遮体。

（20）shatting on one's uppers 是民间的一句俗语，形容人极为贫穷，字面的意思是"穿着掉了底的破鞋大便"。

（21）成语 go broke 的意思是破产了，走到了一文不名的地步。

例：At that rate, he'll go broke soon.

照他那样花钱法，很快就会一文不名。

（22）成语 clean broke 的意思是身无分文。

例：1 was clean broke in less than four days.

不到四天我就一个钱也没有了。

（23）成语 dead broke 的意思是身无分文。

例：Cheap enough, but I'm dead broke.

便宜倒是便宜，可是我身上一个钱也没有。

（24）成语 stone（或 stony）broke 的意思是穷困潦倒，不名一文。

例：That is the money made out of stone broke tramps.

那是一笔从穷得叮当响的流浪汉身上刮来的钱。

（25）成语 flat broke 的意思亦是身无分文，一贫如洗。

例：I unfortunately am short of funds, flat broke, busted, collapsed.

我不幸手头拮据，身无分文，破了产，全部崩溃了。

（26）成语 Tap City 之意为分文皆无。

例："You're Tap City?"——"No problem."

"你没钱了?"——"不要紧。"

（27）成语 tapped out 之意为钱财散尽，不名一文。

例：Tapped out, the bank goes under.

财穷金尽，那家银行就此倒闭。

（28）成语 be cleaned out 的意思正是一贫如洗。

例：I haven't got a penny, I'm quite cleaned out.

我身上一个子也没有，真正的一贫如洗了。

（29）成语 broke to the world（或 wide）之意为穷到一个钱也没有了。

例：I believe you good people think I've come back broke to the world.

我相信各位乡亲以为我这次回来已经一贫如洗了。

（30）成语 flat on one's ass 除有"萎靡不振"之义外，还有"一贫如洗"或"穷困潦倒"的意思。

例：He blew his pay pack and he's flat on his ass.

他丢了饭碗，现在一贫如洗。

（31）成语 down and out 的原意是指在拳击比赛中，被对方打倒在地，不能继续比赛而下场。后转义为在生活中完全失败，变得贫困潦倒，不名一文。

例①："You've never been down and out, I imagine, Mr. Forsyte?" "No," answered Soames. (John Galsworthy, *Swan Song*)

"福赛特先生，我想你从来没有贫困过吧？"索米斯回答道："没有。"（约翰·高尔斯华绥，《天鹅之歌》）

例②：As long as you're up and around and have money, everybody's your friend. But once you're down and out, no one wants to see you any more—see? (Theodore Dreiser, *Twelve Men*)

只要你有权势有金钱，任何人都是你的朋友；要是一旦你落魄贫困潦倒了，再也没人想见你——这你明白吗？（西奥多·德莱塞，《十二个男人》）

（32）成语 down on the knuckle-bone 之意为穷困潦倒，一贫如洗。

例：Diana spent her money to save his life and is now down on the knuckle-bone.

为了救他的命，黛安娜花光了自己的钱，现在已经一贫如洗了。

（3）成语 hard up 之意为不名一文，一贫如洗。

例①：It was no disgrace to be hard up in those times.

在那个年代，穷困潦倒并不丢人。

例②：Ever since Smith lost his job, the Smiths have been hard up.

史密斯失业以后，全家人就没钱花了。

(34) 成语 in low water 的本义是陷入浅水之中，转义为手头拮据，经济困难。

例①：I told you Peru was a delightful country to live in; but it's not quite so nice for people that happen to be in low water, as l was. (Ethel Voynich, *The Gadfly*)

我刚才说过，秘鲁是一个居家最妙的地方，可是你要碰到身无分文，像我当时那样，就有些不妙了。(艾捷尔·伏尼契，《牛虻》)

例②：He was in very low water when I saw him last week—he even asked if I could lend him some money to pay the rent.

我上星期见到他时，他已身无分文——甚至问我能否借点钱给他付房租。

(35) 成语 in the barrel 为美国黑人俚语，意为穷得分文皆无。

例：A red hot pimp like you ain't got no business being in the barrel.

像你这种拉皮条的人，买卖兴隆，不至于两手空空，身无分文吧。

(36) 成语 soldier's thigh 的字面意思是"士兵的大腿"，转义为囊空如洗，贫穷之至。

例：He had only the soldier's thigh.

他口袋里连一个子也没有。

(37) On the breadline 是一句起源于美国的成语，breadline 是指等待救济食物的队伍。1870 年纽约市有一间弗莱舍曼

(Fleischmann) 家庭经营的面包店，以食品新鲜远近驰名。据说，这家店每天到了打烊之前，都会将当天未卖出的面包摆在架上，任凭该市的贫户来领取。因此，每天到了歇业时刻，总会出现一群衣衫褴褛的贫民在店前排队，待候分配救济食品。不消说，一个人如果必须排队等待救济，自然是非常贫穷了。

例：According to recent research in Bangladesh, one family in four was on the breadline or just above it.

根据最近的研究，在孟加拉国四个家庭中就有一个处于赤贫。

（38）成语 out of pocket 的意思是囊空如洗，身无分文。

例：He was both out of pocket and out of spirits by that catastrophe, filed in his health, and prophesied the speedy ruin of the empire. (W. M. Thackeray, *Vanity Fair*)

经过这次灾难，他一贫如洗，总是无精打采的，身体也不好，时常预言英帝国不久便会垮台。(威廉·梅克比斯·萨克雷，《名利场》)

（39）成语 be poorly（或者 badly）off 的意思是生活贫困，穷困潦倒。

例：She's been poorly off since her husband died.

她自从丈夫死后，生活一直很贫困。

（40）成语 abject poverty 的意思是赤贫，一贫如洗。

例：He has fallen into abject poverty.

他已经落得一贫如洗。

（41）成语 poor as a rat 犹如 poor as a church mouse，亦为穷到极点之义。

（42）成语 on the rocks 意为手头拮据，身无分文。

例："1 gather from Mrs. Bergfeld that you're on the rocks." "Fast." said the shaking lips. (J. Galsworthy, *The Silver Spoon*)

"从伯格菲尔德太太处我得知你现在手头拮据。""十分拮据。"伯格菲尔德双唇颤抖着说。(约翰·高尔斯华绥，《银匙》)

（43）成语 walk on one's shoe strings 的意思是陷入贫困，缺衣少穿，一贫如洗。

（44）成语 not a stiver 的意思是没有一分钱，喻身无分文，贫穷至极。

汉语成语例解：

（1）"不名一钱"语出汉代王充《论衡·骨相》："通有盗铸钱之罪，景帝考验，通亡，寄死人家，不名一钱。"此处之名，为拥有之意。不名一钱，谓一个钱也没有，形容贫穷已极。

例①：臣患病乞归，不名一钱。以授徒终于家。(清·纪昀，《阅微草堂笔记·姑妄听之四》)

例②：《新生》的出版之期接近了，但最先就隐去了若干担当文字的人，接着又逃走了资本，结果只剩下不名一钱的三个人。(鲁迅，《呐喊·自序》)

不名一钱"亦作"不名一文"或"一文不名。

（2）成语"一寒如此"语出《史记·范雎蔡泽列传》："范叔一寒如此！乃取其一绨袍以赐予之。"在这句话里，一表示竟然的意思，寒表示贫寒潦倒。

战国时魏国的大夫范雎（字叔），被中大夫须贾和宰相魏齐诬陷，惨遭毒打，后被丢在厕所。众人以为他死了，谁知他死里逃生，跑到秦国，并更名张禄，被秦王重用，成了秦国的宰相。

后来秦国要发兵讨伐魏国，魏国国君派须贾到秦国求情。须贾到了秦国，范雎换上了破烂的衣衫，扮成狼狈不堪的模样，去驿馆见须贾。须贾见到范雎，惊讶于他还活着，并问道："你现在生活得怎么样？在做什么？"范雎骗他说："我现在给人家帮工为生。"须贾怜悯他，请他吃饭，同情道："范叔一寒如此（范叔竟然困难到了这般地步）！"还在临别的时候取了件绸缎袍子送给了他。

结果须贾到了宰相府才发现原来张禄就是范雎，惶恐不安，立刻伏地请罪。范雎表示看在须贾还念旧情，送绸缎给他的分上姑且饶他性命，但他要代为通知魏王把魏齐的人头送来。

最后魏齐被迫自我了断。

在这句成语中，一是竟然之意，寒表示贫寒潦倒，谓贫困潦倒之极。

例：范叔一寒如此，刘郎前度曾来。（宋·范成大，《再游上方》）

（3）成语"家徒四壁"语出《汉书·司马相如传上》："文君夜亡奔相如，相如与驰归成都，家徒四壁立。"

例：好在书携一束，莫问家徒四壁，往日置锥无。（宋·辛弃疾，《水调歌头》）

（4）成语"阮囊羞涩"典出宋代阴时夫《韵府群玉·阳韵·一钱囊》："客问囊中何物，曰：'但有一钱守囊，恐其羞涩。'"成语由此演化而成，意思是说口袋里没钱，形容生活过得窘迫。

例：拟住江西玉山县投亲，道经申浦，阮囊羞涩，行止两难。"（清·百一居士，《壶天录》卷上）

（5）成语"一贫如洗"形容穷得一无所有，像被洗劫过一样。

例：第二日，这些质当的人家都来讨当，又不肯赔偿，结起讼来，连地都卖了，矫大户一贫如洗。（明·冯梦龙，《警世通言》第十五卷）

（6）成语"囊空如洗"形容人的口袋空得像被洗过一样，分文皆无。

例：我非无此心，但教坊落籍，其费甚多，非千金不可，我囊空如洗，如之奈何！（明·冯梦龙，《警世通言》第三十二卷）

（7）成语"一无所有"谓什么都没有，岂止是贫穷。

例：如水中之月，空里之风，万法皆无，一无所有，此即名为无形。（《敦煌变文集·庐山远公话》）

（8）成语"室如悬磬"是古代人形容家境极其贫寒的一种说法。最早见于《国语·鲁语上》："室如悬磬，野无青草，何恃而不恐？"原本指国库空虚，后来转用于形容家境贫寒。

磬是古代石制的一种打击乐器，光溜溜的。要说一个人家穷到了就像挂在架上供人演奏时打击的石磬，那就说明他已穷到了极点。

例：室如悬磬，难堪原宪之贫；地无立锥，敢恢史鱼之苦。（明·沈采，《千金记·遇仙》）

(9) 成语"捉襟见肘"原意为"整理一下衣襟,就露出了胳膊肘",形容衣服之破旧,反射生活之困苦。现也转义为顾此失彼、手忙脚乱。此成语原见于《韩诗外传》:"正冠则缨绝,振襟则肘见。"后演化成"捉襟见肘"。

例:捉襟见肘,免类于前哲;裂裳裹踵,无取于昔人。(唐·李商隐,《上尚书范阳公第三启》)

12　"ambitious as Phaethon"
　　与"自命不凡"

英语成语：

1. ambitious as Phaethon

2. feel one's oats

3. proud as a peacock

4. ride the high horse

5. too big for one's boots

6. big head

7. lift up the horn

8. The fly that stands on the cow's back thinks that it is taller than the cow.

9. go about with one's head in the air

10. swelled head

11. get on the high horse

12. proud as Lucifer

13. too big for one's shoes

14. put on side

15. be stuck up

16. proud stomach

17. act lordly

18. blow one's own horn

19. give oneself airs

20. have one's nose in the air

21. high and mighty

22. on the high ropes

23. turn up one's nose at

汉语成语：

1. 趾高气扬 2. 目中无人 3. 自高自大 4. 不可一世
5. 自命不凡

英语成语例解：

（1）ambitious as Phaethon 之意为"自命不凡""骄傲自大"。法厄同（Phaethon）是太阳神阿波罗与美丽的人间女子克吕墨涅（Clymene）生下的儿子。法厄同十分骄傲，常常在朋友面前夸耀自己是神的后裔，但是朋友们根本不信。为了顾全面子，法厄同求父亲让他驾驶日轮，出于父子之情，阿波罗便答应了。哪知他技术欠佳，日轮擦撞地球，引起一场大火，据说非洲受害最深，当地人的皮肤都被熏黑了。

宙斯见到这种情形，盛怒之下拿起雷矢射死法厄同，这才中止了一场大灾难。从此"法厄同"便被用来指"自命不凡"的家伙，而 ambitious as Phaethon 就用来表示"自命不凡""骄傲自大"的意思。

例：You have made mess of it by relying on that ambitious Phaethon.

就因为你信任那个自命不凡的家伙，才把事情弄得一团糟！

（2）成语 feel one's oats 原用以形容马的心态，指吃了燕麦的马活泼欢跳、精神饱满的样子。1843 年首次出现于以创造山姆·斯利克（Sam Slick）这一人物著称的加拿大作家哈利伯顿（Thomas Chandler Haliburton，1796—1865）的作品中，此成语除用于表示人"兴高采烈""精神饱满"之外，还可表示"自命不凡"和"趾高气扬"。

例：The new gardener was feeling his oats and started to boss the other men.

新园丁自命不凡，开始指挥起他人来了。

（3）成语 proud as a peacock 的意思是"高傲非凡""不可一世"。英王乔治三世（George Ⅲ，1738—1820）精神失常后，在他所有的讲话中每个句子都坚持用 peacock（孔雀）一词结尾。大臣们对他说，peacock 是个美丽而高贵的字眼，在臣民面前只宜悄声说，不能让臣民听见，这才把他的毛病改过来，使他的讲话不那么滑稽可笑了。孔雀行走时总是一副神气活现的样子，且爱炫耀那一身艳丽的羽毛。所以形容一个人非常高傲，人们常以孔雀作比。Proud as a peacock 这一比喻始用于 14 世纪。英国诗人乔叟（Geoffrey Chaucer，1340—1400）曾在《采邑总管的故事》（*Reeve's Tale*）中用过。

例：He was proud as a peacock when he passed his driving test at the first attempt.

他第一次尝试就通过了驾驶测试，于是便得意扬扬。

（4）成语 ride the high horse 表示"趾高气扬""目空一切""盛气凌人"之义。相传古代有七个骑士争夺波斯国王的宝座，后来他们决定：谁的马匹最先嘶鸣，谁就当国王。结果大流士（Darius，公元前548—前486）的坐骑最先发出嘶叫声，于是他就被授予王冠，成为波斯帝国最伟大的君主之一。

以一马而得天下，可以想见当时马的地位有多重要了。根据威克利夫（John Wickliffe，1330—1384）的记载，公元 14 世纪时，皇家和显贵高官在庆典游行期间，总是骑着高头大马（ride the high horse），居高临下，对臣民展示权力和地位，大有耀武扬威、目空一切的架势。

虽然这种习俗已不复存在，但是以 ride the high horse 来比喻"趾高气扬""目空一切""盛气凌人"的说法却沿用至今。

例：I have no objection to his joining our group, but he is a bit too fond of riding the high horse.

我不反对他参加我们这一组，不过他未免有点太盛气凌人了些。

（5）成语 too big for one's boots 的意思是"妄自尊大""目中无人""自高自大"。Boots 在这里是象征一个人所居的职位，他自命不凡而觉得他的脚已大到穿不上原来的靴子的程度。这一成语常与动词 be、get 或 grow 连用。

例：Look at that young man going around giving everybody orders. He's too big for his boots, that's his trouble.

瞧瞧那个年轻人，到处指手画脚，发号施令。他真是目中无人，早晚会出问题。

（6）成语 big head 的字面意思是"发胀的头脑"。这句成语的来源有几种不同的说法，有人以为它与牛和其他牲畜食了金丝桃（Saint-John's-wort）以后生的一种叫作骨质疏松症的病有关。患这种病的病畜头部肿大，由此产生了 big head 这一短语。但也有人认为它出自妄自尊大者之口，这种人认为自己智力超群，必须有一个"大脑袋"才能装得下那么多的智慧。

例：A boss with a case of big head will fill an office full of sore heads.

一个老板如果妄自尊大，那他的办公室里就都是感到头痛、牢骚满腹的人了。

（7）成语 lift up the horn 的意思是"狂妄自大""趾高气扬""不可一世"。其字面意思是"举角"，出自《圣经·旧约·诗篇》，上帝说："我已定下了审判的日期；我要以公道施行审判：叫骄傲的人不要狂妄，叫邪恶的人不要傲慢；我叫他们不要夸张，不要再狂妄自大（lift not up your horn on high）"。Horn 在《圣经》中是"力量""权威""光荣"的象征。这句成语原指从公牛或其他用角进攻的动物头上将角拔出，高高举起，显示自己的胜利，亦作 raise the horn。

例：Pride, when it has lowered its horn as it skirted by ruin, now raises it again as it touches success.

骄傲的人在处于覆灭边缘的时候，垂头丧气不敢自夸，到了接近胜利之日就趾高气扬，大吹大擂起来。

（8）The fly that stands on the cow's back thinks that it is taller than the cow. 是一句谚语，意为停落在牛背上的苍蝇总认为自己比牛高，喻狂妄自大。

（9）成语 go about with one's head in the air 的意思是摇头晃脑地四处走，喻摆架子，自高自大。

（10）swelled（或 swollen）head 意为自高自大、妄自尊大。

例：He has suffered from a swelled head ever since his first success.

自从获得初步成就以后，他就自高自大起来。

（11）成语 get on the（或 one's）high horse 的意思是骑着高头大马，喻耀武扬威、趾高气扬、目空一切。

例：He at once got on his high horse.

他顿时高傲起来。

（12）成语 proud as Lucifer 之意为目空一切、狂妄自大。Lucifer（路西法）即魔王撒旦，堕落以前为天使长。

（13）成语 too big for one's shoes（或 boots）意为自高自大、目中无人。

例：When the teacher made Bob a monitor, he got too big for his boots and she had to warn him.

老师叫鲍勃做班长，他就神气得不得了，因而老师不得不告诫他。

（14）成语 put on side 的意思是拿架子、妄自尊大、傲慢。

例：He puts on so much side that he makes himself ridiculous.

他大摆架子，显得滑稽可笑。

（15）成语 be stuck up 的意思是自命不凡、自高自大。

例：She is so stuck up that she refuses to have anything to do with her neighbours.

她非常傲慢，不同邻居来往。

（16）成语 proud（或 high）stomach 的意思是倨傲、傲慢。

例：He has a proud stomach; he acknowledges no one in the office lower than the chief cashier.

他为人倨傲，在办公室里不跟地位比出纳主任低的人打招呼。

（17）成语 act lordly 的意思是摆出王公贵族的架式，气派十足，形容人狂妄自大、不可一世。

（18）成语 blow（toot）one's own horn（trumpet）的意思是自吹号角（或喇叭），喻自吹自擂、自我赞美。

例：One who blows his own horn commonly gets little praise.

愈是自吹自擂，愈是无人赞美。

（19）成语 give oneself airs 的原意是摆出神态，作出样子，转义为摆架子、高傲、自负。

例：Mary gave herself airs when she wore her new dress.

玛丽穿上新装时神气活现。

（20）成语 have one's nose in the air 的意思是鼻子翘到天

上,喻目空一切、骄傲自大。这句成语始用于1579年,但现在少有人用。

(21) 成语 high and mighty 的原意是位尊权大,转义为傲慢、盛气凌人、不可一世。

例:Mary became high and mighty when she won the prize, and Joan would not go around with her any more.

玛丽获奖后变得十分傲慢,琼不再与她来往了。

(22) 成语 on the high ropes 的原意是高立于钢丝之上,转义为得意扬扬、傲视他人。这句成语源于走钢丝杂技演员的神情,他们在高高的钢丝上行走或表演特技,俯视观众,神采奕奕、洋洋自得。

例:Yes, I went there the night before last, but she was quite on the high ropes about something, and was so grand and mysterious that I couldn't make anything of her.

是的,我前天晚上去了她那儿,也不知道她为什么非常得意,又威风又神秘,弄得我莫名其妙。

(23) 成语 turn up one's nose at 的字面意思是翘起鼻子,鼻子朝天,喻傲慢、不屑一顾、目空一切。

例:This Hornblower hates us; he thinks we turn up our noses at him.

霍恩勃罗这家伙恨透了我们,他以为我们瞧不起他。

汉语成语例解:

(1)"趾高气扬"语出《左传·桓公十三年》:"莫敖必

败。举趾高，心不固矣。"后来逐渐演变成趾高气扬，意思是高高举步，特别神气，形容骄傲自满、不可一世的样子。

例：正说话时，便来了两个人，都是趾高气扬的，嚷着叫调桌子打牌。（清·吴趼人，《二十年目睹之怪现状》第四十四回）

（2）"目中无人"谓眼里没有旁人，形容骄傲自大、看不起人。

例：尝与父奢论兵，指天划地，目中无人，虽奢亦不能难他。（明·冯梦龙，《东周列国志》第九十六回）

（3）"自高自大"谓把自己看得又高又大，自以为了不起。语出《颜氏家训·勉学》："见人读数十卷书，便自高大，凌忽长者，轻慢同列。"

（4）"不可一世"谓不轻易赞许任何同时代的人，认为当今世界没有一个人能比得上他，形容目空一切，狂妄自大到了极点。语出宋代罗大经《鹤林玉露补遗》第十五卷："王荆公少年，不可一世士。"

例：而朋侪邻里，有称其肝肠如火，侠气如云，不可一世者。（明·张岱，《赠沈歌叙序》）

（5）"自命不凡"喻自以为了不起。形容高傲自负的态度。

例：大洪杨先生涟，微时为楚名儒，自命不凡。（清·蒲松龄，《聊斋志异·杨大洪》）

13 "Dame Partington and her mop" 与 "螳臂当车"

英语成语：

1. Dame Partington and her mop
2. kick against the pricks
3. throw straws against the wind
4. bite off more than one can chew
5. finish Aladdin's window
6. run one's head against a brick wall
7. A fog cannot be dispelled with a fan.

汉语成语：

1. 螳臂当车 2. 以卵击石 3. 蚍蜉撼树 4. 不自量力
5. 夸父逐日

英语成语例解：

（1）成语 Dame Partington and her mop 的字面意思是"帕廷顿夫人和她的拖把"。这一成语来自这样一个故事：1824年11月，住在海边的一位妇女，在暴风雨中企图用一个拖把挡住涌向她房子的海水。显然这个办法不可能奏效，这位妇女最后也只得悻悻离去。1831年10月，一位叫作史密斯（Sydney Smith）的记者借用了这个故事来支持英国当时的改革法案。他讽刺试图阻止潮流的议员说："她对付点污水或泥浆完全没问题，但是压根对抗不过暴风雨呀。"（She was excellent at slop or puddle, but should never have meddled with a tempest.）后来这个说法被广泛流传，用来表达"螳臂当车""不自量力"的意思。1851年1月16日，报纸《剑桥编年史》第六版还曾特意用一个专栏考证"帕廷顿夫人和她的拖把"的故事原型。

例：Meanwhile, here she sat face to face with a moral lunatic, who had not even enough sense of humour to see the absurdity of his own request, that she should go out to the shore of this ocean of corruption, and repeat the ancient role of…Dame Partington with her mop and her pail. (Henry Adams, *Democracy*: *An American Novel*, Chapter XIII)

同时，她面对的是个道德疯子，这疯子甚至缺乏足够的幽默感以至于看不出自己要求之荒唐，即她得跑去到这个腐败的汪洋大海的岸边，重演古时……拿着拖把和提桶的帕廷顿夫人的角色。(亨利·亚当斯，《民主：一部美国小说》第13章)

（2）成语 kick against the pricks 原意为"用脚踢刺"，引申

意为作无益的抵抗,以卵击石,自讨苦吃。典出《圣经·新约·使徒行传》第 26 章第 14 节:保罗原名扫罗,早期反对并迫害耶稣的门徒,把许多圣徒囚在牢房,施以重刑,甚至处死。一天,他把信奉耶稣的人绑起来押解到耶路撒冷去,快走到大马士革时,天上突然发出一道比太阳光还要强烈的光照在他的周围。他扑倒在地,听到有声音对他说:"扫罗,你为什么迫害我,你用脚踢刺是难的。"(It is hard for thee to kick against the pricks.)扫罗问:"主啊,你是谁?"回答是:"我是你所迫害的耶稣。"而后有人拉他进城,由亚拿尼亚给他施洗,于是他改信耶稣,并改名保罗。

例:He found it hard to kick against the pricks, yet, for that reason. Kicked every day the harder. (*The Times*)

他感到作无益的反抗是很难的,但是,正因为这个原因,他每天反抗得更激烈了。(《泰晤士报》)

(3) 成语 throw straws against the wild(扔草抵风)也是不自量力的意思。

例:You'll throw straws against the wind if you try to fulfil such a difficult task all by yourself.

如果你想单独完成这一项艰巨工作的话,那恐怕是有点不自量力了。

(4) 成语 bite off more than one can chew 的意思是说,一个人太贪婪,咬下一块他根本没法咀嚼的东西。相当于汉语成语贪多嚼不烂。该成语起源于美国,原指咬嚼烟草。

例:John bit off more than he could chew when he decided to have a race with the best runner in the school.

约翰不自量力，竟然决定同学校里最优秀的赛跑运动员进行比赛。

（5）成语 finish Aladdin's window 的字面意思是"装修好阿拉丁的窗口"，语出《天方夜谭》里阿拉丁与神灯的故事。阿拉丁得到神灯和巨魔以后，吃穿不愁。一天，他看上了苏丹王的女儿，便向苏丹王提婚，并答应给苏丹王造一座王宫。阿拉丁依靠神灯和巨魔建造的苏丹王宫有 24 个窗户，这些窗户都是用宝石镶嵌的，只有一个窗户除外，是留给苏丹王自己去装修的。苏丹王耗空了国库也未能将窗装饰好。后来此语引申为不自量力之意。

（6）成语 run one's head against（或 into）a brick（或 stone）wall 的本义是"将自己的脑袋往砖墙上撞"，这不是不自量力、自讨苦吃吗？

例：To try to change the political convictions of these people would be like running your head into a brick wall.

要想改变这伙人的政治信仰，无异于把你脑袋往砖墙上撞，枉费心机，不自量力。

（7）A fog cannot be dispelled with a fan. 是一句谚语，意为一把扇子扇不走大雾，喻不自量力。

汉语成语例解：

（1）"螳臂当车"典出《庄子·人间世》："汝不知夫螳螂乎，怒其臂以当车辙，不知其不胜任也。"比喻不自量力，冒充英雄和妄图抵抗某种强大力量的人。

《韩诗外传》中,有介绍"螳臂当车"的故事:

春秋时期,齐庄公酷爱打猎。一次,他带随从乘马车到郊外打猎。马车行进过程中,他看见路边有一只小小的爬虫,伸出两只臂膀向滚滚车轮直扑过来,力图阻挡车轮的前进。齐庄公赶忙叫停马车,想仔细看看这是只什么虫子。他发现这只虫子个头很小,却毫不畏惧地扑向数倍于自己身体大小的车轮,顿觉惊奇,就问车夫:"这是什么虫子?"车夫答道:"这是只螳螂。虽然身体很小,却只知前进不知后退。它根本不知晓自己到底有多大力量,只知道一个劲地冲向马车。您看他现在又举起了像刀一样的两条前腿,看见我们的马车过来,也不知道赶紧逃跑,却挥舞着前腿,妄图挡住车轮,真是自不量力!"齐庄公笑着说:"好一个出色的勇士,我们不要伤害它。"说着就让车夫去捉住螳螂,把它放到路边的草丛里。

后来这件事传开了。人们都说齐庄公尊重爱惜勇士。于是就有很多人投奔齐国而去。

例:正是泰山压卵,不须辗转之劳;螳臂当车,岂有完全之理。(清·俞万春,《荡寇志》第一一二回)

(2)"以卵击石",语见《墨子·贵义》:"以其言非吾言者,是犹以卵投石也。尽天下之卵,其石犹是也,不可毁也。"后"以卵击石"与"以卵投石"并用,其意相同,比喻对立的双方力量相差悬殊,用鸡蛋碰石头,不自量力。

例:今将军将不过十员,兵不足二十万,真如群手斗虎,以卵击石,未有不败者也。(明·许仲琳,《封神演义》第五十

三回)

（3）"蚍蜉撼树"语出韩愈《调张籍》诗："李杜文章在，光焰万丈长。不知群儿愚，那用故谤伤。蚍蜉撼大树，可笑不自量。"成语之意，不释自明。亦作"蚍蜉撼大树"。

例：近有文侩，勾结小报，竟也作文奚落先生以自鸣得意，真可谓"小人不欲成人之美"而且"蚍蜉撼大树，可笑不自量"了！(鲁迅《且介亭杂文末编·关于太炎先生二三事》)

（4）成语"不自量力"亦作"自不量力"，是说不能正确估计自己的力量，尤指过高地估计自己，语出《左传·隐公十一年》："不度德，不量力。"

例：是则系国家之安危，生民之性命，某岂可不自量力。(宋·范仲淹,《上吕相公书》)

（5）成语"夸父逐日"的故事见《山海经·海外北经》，故事表现了人类想战胜自然的信念与顽强拼搏的精神，但多被用来比喻不自量力。

例：真谓夸父逐日，必渴死者也。(南朝·宋·僧愍,《戎华论折顾道士夷夏论》)

14 "talk nineteen to the dozen" 与 "喋喋不休"

英语成语：

1. talk nineteen to the dozen

2. talk one's head off

3. harp on one string

4. talk one's ear off

5. talk the bark off a tree

6. talk a dog's hind leg off

7. oral diarrhea

8. wag one's jaw

9. chatter like a magpie

10. rattle away

11. rattle on

12. run on

13. loose one's tongue

14. wag one's tongue

15. waffle on

汉语成语：

> 1. 喋喋不休　2. 呶呶不休　3. 唠唠叨叨

英语成语例解：

（1）成语 talk nineteen to the dozen 起源于蒸汽机时代，成语中的数字是表示蒸汽泵的抽水量和燃料的消耗量。Nineteen to the dozen 即是抽水 1.9 万（nineteen thousand）加仑，需要烧煤 12 蒲式耳（bushel，一蒲式耳等于 36 升）。这句话几经转义，现在用来比喻人讲话的速度很快，或是连续讲个不停，恰如当时的蒸汽机在运转一样，喻人讲话喋喋不休。

这一成语，在使用过程中产生不少变异，如动词 talk 可用 go 或 speak 代替，nineteen 可用 twenty 或 forty 代替，其意思不变。

例：She is talking nineteen to the dozen about that traffic accident she has witnessed.

她正喋喋不休地叙述目睹的那场意外。

（2）成语 talk one's head off 是形容一个人说话絮叨到使人烦到脑袋痛得几乎要掉下来的程度。

例：Lady Britomart：Andrew, you can talk my head off, but

you can't change wrong into right. (George Bernard Shaw, *Major Barbara*)

薄丽托玛夫人：安德鲁，随你怎么说得天花乱坠，你也不能把错的说成对的。(萧伯纳，《巴巴拉少校》)

(3) 成语 harp on one string 或 harp on the same string，乃至缩略形式 harp on 都表示说话唠叨没完没了，喋喋不休。这句成语的出现时间可追溯到 16 世纪。据说古代的竖琴师为了充分显示他们的高超技艺，常常只在一根琴弦上弹奏。格拉夫顿 (Richard Grafton) 认为这一成语是托马斯·莫尔 (Thomas More, 1478—1535) 的创造。

例：The Cardinal made a countenance to the Lord Howard that he should not harp on more upon that string.

红衣主教对霍华德使了个眼色，示意他不要再在这件事上唠叨不止了。

(4) 成语 talk one's ear off 的字面意思是说话絮烦得让人的耳朵快掉下来了，意即说个不停、喋喋不休。

例：All I wanted was a chance to read my book, but my seatmate talked my ear off.

我巴不得能有机会看书，但我邻座的人却唠唠叨叨地说个不停。

(5) 成语 talk the bark off a tree 的字面意思是人唠叨得让树皮都忍受不了，从树干上脱落下来，何况人乎。此成语极言唠叨之甚。

例：Tom talks the bark off a tree, I can't say a word.

汤姆口若悬河说个没完,我插不进一句话。

(6) 成语 talk a dog's (或 donkey's, horse's) hind leg off (亦作 talk the hind leg off a dog/donkey/horse) 的字面意思是人说话唠叨到能使狗、驴或马的后腿折掉的程度,极言絮叨之甚。形容人说话滔滔不绝、喋喋不休,令人烦得要死。

例:For goodness sake don't let that woman start arguing. Once she starts, she'd talk the hind leg off a donkey.

看在老天爷面上,辩论时别让那个女人先讲,她一讲起来,就会唠叨个没完。

(7) 成语 oral (或 verbal) diarrhea 亦作 diarrhea of the mouth 的字面意思是"嘴里发生了腹泻",喻指人说话喋喋不休,失去控制。

例:You've got again oral diarrhea.

你又犯了喋喋不休的毛病。

(8) 成语 wag one's jaw (亦作 wag the jaws) 之意为喋喋不休。

(9) 成语 chatter like a magpie 的意思是像喜鹊一样饶舌,喻喋喋不休。

例:No one wants to sit next to Miss Weleh at the Sewing; she chatters like a magpie, all the time.

在缝纫联谊会上,谁也不想坐在韦尔奇小姐身边,她整天喋喋不休。

(10) 成语 rattle away 意为喋喋不休地讲。

例:She rattled away for the next ten minutes.

她接着喋喋不休地讲了十分钟。

(11) 成语 rattle on 亦为喋喋不休、唠叨不停之意。

例：I always found her company unendurable. She could rattle on for hours about absolutely nothing at all.

我觉得跟她在一起真够受，她会没话找话唠叨个大半天。

(12) 成语 run on 原意为时间流逝，转义为讲个不停、喋喋不休。

例①：He kept running on and on, telling me the same story over and over again.

他喋喋不休地讲着，反复地对我讲那回事。

例②：And in the meantime, while you are running on with your jokes, the money is still here. (Mark Twain, *The Man that Corrupted Hadleyburg*)

而且正当你津津有味地谈着笑话的时候，钱却仍然摆在那儿。(马克·吐温，《败坏了哈德莱堡的人》)

(13) 成语 loose one's tongue 的意思是放开某人的舌头，喻喋喋不休。

例：Wine loosed his tongue.

喝了酒他就喋喋不休地谈开了。

(14) 成语 wag one's tongue 的意思是摇唇鼓舌，唠叨不停，喋喋不休。

例：It is too bad to wag your tongue in the presence of teachers.

你在老师们面前唠唠叨叨是不大好的。

(15) 成语 waffle on 之意为唠唠叨叨，喋喋不休。

例：He waffled on for twenty minutes, and at the end of it, had said very little of any importance.

他唠叨了二十分钟，结果什么要紧的事也没说出来。

汉语成语例解：

（1）"喋喋不休"形容人说话唠叨，令人厌烦，这一成语最早见于《汉书·匈奴传》。

例①：浴已，飞檐间，梳翎抖羽，尚与王喋喋不休。（清·蒲松龄，《聊斋志异·雏鸽》）

例②：宾客会赏，一俗士言词猥鄙，喋喋不休，殊败人意。（清·纪昀，《阅微草堂笔记·滦阳消夏录一》）

（2）"呶呶不休"意同"喋喋不休"，也是形容话多，说起来没完。最早见于唐代著名文学家韩愈的短文《言箴》。

在唐德宗和唐宪宗年间，韩愈曾官至"监察御史""国子""博士""考功郎中"等职位。但他秉性正直、不善逢迎，多次上书进谏，指责政弊，得罪了统治者，又遭谗言陷害，屡次被贬降职。于是作一题为《言箴》的短文：

不知言之人，乌可与言？知言之人，默然而其意已传。幕中之辩，人反以汝为叛；台中之评，人反以汝为倾。汝不惩邪，而呶呶以害其生耶！

大意是说：跟不讲道理之人沟通，何必同他多讲道理？通晓道理之人，不必开口他就懂你的意思了。在官场中争论几句，人家就觉得你心怀反叛；在衙门中提出异议，人家就觉得你存心拆台。难道你还不接受教训吗？还要不停唠叨，难道命都不要了么！

"呶呶"形容的是话多，"呶呶不休"指的是话多得过分。另一位唐代著名文学家柳宗元在《答韦中立论师道书》中，也曾有过类似的表达："岂可使呶呶者，早暮咈吾耳、骚吾心？"

(3) "唠唠叨叨"谓说话啰唆，说起来没完，多含贬义。语出宋代郑思肖《答吴山人问远游观地理书》："古人胸中高明，一见便了……未若后世唠唠叨叨，支支离离，弃本逐末，侈为乖谬。"

15 "shut the stable-door when the steed is stolen" 与 "亡羊补牢"

英语成语：

shut the stable-door when the steed is stolen

汉语成语：

亡羊补牢

英语成语例解：

成语 shut the stable-door when the steed is stolen 出自古罗马政治家西塞罗（Cicero，公元前 106—前 43）的名著《论友谊》(*On Friendship*)，表示贼去关门，为时已晚。亦有用作 lock the stable door when the horse is stolen 或 lock the barn door after the horse is stolen 的。它的引申意思是在遭受重大损失之后才采取防预措施,为时已晚。

例①: When the Spaniards came to view their crop they could not see it in some places for weeds, the hedge had several gaps in it, where the wild goats had got in and eaten up the corn, perhaps here and there a dead bush was crammed in, to stop them out for the present, but it was only shutting the stable-door after the steed was stolen. (Daniel Defoe, *Robinson Crusoe*)

当西班牙人来看他们的庄稼时,他们在一些杂草丛生的地方却看不到作物,树篱那儿有多处缺口,因此野山羊得以进入吃掉谷物;各处所塞的枯死灌木也许是为了暂时堵住它们,这不过好比马给偷了才去关栅栏罢了。(丹尼尔·笛福,《鲁滨孙漂流记》)

例②: I carried my gold loose in a pocket with a button. I now saw there must be a hole, and dapped my hand to the place in a great burry. But this was to lock the stable door after the steed was stolen. (Robert Louis Stevenson, *Kidnapped*)

我在一个有扣子的口袋里零散放着我的金子。现在我看那里一定是有一个洞,便赶快用手捂住那个地方,不过为时已晚。(罗伯特·路易斯·斯蒂文森,《绑架》)

汉语成语例解:

"亡羊补牢"出自《战国策·楚策四》:"臣闻鄙语曰:'见兔而顾犬,未为晚也;亡羊而补牢,未为迟也。'"亡之意为丢失，牢为关牲口的圈。此成语是说，羊丢失以后，才修补羊圈。其引申意义为出了差错，设法补救，免得再受损失。

例①：惩羹吹齑岂其非，亡羊补牢理所宜。(宋·陆游，《秋兴诗之八》)

例②：及今早图，示万国以更新之端，作十年保太平之约，亡羊补牢，未为迟也。(梁启超，《变法通议·论不变法之害》)

这两句成语，无论是从形式结构，还是从思维模式上看，都近乎同理。英国人用的是马和厩门，中国人用的是羊和羊圈，但说明的都是一个道理。道理虽相同，可用法正好相反。英语成语说贼去关门，为晚已晚，无法补救。而汉语成语的意思却是，虽然丢了羊，但是如果及时修补羊圈，就会免遭继续损失，中心意思是为时不晚，这与为时已晚正好相反。所以，在比较之中，我们要认识到它们的共同之处，也要了解它们的相异之处，尤其是在用法上。

16 "Spilled water is not picked up again" 与 "覆水难收"

英语成语：

1. Spilled water is not picked up again.
2. What's done is done.
3. What's done cannot be undone.
4. There's no use crying over spilt milk.
5. That's water over the dam.
6. Spilled water never returns to its tray.
7. What's lost is lost.
8. The lot is cast.
9. You can't unscramble eggs.

汉语成语：

覆水难收

英语成语例解：

（1）Spilled water is not picked up again. 是一句谚语，意思是一旦水泼出，就再也收不回，喻覆水难收。

（2）成语 What's done is done. 最早见于英国作家为海伍德（J. Heywood, 1497—1580）的《谚语集》（*Proverbs*, 1546）。英国剧作家威廉·莎士比亚（1564—1616）的悲剧《麦克白》（*Macbeth*, 1605）的主人公麦克白是位战功赫赫的苏格兰大将，由于受女巫和夫人的诱惑和野心的驱使，杀死了慈祥的国王，而后引起一连串的犯罪，最后导致灭亡。在剧中第三幕第二场，有这样一句话：Things without all remedy should be without regard; what's done is done。（无法挽回的事，只好听其自然；事情干了就干了。）这句成语表示事已定局，不可以更改，更无可挽回。与汉语成语"覆水难收"意同。

例：Don't do anything rash until you've heard what he has to say. You can only cause a lot of trouble. What's done is done. (Mario Puzo, *The Godfather*)

在你听到他的报告之前，切莫鲁莽行动。不然，你只能引起许多麻烦，生米已经煮成熟饭了。（马里奥·普佐，《教父》）

（3）还有另外一种说法：what's done cannot be undone. （已做的事情不可能挽回。）这种说法也成为流行的同义成语。

例①："If it's done and can't be undone," he said cheerfully, "I don't see that advice is needed." (David Graham Phillips, *The Cost*)

"要是说已做的事情不可能挽回，"他愉快地说，"我看这

建议就没什么必要了。"（大卫·格雷厄姆·菲利普斯,《代价》）

（4）There's no use crying over spilt milk. 或缩略式 cry over split milk 原意为"牛奶泼了,哭也无济于事"。这是在英美广泛应用的一句成语。它最早出自加拿大幽默作家哈利伯顿（Thomas C. Haliburton）的《钟表匠》（*The Clockmaker*, 1835）一文中。书中主人公的朋友对他说："What's done, Sam, can't be helped, there is no use in crying over split milk."（山姆,已经做了的事不可挽回了。牛奶泼了,哭也没用。）

（5）That's water over the dam. 的意思是"溢过堤坝的水"。溢过堤坝的水是再也不会流回去的,喻指事已过去,已成定局,无可挽回。有时亦作 that's water under the bridge。

例：Since the sweater is too small already, don't worry about its shrinking, that's water over the dam.

既然毛线衫太小,就不必担心它会缩水,因为已经无法挽回了。

（6）Spilled water never returns to its tray. 是一句谚语,意思是水从盘中洒出,再也收不回,喻覆水难收。

（7）What's lost is lost. 是一句谚语,意为失者不可复得,喻覆水难收。

（8）成语 The lot is cast. 意为大局已定,木已成舟。

（9）成语 You can't unscramble eggs. 是一句谚语,意思是蛋碎了是无法复原的,喻覆水难收。

汉语成语例解：

（1）"覆水难收"亦作"反水难收"，是说泼出的水无法收回来，比喻事成定局，不可挽回。典出《后汉书·光武帝纪上》："反水不收，后悔无及。"

（2）"木已成舟"比喻事情已成定局，无法挽回。典出《墨子·非乐》："舟车既已成矣！吾将恶许用之！"民间俗语"生米做成熟饭"亦谓既成事实，无法挽回、更改。

例①："到了明日，木已成舟，众百姓也不能求我释放，我也有词可托了。"（清·李汝珍《镜花缘》第三十五回）

例②："如此才人，足为快婿尔女已是覆水难收，何不宛转成就了他。"（明·凌濛初《初刻拍案惊奇·通闺闼坚心灯火》）

例③："就是婶子，见'生米做成熟饭'，也只得罢了，再求一求老太太，没有不完的事。"（清·曹雪芹《红楼梦》第六十四回）

17 "in the altogether" 与 "一丝不挂"

英语成语：

1. in the altogether
2. in the buff
3. birthday suit
4. in one's skin
5. naked as my mother bore me
6. naked as one's nail
7. naked as a worm
8. naked as a needle
9. with nothing on
10. in a state of nature

汉语成语：

1. 赤身裸体 2. 一丝不挂

英语成语例解：

（1）成语 in the altogether 的意思是"裸体"或"一丝不挂"。这是口语中表示"裸体"的一种委婉说法。它可以追溯到 19 世纪 90 年代。1894 年英国小说家杜莫里埃（George du Maurier, 1834—1896）在其小说《特里尔比》(*Trilby*) 中首先使用 altogether 一词表示油画中的裸体人。书中艺术家的模特儿说："I sit for the altogether."（我给裸体画当模特儿）。1895 年《纽约信使报》(*New York Mercury*) 在一条标题中用了 in the altogether 一语表示"裸体"。该标题为："Will the next fad be photographs of modern woman taken in the 'altogether'?"（现代派妇女拍裸体照将会成为流行的风尚吗？）由于搭配需要，介词 in 有时候用 into。

例①：Don't stand by the window in the altogether. Someone might see you.

不要光着身子站在窗边，可能会被别人看到。

例②：The model posted in the altogether.

那个模特儿一丝不挂地摆好姿势。

（2）成语 in the buff 的意思是"赤身裸体"。19 世纪在美国，水牛（buffalo）大量的被捕猎，用水牛皮制的上衣曾经风靡一时。Buff 原指用黄牛或水牛皮制的坚韧柔软的暗黄皮革，它源于拉丁语 bufalus，也可以说是 buffalo 一词的缩略形式。人的皮肤经过日晒也会变成这种颜色，故 buff 常喻指"人的皮肤"，in the buff 因此被用来表示"赤身裸体"。

例①：They enjoy sunbathing in the buff.

他们喜欢光着身子晒日光浴。

例②：Jim came out of the bedroom in the buff.

吉姆一丝不挂地从卧室里走出来。

（3）成语 birthday suit 的意思是"一丝不挂""赤身裸体"。这是表示光着身子的一种委婉说法。婴儿呱呱坠地降临人世时，总是赤身裸体、一丝不挂的，就像亚当、夏娃最初光着身子一样，因此人们就以 birthday suit（生日服装）来作比。这种用法多少带有诙谐色彩。另有一种解释认为，此语可能源于旧时英国国王在生日时为侍臣、侍从定制新衣的习俗。此语在历史上曾有若干异体，如 1731 年以 birthday gear 的形式出现在英国作家斯威夫特的作品中。1771 年以 birthday suit 的形式出现在作家斯摩莱特（Tobias George Smollett, 1721—1771）的书信体小说《亨佛利·克林克》（*Humphry Clinker*）里，书中有这样一句：We bathed in our birthday suit.（我们光着身子游泳。）19 世纪 60 年代英国贵族用 birthday attire 来表示赤身裸体，而现今不论在英国还是在美国、加拿大似乎只通用 birthday suit 这一形式。此语常与介词 in 连用，作 in one's birthday suit。

例①：Here's a snapshot of me at six months old, wearing my birthday suit.

这是我六个月时光着身子的一张快照。

例②：He ran along the corridor to the bathroom in his birthday suit.

他一丝不挂地穿过走廊跑到浴室。

（4）成语 in one's skin 的字面意思是"穿着皮肤"，喻指人一丝不挂。

例：The boy stood in his skin.

那男孩赤身裸体地活着。

（5）成语 naked as my mother bore me（亦作 as naked as I was born）意为赤身裸体、一丝不挂。

（6）成语 naked as one's nail 的意思是像人的指甲一样裸露着，喻赤身裸体、一丝不挂。

（7）成语 naked as a worm 的意思是赤裸得像一个虫子，喻赤身裸体、一丝不挂。

（8）成语 naked as a needle 的意思是光得像一根针，喻赤身裸体、一丝不挂。

（9）成语 with nothing on 的意思是赤裸裸、一丝不挂。

例①：I cannot help blushing when I am rung-up by women—with nothing on but spectacles and a bath-towel.

当我光着身子，只戴着一副眼镜和围着一条浴巾时，女人打来电话，我就禁不住要面红耳赤。

例②：We always swam here with nothing on.

过去我们在这儿游泳总是全身脱得精光。

（10）成语 in a state of nature 的原意是处于自然状态，处于原始状态，转义为裸体、一丝不挂。

例：The insane man came out of his house in a state of nature.

那个疯子赤身裸体地跑出屋外。

汉语成语例解：

（1）"赤身裸体"谓光着身子、一丝不挂，形容粗俗无礼，有失文明。

例：吴班引兵到关前搦战，耀武扬威，辱骂不绝，多有解衣卸甲，赤身裸体，或睡或坐。(元·罗贯中，《三国演义》第八十四回)

（2）"一丝不挂"原为佛教用语，比喻人没有一点牵挂。后指不穿衣服、赤身裸体，形容粗俗无礼，有失文明。

例：放闸老兵殊耐冷，一丝不挂下冰滩。(宋·杨万里，《清晓洪泽放闸四绝句》)

18 "In the country of the blind, the one-eyed man is king." 与"山中无老虎,猴子称大王"

英语成语:

1. In the country of the blind, the one-eyed man is king.
2. When the cat's away, the mice will play.
3. Monoculus may be king in Caecus country.
4. For want of a wise man, a fool is set in the chair.
5. If the elephant were not in the wilderness, buffalo would be the greatest.
6. In the valley where there is no tiger, the hare is the master.
7. Cat mighty dignified till the dog come by.
8. The good looking man is king, if there is no rich man near.

汉语成语:

> 山中无老虎,猴子称大王。

英语成语例解：

（1）In the country of the blind, the one-eyed man is king. 的意思是"盲人国里，独眼龙称王"。这句成语最早见于英国诗人斯科尔顿（John Skelton, 1460—1529）抨击红衣主教沃尔西（Thomas Wolsey, 1475—1530）的一首诗。荷兰人文主义者伊拉斯摩斯（Erasmus, 1466—1536）也把这一诗句收入他编纂的《格言集》（*Adagia*, 1500）里。这句成语的含义是矮子里面拔大个，在一群无能之辈中，即使平平庸庸的人也可以被看作杰出的人物，类似汉语中的"山中无老虎，猴子称大王"。

例：Almost nobody's competent, Paul. It's enough to make you cry to see how bad most people are at their jobs. If you can do a half-assed job of anything you're a one-eyed man in the kingdom of the blind. (Kurt Vonnegut, *Player Piano*)

保罗，这儿几乎没有人能胜任的。见大多数人的工作如此糟糕，这就足以让你哭起来。只要你能做点屁大的事情，你就是瞎子圈里有一只眼睛能看见东西的人了。（库尔特·冯内古特，《自动钢琴》）

（2）When the cat's away, the mice will play. 是一句谚语，谓猫儿不在，老鼠成精，近于汉语的大王外出，小鬼跳梁。这句谚语最早见于17世纪约翰·雷（John Ray）的《谚语集》（*Collection of Proverbs*），含义是当有威慑力的人不在时，下面的人就可能忘乎所以、为所欲为，颇有山中无老虎，猴子称大王之意。

例：Play up to her, won't you? Be the husband who's taking

a holiday—playing while the cat's away. (L. P. Hartley, *A Perfeet Woman*)

你和她配合表演，好吗？你扮演正在度假的丈夫——猫儿不在，耗子逍遥自在。(莱斯利·珀斯·哈特利，《一个完美的女人》)

（3）Monoculus may be king in Caecus country. 的意思与 In the country of the blind, the one-eyed man is king. 完全相同，区别只在于用拉丁语 monoculus 替换了英语中的 the one-eyed man（独眼人），用拉丁语 caecus 替换了英语中的 the blind（盲人）。

（4）For want of a wise man, a fool is set in the chair. 是一句谚语，意为皆因能人缺乏，交椅轮到一个傻瓜。意即山中无老虎，猴子称大王。

（5）If the elephant were not in the wilderness, buffalo would be the greatest. 是一句谚语，意为荒野若无大象，奶牛就称大王，喻山中无老虎，猴子称大王。

（6）In the valley where there is no tiger, the hare is the master. 是一句谚语，意思是山谷中无老虎，野兔是其主。其义与山中无老虎，猴子称大王相同。

（7）Cat mighty dignified till the dog come by. 意思是狗不在场的时候，猫神气十足。相当于汉语成语山中无老虎，猴子称大王。

（8）The good looking man is king, if there is no rich man near. 是英语谚语，意思是富翁不在，俊者为王。相当于汉语成语山中无老虎，猴子称大王。

汉语成语例解：

"山中无老虎，猴子称大王"喻指当首领的不是由于本领高明，而是因为没有更好的，不得已而为之，类似的成语还有"山中无鸟兽，螳螂自称王""山中无大树，茅草也称王"。

英语成语"盲人国里，独眼龙称王"，以人的差异类比。汉语成语"山中无老虎，猴子称大王"以动物相类比。虽比拟有所不同，但说明的事理是完全一样的，堪称异曲同工。

19 "Castor and Polydeuces" 与 "刎颈之交"

英语成语：

1. Castor and Polydeuces
2. Damon and Pythias
3. David and Jonathan

汉语成语：

1. 刎颈之交　2. 生死之交　3. 莫逆之交

英语成语例解：

（1）成语 Castor and Polydeuces 中的卡斯托耳和波吕丢刻斯兄弟俩在希腊神话中合称狄俄斯库里兄弟（Dioscuri），为仙女勒达（Leda）所生。其实他们是一对同母异父的兄弟，卡斯托耳的父亲是斯巴达王廷达瑞俄斯（Tyndareus），而波吕丢刻斯的父亲则是主神宙斯。由凡人所生的卡斯托耳是会死的，而由神所生的波吕丢刻斯是永生的。这两人以其亲密情谊著称。当卡斯托尔战死后，波吕丢刻斯向宙斯请求，希望也赐他一死。宙斯要他作个选择：要么一个人永远和众神在奥林匹斯山生活；要么和兄弟在奥林匹斯过一天，在阴间过一天。波吕丢刻斯选择了后者。因此他们的名字成了亲密朋友的象征，刎颈之交的代用语。也做 Castor and Pollux。

例：Dr. Leo Newmark wrote me asking for Stillman's address, saying that when one wishes to know about Castor, he naturally calls on Polydeuces, I could only reply that my relation with Stillman was not that of Polydeuces, to Castor but rather that of Chauvin to Napoleon. (*Bulletin of San Francisco Medical Society*)

纽马克博士写信向我要斯蒂尔曼的地址，说人们想知道卡斯托耳的情况自然就会找波吕克斯。我只能回答说我和斯蒂尔曼的关系并不是卡斯托耳和波吕克斯的关系，而是沙文和拿破仑的关系。(《旧金山医学会通报》)

（2）成语 Damon and Pythias 典出希腊神话。达蒙（Damon）和皮西厄斯（Pythias 亦作，Phintias）象征着愿为彼此牺牲自己的朋友。

关于这两位朋友的故事有诸多不同的版本，但其中最著名的是西塞罗在 De Officiis (《论义务》) 中讲述的版本。皮西厄斯被锡拉丘斯的暴君狄奥尼修斯一世判处死刑，他要求得到一些时间来处理私事。狄奥尼修斯傲慢拒绝。于是达蒙提出如果他的好友皮西厄斯不在指定时间返回,自己愿代他受死。当判死之人皮西厄斯如约在指定时间返回时,狄奥尼修斯被他们的友谊感动,释放了他们。英国剧作家爱德华兹(Richard Edwards,1522—1566)以他们的故事为原型创作了《达蒙和皮西厄斯》(1564),使这个故事广为人知。

例①:We have developed a friendship like Damon and Pythias.

我们已经建立起患难与共的友谊。

例②:The Damon and Pythias of the establishment were Damon and Pythias no longer, they were ready to fly each at the other's throat.

这家公司的两位生死之交已经再也称不上莫逆了,他们已经成了不共戴天的仇人。

(3)成语 David and Jonathan 典出《圣经・旧约・撒母耳记上》:大卫赤手空拳打败歌利亚后,扫罗便委他以都督重任,成为以色列历史上一位最年轻的军事将领。扫罗的儿子、王位继承人约拿单非常敬佩大卫,两人一见如故,成为莫逆之交。约拿单虽然很清楚地知道,大卫是他将来争夺王位的劲敌,但在他父亲扫罗要杀害大卫的关键时刻,甘冒父王动怒的风险,毅然挺身而出,搭救大卫脱险,躲进深山老林。尽管父亲警告他,如果他继续帮助大卫,就将失去王位,但这并不能影响他对朋友真诚无私的友谊。约拿单痛苦地问父王:"为什么要杀大卫,他犯了什么罪?"扫罗气得发疯,提起枪来就刺约拿单,但未刺中。约拿单大怒,当即离席而去。傍晚,他又偷偷会见大卫,叫他永远不要让王看见。临别时,大卫伏在地上向好友拜了三拜,然后两人抱头大哭,难舍难分,发誓永远忠于友谊。此成语喻同生共死的朋友,莫逆之交。

例:The two had had an almost classic friendship, David and Jonathan, wherein Brangwen was the Jonathan, the server. (David Herbert Lawrence, *The Rainbow*)

他们俩之间的友谊,近乎大卫和约拿单之间的古典式友谊,布兰温是约拿单,甘愿为对方效力。(大卫·赫伯特·劳伦斯,《虹》)

汉语成语例解:

(1) 成语"刎颈之交"语出《史记·淮阴侯列传》:"始常山王、成安君为布衣时,相与刎颈之交。"意思是以生命相许的好朋友,比喻同生死、共患难。

例:卒相与欢,为刎颈之交。(汉·司马迁,《史记·廉颇蔺相如列传》)

(2) 成语"生死之交"指同生死共命运的朋友或友谊。

例①:无二鬼叹了一口气道:"今日众兄弟幸会,又结了生死之交,月下谈心,酒逢知己,正可作彻夜之饮。"(清·东山云中道人,《平鬼传》第二回)

例②:就供案香,二人结为生死之交。(清·鸳湖渔叟,《说唐》第二十二回)

(3) 成语"莫逆之交"谓情投意合、至好无嫌的朋友之间的友谊。莫逆指彼此心意相通,没有抵触。

例①：膺之所与游集，尽一时名流，与邢子才、王景等为莫逆之交。(李延寿，《北史·司马膺之传》)

例②：后来我发现其中有几位还是我的读者，我们更成了莫逆之交了。(邹韬奋，《经历·再被羁押》)

20 "the pot calling the kettle black" 与 "老鸹嫌猪黑"

英语成语：

1. the pot calling the kettle black.
2. A dog soiled with excrement laughs at another soiled with bran.
3. A damaged plate laughs at a broken plate.
4. The plate kiln calls the oven burnt house.
5. The camel does not see his own hump, he sees only the hump of his brother.

汉语成语：

> 1. 老鸹嫌猪黑 2. 五十步笑百步

英语成语例解：

（1）The pot calling the kettle black. 古代人以柴薪为燃料，

20 "the pot calling the kettle black" 与 "老鸹嫌猪黑"

不论什么加热器皿经烟熏火燎都会变黑。用被烧黑的饭锅来讥笑被烧黑的水壶,岂不是只看见了人家黑,没有看见自己黑。这句谚语讽喻一个人嫌恶或指责存在于别人身上的缺点和毛病,忽视了自己正好也有这种缺点和毛病,如果说有差别,也只是程度上的不同。这句成语最早见于西班牙作家塞万提斯(Cervantes,1547—1616)的名著《堂·吉诃德》(*Don Quixote*),书中主人公堂·吉诃德的仆从桑丘(Sancho)提到过这句古老的谚语。

例①:"My goodness, I didn't start this war and I don't see any reason why I should be worked to death and…" "A traitor to Our Glorious Cause!" "The pot's calling the kettle black…" (Margaret Mitchell, *Gone with the Wind*)

"天晓得,这个仗又不是我要打的,我看不出有什么理由让我累得要死,而且……""你背叛我们的光荣事业了!""你不过是饭锅讥笑水壶黑罢了……"(玛格丽特·米切尔,《飘》)

例②:Stop criticizing the others. What you're doing is like pot calling the kettle black.

不要批评别人了。你是看见了别人黑,没看见自己黑。

(2) A dog soiled with excrement laughs at another soiled with bran. 是一句谚语,意为狗自己身上有粪便,还笑人家有糠麸,喻老鸹嫌猪黑。

(3) A damaged plate laughs at a broken plate. 是一句谚语,意思是裂纹的盘子笑话破碎的盘子,喻五十步笑百步。

(4) The kiln calls the oven burnt house. 是英语谚语,意思

是窑管炉灶叫烧焦了的炉膛，喻老鸹嫌猪黑。

（5）The camel does not see his own hump, he sees only the hump of his brother. 是英语谚语，意思是骆驼不见自己峰，只见同伴背不平。喻只见别人缺点，看不见自己的不足，相当于汉语熟语老鸹笑猪黑。

汉语成语例解：

（1）"老鸹嫌猪黑"是一句熟语，老鸹是乌鸦的俗称，全身羽毛呈黑色。猪通常都是黑色的，乌鸦和猪都是黑色的，但乌鸦偏偏嫌猪黑。人们用这句成语喻指有人只看见或指责别人的缺点或不足，看不见自己的缺点或不足。这句成语也多用来嘲笑或讽刺只挑剔别人，不检讨自己的人。有时也说成老鸹落在猪身上，看见人家黑，看不见自己黑。

例①：俗语对：老鸹嫌猪黑，乌龟笑鳖跛。（清·缪莲仙，《梦笔生花》初编八卷）

例②：老鸹骂猪黑，你就不是牛贩子吗？（克非，《春潮急》）

（2）"五十步笑百步"比喻事情的缺点或错误，只有程度上的不同，而无本质上的差别，典出《孟子·梁惠王上》。

例①：昔之所谓道者，于形为无形，于事为无事，恬漠冲粹，养智怡神。岂独爱欲未除，宿缘是畏，唯见其有，岂复是过，以此嗤齐侯，犹五十步笑百步耳。（南朝·齐·僧祐，《弘明集·何承天〈答宗居士书〉》）

例②：他觉得即使自己的手不是那么白软，也不能去打瑞

丰了;他和瑞丰原来差不多,他看不起瑞丰也不过是以五十步笑百步罢了。(老舍,《四世同堂·第二部·偷生》)

从英汉这两句成语的概念看,西方人和东方人在思维观念中都把黑色看成是不光彩的象征,所以都把别人的不足比喻成黑色。但成语要表达的并不是谁足谁不足,而是用以批判人性的一种弊病或某些人的不良倾向。西方人以器类比,东方人以动物类比,殊途同归。世界各个民族几乎都有意义类似的成语。比如,俄罗斯谚语有"大破口笑小窟窿";孟加拉国谚语有"筛子笑粗箩,满身是窟窿"。

21 "Talk of the devil, and he is bound to appear."
与"说到曹操，曹操就到"

英语成语：

1. Talk of the devil, and he is bound to appear.
2. Talk of an angel and you′ll hear his wings.
3. Talk about the devil and his imps will appear.
4. Talk of the devil and you hear his bones rattle.
5. Sooner named sooner come.
6. Talk about the wolf, and the wolf is here.
7. Talk of the devil and he shows up.

汉语成语：

说到曹操，曹操就到

英语成语例解：

（1）Talk of the devil, and he is bound to appear. 是一句谚语，最早见于荷兰人文主义者埃拉斯穆斯的《格言集》(*Adages*)，意即当人们谈及某人时，碰巧这个人就出现了，它的模式与含义同汉语说曹操，曹操到几乎没什么两样。

例：The unexpected appearance of Mrs. Rainscourt made him involuntarily exclaim, "Talk of the devil…" "And she appears, sir," replied the lady, rising, and making a profound courtesy. (Frederick Marryat, *The King's Own*)

赖恩斯科特太太意外地出现使他不由自主地喊起来，"说魔鬼……""她就到了，先生，"这位太太回答说，她站立起来，显出非常谦恭有礼的样子。（弗雷德里克·马里亚特，《国王自己的东西》）

（2）Talk of an angel and you'll hear his wings. 是一句谚语，意即说到天使，你马上就会听到他鼓动翅膀的声音。

（3）Talk about the devil and his imps will appear. 是一句谚语，意即谈到魔鬼，魔鬼的子孙就到。

（4）Talk of the devil and you hear his bones rattle. 是一句谚语，意即谈到魔鬼，你马上就会听到他的骨头格格响，亦即说鬼鬼到，说人人到。

（5）Sooner named sooner come. 是英语谚语，意思是说到谁，谁就到，相当于汉语说曹操，曹操到。

（6）Talk about the wolf, and the wolf is here. 是英语谚语，意思是说到狼来，狼就到此，相当于汉语说曹操，曹操到。

(7) Talk of the devil and he shows up. 是英语谚语，意思是说到魔鬼，魔鬼就到，相当于汉语说曹操，曹操到。

汉语成语例解：

成语说到曹操，曹操就到，是真有其人其事，曹操是三国时期的政治家、军事家、诗人，先为东汉丞相，后来，曹丕称帝，建立魏国，追尊曹操为魏武帝。当时，有一次，众人正在议论曹操的时候，曹操突然闯了进来。后人就把这一情景传播开并把这一说法延续下来，成为在谈论某人时，这人恰巧就来了的表示凑巧的固定表达方式。

例①：小王跟余兰一边打招呼，一边笑着说："我们正说你呢，真是说曹操，曹操就到。你这些天忙什么呢？怎么老看不见你！"

例②：丁海川怀着激动的心情走进郭师傅的院子。郭师傅老伴一见，两手往衣襟上一拍，拍出十个白面手印，笑着说："哟，真巧！说曹操，曹操就到。老头子正张罗去请你呢！"

这两句成语的思维方式和叙述方式是完全一致的，不同的只在于英语成语中的"魔鬼"用的是泛指，汉语成语中的"曹操"用的是专指，但对于整个成语来说，表达的概念是完全相同的，有时可互译。

22 "Walls have ears."
与"隔墙有耳"

英语成语：

Walls have ears.

汉语成语：

隔墙有耳

英语成语例解：

据说法国卢浮宫在凯瑟琳皇后（Catherine de Medici, 1519—1589）时代有的房间设计得可以听到另一个房间里人们讲的话，因此这位多疑的皇后得以获悉许多国家秘密和阴谋事件。英国早在乔叟《坎特伯雷故事集》的《武士的故事》(*Knight's Tale*, 1387) 中就有"fields have eyes and woods have ears"（田野里有眼，树林里有耳）的说法。1546年海伍德的《谚语集》（*Proverbs*）也收有这说法。这句成语的意思是：说话一定要小心谨慎，附耳低语，否则最秘密的事情也可能被人听去。人们常以此成语提醒人凡事要多加提防。

例①："It is not good to speak of such things," said Heriot, "especially of the great; stone walls have ears, and a bird of the air shall carry the matter." (Walter Scott, *Fortunes of Nigel*) "谈这样的事情是不好的，"赫里奥特说："特别是大事：石头墙也有耳朵，天空的鸟儿也会传出去的。"（沃尔特·司各特，《奈吉尔的命运》）

例②："Mr. Baker gave me hell for letting you spend a thousand dollars," "Why, that old goat!" "Mary—Mary! The walls have ears." (John Steinbeck, *The Winter of Our Discontent*) "贝克先生因为我让你花掉一千块钱而臭骂了我一顿。""哎呀，这老混蛋！""玛丽，玛丽，隔墙有耳啊。"（约翰·斯坦贝克，《烦恼的冬天》）

汉语成语例解：

"隔墙有耳"是说隔着墙也会有人听，比喻说话要防有人听去，走漏消息。语出《管子·君臣下》"墙有耳，伏寇在侧。墙有耳者，微谋外泄之谓也。"《元曲选·孟德耀举案齐眉》第二折有"隔墙须有耳，窗外岂无人"之说，"隔墙有耳"可能是由这两句话缩略而成，这也符合汉语四字成语的传统形式。

例①：休得再提。常言道："隔墙须有耳，窗外岂无人。"

只可你知我知。(明·施耐庵,《水浒传》第十六回)

例②：隔墙须有耳,窗外岂无人。柳氏镇日在家中骂媒人,骂老公,陈青已自晓得些风声。(明·冯梦龙,《醒世恒言·陈多寿生死夫妻》)

英汉这两句成语,几乎完全相同,表达的也都是同一个道理。其中只是由于形成这种说法的情境不同,才有些许差别。英语说墙上有耳,汉语说墙外有耳,在翻译中完全可以互译。

23 "Love me, love my dog." 与 "爱屋及乌"

英语成语：

1. Love me, love my dog.
2. He that loves the tree loves the branch.
3. If you love the boll, you cannot hate the branches.
4. Love the ground he treads.

汉语成语：

1. 爱屋及乌 2. 屋乌推爱

英语成语例解：

（1）成语 Love me, love my dog 最早见于法国的神学家和宗教改革家圣贝尔纳（Bernard of Clairvaux，1090—1153）的布道

词，1546年收入海伍德的《谚语集》(*Proverbs*)，意思是"爱吾之人亦将爱吾之犬"。引申意思是"如果你爱我，就要对我所有的一切也采取保护的态度，不要因为我有缺点就厌恶我"，极近汉语"爱屋及乌"之义。

例①：And Melanie, with a fierce "Love-me-love-my-dog" look on her face, made converse with astounded hostesses. (Margaret Mitchell, *Gone with the Wind*)

媚兰以一种强烈的"爱屋及乌"的表情看着斯嘉丽，跟那些对此大为惊讶的女主们交谈着。(玛格丽特·米切尔,《飘》)

例②："She'd take it as a personal insult if I said those regular Sunday visits to her parents were getting a bit of a bore."

"Love me, Love my dog. Eh?"

"我要是说我对星期天定期看望她的父母感到有些厌烦，那她就会当作是对她本人的侮辱。"

"爱屋及乌嘛，是吧？"

(2) He that loves the tree, loves the branch. 是英语谚语，意思是爱树者必惜枝，喻爱屋及乌。

(3) If you love the boll, you cannot hate the branches. 是英语谚语，意思是你要爱果就不会恨枝，喻爱屋及乌。

(4) Love the ground he treads. 是英语谚语，意思是爱一个人，就连他踩过的地都爱，喻爱屋及乌。

汉语成语例解：

(1) "爱屋及乌"出自《尚书大传》："爱人者，兼其屋上之鸟",成语由此概括而来,形容喜欢一个人或物,对与其有关的事物也有感情。

例①：他们都是你舅舅的相识,你何无爱屋及乌情？(明·许自昌,《水浒记·投胶》)

例②：杨妃平日爱这雪花女,虽是那鹦鹉可爱可喜,然亦因是安禄山所献,有爱屋及乌之意。(明·褚人获,《隋唐演义》第八十七回)

(2) 成语"屋乌推爱"谓因为爱某人而推及爱与他有关联的人或物。

例：蒙尊嫂留小生进里面来坐,这个都是看宋公明的分上,屋乌推爱,一时相缱绻。(明·许自昌,《水浒记·渔色》)

英汉这两句成语都有自己各自形成的年代和环境,可以说都有千年以上的历史了。成语的含义也基本相同,所不同的是英语成语以第一人称说起,以人及物。汉语成语没有人称,并以物及物。虽叙述方式略有不同,但用法和含义相差无几。

24 "a flash in the pan" 与 "昙花一现"

英语成语：

1. a flash in the pan
2. nine day's wonder

汉语成语：

> 昙花一现

英语成语例解：

（1）成语 a flash in the pan 中的 pan 指旧式火枪的火药池。旧式火枪始于 17 世纪，扣动扳机时，击锤碰击燧石，产生火花。点燃火药池内的火药，进而引燃枪膛内的主装药，将弹丸射出。可是，由于主装药受潮或火门受阻，火枪往往会打不响，只是在火药池内有火一闪而已。这就是 a flash in the pan 一语的来源。后来，人们就用此语喻指"昙花一现""一时的成功"或"昙花一现的人物"。

例①：That novel of hers was a flash in the pan, and she hasn't written anything decent since.

她那部小说只不过是昙花一现，此后她再没写出像样的东西。

例②：His son did pass one exam but it was just a flash in the pan.

他儿子的确是通过了一门考试，但那只是一时的成功。

（2）成语 nine day's wonder 原意为"九天的惊讶"，喻指轰动一时的事物，昙花一现。这句成语可能源自中世纪时重大宗教节日的庆典活动。这些活动通常持续九天，称作 novena（连续九天的祈祷式），伴有游行以及各种庆祝活动。九天后，人们的生活恢复正常。另有一说认为，这一成语源自古谚语 A wonder lasts nine days, and then the puppy's eyes are open.（九天的惊讶后幼犬睁开了眼。）意思是说小狗出生九天后才睁开眼，有了视力，比喻人们会暂时顺应于轰动一时的某个人或某一事件，但是一旦他们看清了事物的本来面目，惊奇就会随之消失。莎士比亚在历史剧《亨利六世》（下篇）第三幕第二场中使用了这一短语：当爱德华王（King Edward）告诉葛罗斯特（Gloucester）公爵他将娶寡妇葛雷夫人（Lady Grey）为王后时，公爵吃惊地说："That would be ten days' wonder at the least."（那至少要让我们惊奇十天。）克莱伦斯公爵接着说："That's a day longer than a wonder lasts."（这比一桩普通的奇闻还能多维持一天的寿命。）

1385 年，英国诗人乔叟曾在其诗作《特洛勒斯和克丽西德》(*Troilus and Criseyde*)中提到这一点，其中有这样一句话："For wonder last but nine nights…"（什么事都新鲜不了九天）。成语 nine day's wonder 不是从乔叟的诗句便是从上面提到的一句古谚演变而来的。而莎士比亚只不过是灵活而诙谐地运用了这一成语。

英国第 22 届"桂冠诗人"梅斯菲尔德（John Masefield, 1878—1967）写过一首诗，生动地记述了 1940 年英军从敦刻尔克（Dunkirk）撤退的情景，歌颂了士兵的勇敢坚毅精神。该诗便是以《轰动一时的奇闻》(*The Nine Day's Wonder*)为题的，但此语在此不带任何贬抑含义。第二次世界大战期间还有人仿此语创造了 ninety-day wonder 一语来揶揄那些只经过三个月培训便成为候补军官的事。

例①：Every great event of contemporary polities is a nine day's wonder.

当代政治中的每一件大事都不过是昙花一现，很快就会销声匿迹。

例②：Last year the art critics praised Jonas as if he were a master, but he turned out to be a nine day's wonder.

去年艺术评论家们还赞颂乔纳斯为大师呢，但后来证明他只是一个昙花一现的人物。

汉语成语例解：

"昙花一现"通常认为来自佛教传说，本是形容难得出现的意思，后多用以比喻刚一出现就迅速消逝的人或事物。

昙花原产热带美洲，是属于仙人掌科的一种肉质植物。老茎圆柱形，而新茎扁平、绿色，呈叶状。其花从叶状枝生出，大型、白色、暗香，夜间开放，数小时便萎谢，所以有"昙花一现"的说法。

另一说法，"昙花一现"的昙花，不是上述的那一种，而是产于印度的另一种。这种昙花，枝高丈余，叶长半尺，叶端尖形，雌雄异花，隐藏在花托里，因此常被误认为隐花植物。它的名称古时音译作"优昙钵罗"，简作"优昙钵"或"优昙花"。如苏东坡《赠潇洒信长老》诗云："优钵昙花岂有花，问师此曲唱谁家？"

例①：昙花一现，万事付东流。咳，无限伤心自怨尤。（清·何镛，《乘龙佳话·归里》）

例②：使非中道废弃，能继续其业以至今日，则岂不足以自豪于世界耶！即此昙花一现，已足为我国学术史之光矣。（梁启超，《王荆公传》第十二章）

25 "all my eye" 与 "胡言乱语"

英语成语：

1. all my eye
2. banana oil
3. lie in one's throat
4. talk through one's hat
5. a lot of malarkey
6. talk through one's neck
7. pile of shit
8. talk rot
9. tommy rot
10. apple sauce
11. stuff and nonsense
12. talk wet
13. shoot one's mouth off
14. shoot the bull

汉语成语：

1. 胡言乱语 2. 信口开河

英语成语例解：

（1）成语 all my eye 原意可能指"眼中噙着泪但心中并不悲伤"。这句成语已有 200 多年的历史了，其出处不详。18 世纪的幽默作家乔·米勒（Joe Miller）编了一则滑稽故事，说一个英国水手在国外一教堂做礼拜时听到有人祈祷"Oh mihi, beate Martin"，意思是说 O grant me aid, blessed St. Martin（哦，赐助予我，圣马丁），但那句话听上去却像 All my eye and Betty Martin，所以，后来 all my eye 又有了较长的表达形式——all my eye and Betty Martin，意思完全相同，皆为胡说八道之意。

例：He told me how sorry they were that they were unable to help, but that was all my eye.

他告诉我他们很抱歉不能帮忙，但那完全是胡说八道。

（2）成语 banana oil 原意为"香蕉水"，转义为"胡说八道""废话连篇"。香蕉水是一种化合物，用作油漆溶剂，也用作食品果味添加剂。它的气味与香蕉相似，因此称为香蕉水。它的特征是"太甜""太油腻"，由此产生了"油腔滑调""花言巧语"的喻义。

例①：Cut out the banana oil, flattery will get you nowhere.

别花言巧语胡说八道了，奉承人是没有用的。

例②：It was only the pure banana oil of the propagandist.

这纯粹是那位宣传家的胡说八道。

（3）成语 lie in one's throat 的意思是"撒弥天大谎""胡说八道""信口开河"。此语源自莎士比亚喜剧《第十二夜》第三幕第四场：塞巴斯蒂安（Sebastian）和薇奥拉（Viola）是孪生兄妹，在一次海上航行中哥哥被海浪卷走，妹妹流落到伊利里亚。她女扮男装给伊利里亚公爵奥西诺（Orsino）当侍童，改名叫西萨里奥（Cesario）。不久她爱上了公爵。可是公爵不知道真相，他爱上了一个名叫奥丽维娅（Olivia）的姑娘，公爵派他谈吐高雅的"侍童""西萨里奥"去见她，向她转达爱慕之情，奥西维娅小姐一见这位"侍童"就钟情于"他"，拒绝其他求婚者。公爵遭到拒绝后，写信给"西萨里奥"要求决斗。信中写道："你去见奥丽维娅小姐，她当着我的面把你厚待；但是你喉中的谎言并不是我向你挑战的理由"（But than lies in thy throat; that is not the matter I challenge thee for.）。由此产生这句成语，表示信口开河，胡说八道。亦作 lie in one's teeth。

例①：Well, I do nothing in the world but lie, and lie in my throat.

唉，我这个人除了说谎不会干什么别的，我总是胡说八道。

例②：Whoever charged him with the plot lied in his throat.

不管什么人控告他搞阴谋都是胡说八道。

（4）成语 talk through one's hat 的意思是"信口开河""胡说八道"。据说这一成语是在 19 世纪末美国的一次总统竞选期间出现并开始使用起来的。当时纽约一家报纸《世界报》(*The World*) 刊登了一些漫画，讽刺 1888 年当选总统的共和党候选人哈里森 (Benjamin Harrison, 1833—1901)。哈里森常戴一顶海狸皮高礼帽，漫画就有意把哈里森的那顶帽子画得又高又大，遮住了大半个脸，以此讽刺在这种情况下他不论讲什么，都几乎毫无意义。以后哈里森的民主党对手就用 talk through one's hat（字面义：透过帽子讲话）一语来影射攻击他在全国各地发表的竞选演说都是信口开河、胡说八道。这一比喻说法很快就为广大群众所接受并渐而变为英语成语的一分子，亦作 talk through one's neck。

例①：Don't take any notice of what he says. He knows nothing whatsoever about finance and is just talking through his hat.

别听他的话，他对金融一窍不通，他是在瞎说一通。

例②：He said that her family are emigrating, but he's talking through his hat.

他说她一家人要移居国外，他是在胡说八道。

(5) 成语 a lot（或 bunch）of malarkey 之意为鬼话连篇、胡说八道。

例：That's a lot of malarkey.

那完全是一派胡言。

(6) 成语 talk（或 speak）through (the back of) one's neck 的意思是通过人的脖子后说话，喻乱说一通、胡说八道。

例：Alfred didn't know a thing about it and was almost

certainly talking through the back of his neck.

艾尔弗雷德对此一窍不通，几乎可以肯定他是在胡说八道。

（7）成语 pile of shit 的意思是胡说八道、废话连篇。

（8）成语 talk rot 的意思是胡说八道、满口胡言。

例：He's talking rot when he says that the company is almost bankrupt.

他说这家公司快要破产了，简直是胡说八道。

（9）成语 tommy rot 的意思是胡说八道、乱说一通。

例：Shut up and don't talk such tommy rot!

住口，别再胡说八道了！

（10）成语 apple sauce 原意为苹果酱，转义为胡说八道。

（11）成语 stuff and nonsense 之意为胡说八道。

例："Stuff and nonsense!" said Mr. Fang: "don't try to make a fool of me." (Charles Dickens, *Oliver Twist*)

"胡说八道！"费恩先生说："别想在我面前耍花枪。"（查尔斯·狄更斯，《雾都孤儿》）

（12）成语 talk wet 的意思是胡诌、胡说八道。

例："Oh, don't talk so wet! You make me tired!"

"哦，别胡说八道了，你烦死我了！"

（13）成语 shoot one's mouth off 的意思是信口开河、胡吹一通、胡说八道。

例：One the airwaves, they shoot their mouths off about things they know little about.

在广播节目里，他们信口雌黄谈论几乎一无所知的事物。

(14) 成语 shoot the bull 之意为吹牛、胡说八道。

例：Don't pay much attention to what he says. He likes to shoot the bull.

别听他的,他喜欢吹牛。

汉语成语例解：

(1)"胡言乱语"亦作"胡说八道",皆为丧失理智说胡话或毫无根据地瞎说一气。"胡说"一词,在南宋周密《齐东野语》一书的《诛韩本末》中就出现过。韩侂胄是宋宁宗赵扩的大臣,以外戚执行,权居左右丞相之上,仗势独断,十几年中干了很多坏事。那时,北方的金朝占领着中原一带。韩和他的同党为进一步达到他们夺权篡国的目的,怂勇宁宗下诏出兵攻金,结果却连打败仗,韩吓得急忙向金朝求和,并与金人秘密私通,南宋政府因此把他杀了。因为韩侂胄手握大权,当时逮捕和处死他,也是秘密进行的。他死的前一天,同党周筠得到风声,立刻写了字条悄悄向他报告。可是韩侂胄当时喝得醉醺醺的,根本不信,"视之曰:'这汉又来胡说!'于烛上焚之"。

例：星期日的上午,不得不坐在教室里听那个主教的胡说八道,也是一件苦事。(邹韬奋,《经历·踏进了约翰》)

(2)成语"信口开河"本来应作"信口开合",在"元曲"中有不少这样的话。所谓"信口",是出言不假思索的意思。宋代苏轼诗曰:"杜陵布衣老且愚,信口自比契与稷。"明代杨基诗曰:"我自信口答所问,怪我出语多惊人。"形容说话随便,只管嘴巴一开一合地任意乱说,就叫"信口开合"。

"合"与"河"同音,后来就误写成"信口开河"。

例①:村老老是信口开河,情哥哥偏寻根究底。(清·曹雪芹,《红楼梦》第三十九回)

例②:信口开河是不负责任,存心欺骗更是无耻。(闻一多,《愈战愈强》)

26 "Hair by hair you will pull out the horse's tail."
与"只要功夫深,铁杵磨成针"

英语成语:

1. Hair by hair you will pull out the horse's tail.

2. Soft water constantly striking the hard stone wears it at last.

3. Wholeheartedness will pierce a rock.

4. Little strokes fell great oaks.

5. With time and patience the leaf of the mulberry becomes satin.

6. A drop and a drop cut through the rock.

7. Grinding and grinding wears out the hardest of grindstones.

8. The gutter by dropping wears the stone.

9. Patience pierces the rock.

10. Patience wears out stones.

11. The patient man cooks a stone till he drinks broth from it.

26 "Hair by hair you will pull out the horse's tail." 与 "只要功夫深,铁杵磨成针"

汉语成语:

1. 只要功夫深,铁杵磨成针 2. 水滴石穿 3. 精卫填海

英语成语例解:

(1) Hair by hair you will pull out the horse's tail. 是一句英语谚语,意思是"一根一根地拔,你就能拔光马尾巴上的毛"。这句谚语来源于古希腊传记作家普卢塔赫(Plutarch)记述的一则故事:古罗马统帅塞多留(Sertorius)为了教育士兵认识毅力之可贵,就牵来两匹马,让两个士兵分别去把马尾上的毛拔光,其中一个是身材魁梧的力士,他抓住一匹瘦马尾巴上的毛,一把一把地往下拽,但怎么也拽不净,而另一个士兵是个不起眼的小个子,而他的马很壮,尾巴又粗又大,但他很有耐心,他一次只拔一根毛,不慌不忙地一根一根地拔,最后把马尾上的毛拔得净光,一根不存。这句谚语用来形容慢而稳,可赢得比赛,喻指持之以恒可成大业。

(2) Soft water constantly striking the hard stone wears it at last. 是一句谚语,意思是细水常击顽石,顽石终会磨损,喻滴水穿石。

(3) Wholeheartedness will pierce a rock. 是一句谚语,意思是全神贯注地干能把一块石头打穿,喻只要功夫深,铁杵磨成针。

（4） Little strokes fell great oaks. 或 Little strokes fell down strong oaks. 意思是小劈可以砍倒大树，喻只要功夫深，铁杵磨成针。亦作 Many little strokes fell down strong oaks。

（5） With time and patience the leaf of the mulberry becomes satin. 是一句谚语，意思是有了时间和耐心，桑叶也能变缎子，喻只要功夫深，铁杵磨成针。

（6） A drop and a drop cut through the rock. 是英语谚语，意思是滴水可穿石，相当于汉语成语水滴石穿。

（7） Grinding and grinding wears out the hardest of grindstones. 是英语谚语，意思是磨了一刀又一刀，磨石再硬也会凹，喻只要功夫深，铁杵磨成针。

（8） The gutter by dropping wears the stone. 是英语谚语，意思是滴水穿石。

（9） Patience pierces the rock. 是英语谚语，意为耐心可以穿石，喻只要功夫深，铁杵磨成针。

（10） Patience wears out stones. 是英语谚语，意为耐心可以磨没石头，喻只要功夫深，铁杵磨成针。

（11） The patient man cooks a stone till he drinks broth from it. 是英语谚语，意为只要有耐心，石头也能熬出肉汤，喻只要功夫深，铁杵磨成针。

汉语成语例解：

（1）"只要功夫深，铁杵磨成针"是说只要用功夫，有毅力，任何难做的事也能做成功，亦作"拼得功夫深，铁杵磨成针"。

史书最早记载磨杵成针的故事是宋代祝穆《方舆胜览》卷五十三《磨杵溪》磨杵成针的故事。明代陈仁锡《潜确类书》卷六十:"李白少读书,未成弃去,道逢老妪磨杵,白问其故。曰:'欲作针。'白感其言,遂还卒业。"明代曹学佺《蜀中广记·上川南道彭山县》:志云,县东南二十五里有磨针溪,在象耳山下,相传李白读书山中,学未成弃去,适过是溪,逢老媪方磨铁杵,问何为,曰欲磨作针耳。白感其言,遂还卒业。

(2)"水滴石穿"语出宋代罗大经《鹤林玉露·一钱斩吏》,这是用滴水这一自然现象作的比喻。一滴水,虽然渺小柔弱,碰到石头上就会粉身碎骨,然而日复一日,年复一年地滴下去,终会有那么一天,石头一定会被水给穿透的。

(3)"精卫填海"比喻矢志不移,努力不懈。精卫是古代神话中的鸟名。传说上古炎帝的小女儿女娃到东海边去玩,被海涛淹没,死后化为一只小鸟,发誓要把大海填平,整天不停地去衔西山的树枝、石子抛进大海,后因嘴被木石磨穿而死。因为它叫的声音似"精卫",人们就称其为"精卫"鸟。

例:商蚷驰河河可凭,精卫填海海可平。物情大忌不量力,立志亦复加专精。(宋·刘过,《呈陈总领·其四》)

27 "look for a needle in a haystack" 与 "海底捞针"

英语成语：

1. wild goose chase
2. milk the ram
3. look for a needle in a haystack
4. plough the sands
5. spin one's wheel
6. teach a pig to play on a flute
7. flog a dead horse
8. put a quart into a pint pot
9. go whistling jigs to a milestone
10. bay the moon
11. beat the air
12. burn daylight
13. bark up the wrong tree
14. Sisyphean task

15. It is useless to flog a dead horse.
16. It is no use pumping a dry well.
17. It is very hard to shave an egg.
18. The dog barks at the moon in vain.
19. The dog may bark but the anthill will not run away.
20. The biting fly gets nothing by alighting on the back of tortoise.
21. In vain you show light to the blind.
22. It is a loss of soap to wash the ass's head.
23. A nod is as good as a wink to a blind horse.
24. Water is not carried out in a sieve.
25. Pour water into a sieve.
26. run after two hares
27. seek a hare in a hen's nest
28. bang one's head against a brick wall
29. wash an ass's head
30. try to do the impossible
31. whistle jigs to a milestone
32. all for naught
33. bring to naught
34. go to naught
35. go for nothing
36. to no purpose
37. fight with one's own shadow
38. in vain
39. limn on water
40. lash the waves

41. look for wool on an ass

42. Don´t look for a ram with five feet.

43. He that washes an ass´s head, loses both his soap and his labour.

44. It is in vain to cast your net where there is no fish.

45. It is in vain to lead ox to the water if he is not thirsty.

46. It is lost labour to sow where there is no soil.

47. Don´t try to sell ice to the Eskimos.

48. Fan the sun with peacock´s feather

49. Don´t try to swim where there is no water.

50. Don´t try to pull yourself up by your own bootstraps.

51. He wags a wand in the water.

汉语成语：

1. 水中捞月　2. 海底捞针　3. 缘木求鱼　4. 徒劳无功
5. 枉费心机

英语成语例解：

（1）成语 wild goose chase 的意思是"无望的追求""徒劳的举动""白白浪费时间"。关于这句成语的起源，美国与英国的学者各持不同的看法。美国学者认为，wild goose chase 是一种骑马比赛，参加者两人以上为一组，第一队的人骑着马带头，不论是转弯还是绕道，后面的队伍必须要照他的路线骑，并想办法超过他，成为带头的人。据说这种比赛是依据野鹅群飞行的样式模仿而来的。英国学者则认为，此语与打猎有关。由于生活在水边草丛的野鹅，既会在陆上跑，又会在水里游。即使在天上飞也不是件难事。因此，猎人捕捉到野鹅的机会非常少，经常是白忙一场。所以，"追捕野鹅"根本就是白费心力。而这句成语的意思也与这种来源接近，比喻愚蠢（或毫无希望）的追寻、白费力气的追求。

例：Finding a man to marry Maggie in the next couple of years is a wild goose chase. She is too devoted to her career.

要帮玛姬在几年内找个男人结婚是白费力气的，她把身心都投到工作上了。

（2）成语 milk the ram 的字面意思是"挤公羊的奶"，喻指做徒劳无益的事。此语出自英国牧师约翰·海尔斯（John Hales, 1584—1656）的《短论集》（*Several Tracts*）。它可能来自谚语 Whilst the one milks the ram, the other holds under the sieve.（一个人在上面挤公羊的奶，另一个人在下面用筛子接奶。）此成语有时亦作 milk the bull。

例：Bruce had tried everything training his dog to play tricks but it was like milking the bull.

布鲁斯试图教他的狗玩把戏，但他想尽办法还是徒劳无功。

（3）成语 look（或 search）for a needle in a haystack 的意思是"海底捞针""徒劳无益"。1517 年，英国政治家兼作家托马斯·莫尔勋爵（Thomas More, 1478—1535）首先使用了这句成

语："在他的所有著作中寻找一句话，犹如在干草堆中寻找一根针。"

例：Trying to find one small boy in the large crowds at the football match was like searching for a needle in a haystack.

想在看足球的比赛的人群中寻找一个小男孩，就犹如在干草堆中寻找一根针一样困难。

（4）成语 plough the sands 的意思是"徒劳无功""做不可能奏效的事"。如果在沙子中用犁耕，开出来的沟立刻会恢复原状，这岂不是徒劳无功？莎士比亚在《理查二世》一剧中用了含义相近的另一条成语：Alas, poor Duke! The task he undertakes is numbering sands and drinking oceans dry.（唉，可怜的公爵！他所担负的工作简直是点数沙粒和喝干海水。）

例：After his wife died he began to work longer hours in order to pass the time, but he was really just ploughing the sand.

他在妻子死后为了消磨时间而开始加班加点工作，这实在是徒劳无益。

（5）成语 spin one's wheel 的字面意思是"让轮子空转"，喻指"浪费时间""作无效劳动"。

例：Stop spinning your wheels, get yourself in gear.

别浪费时间了，按部就班干活吧。

（6）成语 teach a pig to play on a flute 的意思是"做不可能奏效的事""徒劳无功"。人如何能教会猪吹笛子呢？不言而喻，是异想天开，白费力气。

例：If you do so, you are teaching a pig to play on a flute.

如果你这样做的话，那是不会有任何结果的。

（7）成语 flog（或 beat/mount on）a dead horse 的字面意思是"抽打死马"，喻指"白费力气""徒劳无益""无济于事"。成语 sing psalms to dead horse（给死马唱赞歌）亦是此意。

例：We discussed some incidents that had happened long ago. It was really flogging a dead horse.

我们讨论了一些很早以前发生的事情，这简直是浪费精力。

（8）成语 put（或 get）a quart into a pint pot 的意思是"以升容斗""以小者容纳大者"，喻指"徒劳无益""白费力气"。

例：Many new people have moved into this small town and they have nowhere to live. You can't put a quart into a pint pot.

许多新居民搬进了这个小城镇，可是没有地方住。你总不能把一斗东西装进一升的容器里。

（9）成语 go whistling jigs to a milestone 的意思是"做不可能成就的事""缘木求鱼"。

例：To ask for help from him is to go whistling jigs to a milestone.

请他帮忙是徒劳的。

（10）成语 bay the moon 的字面意思是"狂犬吠月"，出自莎士比亚悲剧《裘力斯·凯撒》第四幕第三场：勃鲁托斯（Brutus）指责卡修斯（Cassius）"手心很有点痒，常常为了贪图黄金的缘故，把官爵出卖给无功无能的人"，两人因此争吵起来，勃鲁托斯接着说："我们曾经打倒全世界首屈一指的人物，因为他庇护盗贼；难道就在我们中间，竟有人甘心让卑污的贿赂玷污他的手指，为了这样一把金钱，出卖我们伟大的荣誉吗？我宁愿做一只向月亮狂吠的狗，也不愿做这样一个罗马人（I had rather be a dog and bay the moon than such a Roman.）。"这句成语亦作 bark at the moon。

例：You lost Sue entirely through your own fault and now she's gone with someone else. You're just baying the moon if you expect to get her back now.

由于你的错误，你完全失去了苏，她已经跟别人出走了。如果现在你还期望她回来，那只是枉费心机。

（11）成语 beat the air 的字面意思是"打空气"。语出《圣经·新约·哥林多前书》，《哥林多书》分为前后两卷。哥林多教会派系纷争，还犯有乱伦等罪行。圣保罗对此深恶痛绝。便写了这封书信严厉申斥他们。后来，他听说多数教徒已痛改前非，深感欣慰，又写了一封信给他们，表示赞扬，称为《哥林多后书》。在前书中他助人改邪归正，以他为榜样。他说："I therefore so run, not as uncertainly; so fight I, not as one that beateth the air. (所以我奔跑不像无定向的，我打拳不像打空气的。)"后来人们用 beat the air 表示"徒劳无功""白费力气"，亦可写作 beat the wind。

例：He cared little about contemporary politics, which he regarded as beating the wind.

他很少关心当代政治，他认为那是白费力气。

（12）成语 burn daylight 原意为"白天点灯"。典出莎士比亚悲剧《罗密欧与朱丽叶》第一幕第四场：罗密欧受着单恋的折磨而终日闷闷不乐。好友茂丘西奥（Mercutio）和班伏里奥（Benvolio）劝他一起去跳舞，以驱赶心头的烦恼。茂丘西奥对罗密欧说："要是你已经没头没脑深陷在恋爱的泥沼里——恕我说这样的话——那么我们一定要拉你出来。来来来，我们别白日点灯浪费光阴了。"（If thou art Dun, we'll draw thee from the mire of this sir-reverence love, where in thou stick'st up to the ears. Come, we burn daylight, ho!）

例：Burn not daylight about it; we have short time to spare.

不要在这上面浪费光明，我们剩下来的时间不多了。

（13）成语 bark up the wrong tree 原意是"猎犬向无猎物的树乱吠"，以后转义为"找错（或弄错）目标""白费力气""徒劳无益"。此成语一般用于口语。源出流传于英美的狩猎故事。浣熊是美洲特有的一种动物，性喜夜间活动，所以打浣熊通常是在夜里进行。要寻觅浣熊的踪迹，猎人非借助猎犬不可。猎犬把浣熊赶上树之后，就站在树下狂吠不止直至主人到来。但是浣熊非常机灵敏捷，常常在黑暗中悄悄地穿过树枝跳到另一棵树上去，任凭猎犬朝着没有浣熊的树汪汪狂吠，猎人终究还是空忙一场。

例：New evidence suggests that we have been barking up the wrong tree in our search for a cure.

新的证据表明，我们在寻找对策时弄错了目标，白白忙活了一场。

（14）成语 Sisyphean task（或 labour）的意思是"西西弗斯所做的苦工"。引申为"永无休止的苦工"或"徒劳无益"。

这个成语典出荷马史诗《奥德赛》。西西弗斯是传说中的科林斯国王,因生前作恶多端,一说因为得罪了神祇,死后堕入地狱,被罚做苦工。据《奥德赛》卷十一描写,奥德修斯到阴间看到形形色色的鬼魂。他看到西西弗斯用双手向山上推滚大石块,但每当他快要把大石推到山顶时,那块大石就滚落下来,于是他还得重新再推。如此循环不息,西西弗斯弄得满头尘土,浑身汗水,但这艰苦的劳动毫无结果。由此,语言中产生了这一"劳而无功"的成语。这个古老的成语远在公元前一世纪古罗马诗人的作品中就已出现。因此,它在欧洲许多语言中都有。

(15) It is useless to flog a dead horse. 是一句谚语,其意一目了然,死马加鞭,徒劳无益。

(16) It is no use pumping a dry well. 是一句谚语,意为枯井汲水白费力,喻徒劳无功。

(17) It is very hard to shave an egg. 是一句谚语,意为给鸡蛋刮胡须是非常难的事,喻枉费心机、白费力气。

(18) The dog barks at the moon in vain. 是一句谚语,意为狗吠月亮,徒劳无用,喻白费力气。

(19) The dog may bark but the anthill will not run away. 是一句谚语,意为狗可能对蚂蚁洞狂吠不止,但蚂蚁还是不会离开,喻徒劳无功,白费力气。

(20) The biting fly gets nothing by alighting on the back of tortoise. 是一句谚语,意为叮人的苍蝇落在龟背上,什么也没得着,喻徒劳无益。

(21) In vain you show light to the blind. 是一句谚语, 意思是为瞎子打灯, 白费力气, 喻徒劳无功。

(22) It is a loss of soap to wash the ass's head. 是一句谚语, 意思是给驴洗头, 白费肥皂, 喻徒劳无功。

(23) A nod is as good as a wink to a blind horse. 是一句谚语, 意思是对瞎马点头和眨眼都一样无用, 喻瞎子点灯——白费蜡。

(24) Water is not carried out in a sieve. 是一句谚语, 意思是用筛子是舀不上来水的, 喻竹篮打水一场空。

(25) Pour water into a sieve 是一句谚语, 意思是往筛子里注水什么也剩不下, 喻竹篮打水一场空。

(26) 成语 run after two hares 的意思是同时追赶两只兔子, 意为做徒劳无益的事。

例: If you run after two hares, you will catch neither.

如果你要同时追赶两只兔子, 你就会一只也捉不到。

(27) 成语 seek a hare in a hen's nest 的意思是鸡窝里找野兔, 喻做枉然之事。

(28) 成语 bang one's head against a brick wall 的意思是把自己的脑袋往砖墙上撞, 喻白费力气、徒劳无益。

例: She hasn't a hope of getting him to change his mind. She's just banging her head against a brick wall.

她根本不能使他回心转意, 她简直是在枉费心机。

(29) 成语 wash an ass's head (或 ears) 洗驴头 (或耳), 喻白费力气。

（30）成语 try to do the impossible 意为想做不可能做到的事，喻徒劳无益。

（31）成语 whistle jigs to a milestone 的意思是向里程碑用口哨吹奏舞曲，喻徒劳无益。

（32）成语 all for naught 的意思是一切都归于零，喻白费力气。

例：They had all their trouble all for naught.
他们的一切辛劳都白费了。

（33）成语 bring to naught 的意思是使什么白费了，喻徒劳无功。

例：You have brought all my labours to naught.
你使我的全部心血付诸东流。

（34）成语 go to naught 的意思是使什么变得毫无价值，喻白费力气。

例：The dog's attempts to climb the tree after the cat went to naught.
那条狗试图跟着猫爬到树上去，结果是白费力气。

（35）成语 go for nothing 的意思是落得一场空，喻劳而无功。

例：When the company was taken over by a powerful trust, a lot of people lost their jobs. Their loyalty and hard work went for nothing.
这家公司被实力雄厚的托拉斯接收之后，许多人都失业了，他们过去的忠诚和辛劳也都付诸东流。

（36）成语 to no purpose 的意思是徒劳无益。

例：I have tried hard for you, but all to no purpose. (Charles Dickens, *Oliver Twist*)

我已为你出了不少力，可是毫无结果。（查尔斯·狄更斯，《雾都孤儿》）

（37）成语 fight with one's own shadow 的意思是同自己的影子奋战，喻徒劳无益。

例：In this argument he fought with his own shadow.

在这场辩论中，他的发言简直是白说一通。

（38）成语 in vain 之意为徒然、白费力气。

例：The enemy attempted to win over Uncle Chen, but it was in vain.

敌人企图把陈大叔拉过去，但是徒劳无效。

（39）成语 limn on water（亦作 limn the water）的意思是在水上绘画，喻徒劳无益。

（40）成语 lash the waves 的意思是用鞭子抽打水的波浪，喻白费力气，徒劳无益。

（41）成语 look for wool on an ass 的意思是在驴身上找羊毛，犹如缘木求鱼，徒劳无益。

（42）Don't look for a ram with five feet. 是英语谚语，意为不要去寻找有五只脚的公羊。喻莫做徒劳无益的事。

（43）He that washes an ass's head, loses both his soap and his labour. 是英语谚语，意思是为驴洗头，白费肥皂和功夫，喻徒劳无益。

(44) It is in vain to cast your net where there is no fish. 是英语谚语，意思是在没有鱼的地方撒网，是白费力气，喻徒劳无益。

(45) It is in vain to lead ox to the water if he is not thirsty. 是英语谚语，意思是如果牛不渴，你把它领到水边也是枉然，喻徒劳无益。

(46) It is lost labour to sow where there is no soil. 是英语谚语，意思是在没有土的地方播种是徒劳的，亦喻劳而无功。

(47) Don't try to sell ice to the Eskimos. 是英语谚语，意思是不要向爱斯基摩人兜售冰块，喻徒劳无益。

(48) 成语 fan the sun with peacock's feather 的意思是用孔雀的羽毛去扇太阳，喻徒劳无益。

(49) Don't try to swim where there is no water. 是英语谚语，意思是不要企图在没有水的地方游泳，喻徒劳无益，异想天开。

(50) Don't try to pull yourself up by your own bootstraps. 是英语谚语，意思是不要企图靠拉自己的拔靴带把自己拉起来，喻徒劳无益。

(51) He wags a wand in the water. 为英语谚语，其意思是在水中挥棒，喻徒劳无益。

汉语成语例解：

(1) "水中捞月"出自两个典故：其一，唐代释道世《法苑珠林·愚戆篇·杂痴部》载："过去世时有城，名波罗奈，国名伽尸。于空闲处有五百猕猴游行林中，到一尼俱律树下，树下有井。井中有月影现时,猕猴主见是月影,语诸伴言:'月今日死,落在井中,当共出之,莫令世间长夜暗冥。'共作计议言云:'何能出?'猕猴主言:'我知出法,我捉树枝,汝捉我尾,展转相连,乃可出之。'时诸猕猴即如主言,展转相捉。小未至水,连猕猴重,树弱枝折,一切猕猴堕井水中。尔时树神便说偈言:'是等駮榛兽,痴众共相随。坐自生苦恼,何能救出月?'"

另据宋代洪迈《容斋随笔·李太白》云:"世俗多言李太白在当涂采石,因醉泛舟于江,见月影,俯而取之,遂溺死,故其地有捉月亭。"

上述两则文献记载,都与成语"水中捞月"的形成有关。"水中捞月"比喻白费力气,徒劳而无功,有时亦作"水中捉月"。

例:是人非人心不别,是幻非幻如何说。虽则似空里拈花,却不是水中捞月。(明·汤显祖,《还魂记·冥誓》)

(2) 成语"海底捞针",亦作"东海捞针""大海捞针"。言要从海里捞取一根针,形容极难办到,或者根本不可能的事。

例:咳,只是命运低微,人情薄恶,觅利如在大海捞针,揽祸似干柴引火。(明·王錂,《春芜记·定计》)

(3) "缘木求鱼"语出《孟子·梁惠王上》:"以若所为,求若所欲,犹缘木而求鱼也。"缘,攀;木,树;求,寻找。爬到树上去找鱼,比喻做事不会有结果,徒劳无益。

例:作者之意,既其如彼;后学之见,又且如耕石种稻,缘木鱼求,期于有获,难矣。(宋·张君房,《云笈七签》卷七〇)

(4) "徒劳无功"源于"劳而无功"一语,这一易词,加强了语意。这一成语指白白花费功夫,却没有一点成绩,用于贬义。

春秋时管仲《管子》卷一《形势》曰:"毋与不可,毋强不能,毋告不知。与不可,强不能,告不知,谓之劳而无功。"这是春秋齐国宰相管仲从政的经验,意思是说不要给予不可以的,不要强人之所不能,不要语人所不知,否则都是白费事而得不到好处。

例:孟良、岳胜,英勇难敌,且部下皆是强徒,俱能厮杀,若与死战,徒劳无功,不如设计胜之。(明·熊大木,《杨家将演义》一五回)

(5)成语"枉费心机"表示白白地浪费心思与精力。枉,白白地,徒然。

例:所云筑室藏书,此亦恐枉费心力。不如且学静坐,闲读旧书,涤去世俗尘垢之心。(宋·朱熹,《答甘道士书》)

28 "do in Rome as the Romans do" 与 "入乡随俗"

英语成语：

1. do in Rome as the Romans do

2. never wear a brown hat in Friesland

3. go native

4. Wherever you may be, do as you see done.

5. Shut your eyes if you are among the blind.

6. If the natives eat rats, eat rats.

7. When one goes to a town inhabited by squint-eyed people, one must squint one's eyes.

8. Where you are, do as you see done.

9. Cover your eyes in the village where everyone else is blind.

10. If you are sitting on his cart you must sing his song.

汉语成语：

1. 入乡随俗   2. 入境问禁

英语成语例解:

(1) 成语 do in Rome as the Romans do 原意为"在罗马,就照罗马人那样做",喻指入乡随俗。此成语来源于圣安布罗斯(St. Ambrose)给圣奥古斯丁(St. Augustine)的忠告。圣奥古斯丁在《致贾纽埃里厄斯》(*Epistle to Januarius*)中写道:"我母亲来到米兰和我住在一起,发现米兰的教徒不像在罗马那样于星期六实行斋戒,她不知怎么办才好。于是我请教了圣安布罗斯。他回答说:'如果你在罗马,就照罗马的风俗生活。'(If you are in Rome, live after the Roman fashion.)"这句成语常被用来作为改变自己习惯的借口。萧伯纳(George Bernard Shaw)1932年7月11日在纽约的一次广播讲话中,用了这一成语的另一种常见形式:"When in Rome do as the Romans do" is the surest road to success. ("入乡随俗"是通往成功的必由之路。)

例:"One must do at Rome as Romans do," Pen said, in a dandified manner, jingling some sovereigns in his waistcoat-pocket. (William Makepeace Thackeray, *The History of Pendennis*)

"在罗马就得像罗马人一样过活,"小潘摆出一副公子哥儿的派头说道,一边把口袋里几个金币弄得叮当直响。(威廉·梅克比斯·萨克雷,《潘登尼斯》)

(2) 成语 never wear a brown hat in Friesland 之意为"身在弗里斯兰,莫戴棕色有边帽",转意为"入乡随俗""入境问禁"。这句成语来源于这样一个故事:弗里斯兰是荷兰北部沿海省份,西起艾瑟尔湖,北临北海。这里的居民基本上仍保持着自己的传统文化,使用自己的语言。据载,他们曾一度习惯于戴毛线编织的无边帽、无边丝织大边帽、金属无边帽和后来的装饰得华丽无比的大软边帽。一次，有个外地的游客来到弗里斯兰，他戴了一顶普通的棕色有边帽。当地人见了这顶与众不同的棕色有边帽，惊异不已，都来围观、嘲笑和戏弄这位怪客，儿童甚至把他当作怪物，向他投掷石块。后来他竟被当地人强行驱逐出境。

（3）成语 go native 指在殖民地的欧洲人为当地人所同化，采取当地人的生活方式，亦即入乡随俗。

例：The shipwrecked seaman, be friended by the friendly islanders, decided to go native,

那海上遇难的水手，被岛上友好的居民当成朋友，于是决定过当地人的生活。

（4）Wherever you may be, do as you see done. 是一句谚语，意为不管你可能在什么地方，都要按照你看到的去做，喻入乡随俗。

（5）Shut your eyes if you are among the blind. 是一句谚语，意为若是与盲人在一起，你得闭上眼睛，喻入乡随俗。

（6）If the natives eat rats, eat rats. 是一句谚语，意思是如果当地人吃老鼠，你就吃老鼠，喻入乡随俗。

（7）When one goes to a town inhabited by squint-eyed people, one must squint one's eyes. 是一句谚语，意思是走进斜眼人之城，就得斜眼看人，喻入乡随俗。

（8）Where you are, do as you see done. 是一句谚语，意思是你在哪里，你就得按照所看到的去做，意即入乡随俗。

(9) Cover your eyes in the village where everyone else is blind. 是英语谚语，意思是在盲人村，蒙上你的眼睛，喻入乡随俗。

(10) If you are sitting on his cart you must sing his song. 是英语谚语，意思是坐在人家的车上就得唱人家的歌，喻入乡随俗。

汉语成语例解：

（1）"入乡随俗"谓到哪个地方就顺从哪个地方的风俗。语出宋代释普济《五灯会元·大宁道宽禅师》："虽然如是，'且道入乡随俗一句作么生道？'良久曰：'西无梵语，此土唐言。'"

（2）"入境问禁"谓到一个新地方，先要问问那里禁止些什么，以免触犯。语出《礼记·曲礼上》："入境而问禁，入国而问俗，入门而问讳。"

29 "an eye for an eye and a tooth for a tooth"
与"以眼还眼,以牙还牙"

英语成语:

1. pay somebody in their own coin
2. give someone a dose of their own medicine
3. Dose a man with his own physique.
4. an eye for an eye and a tooth for a tooth
5. return like for like
6. serve one with the same sauce
7. go toe to toe
8. answer a fool according to his folly
9. cast out devils through the prince of the devils
10. Happy shall he be, that rewardeth thee as thou hast served us.
11. fight fire with fire
12. measure for measure
13. hair of the dog
14. a Roland for an Oliver

15. dirt will remove dirt, reproach will overcome reproach

16. requite like for like

17. evil must be driven out by evil

18. fire drives out fire

19. get some of one's own medicine

20. give someone a taste of their own medicine

21. give someone a pig of their own sow

22. set a thief to catch a thief

23. beat someone at their own weapon

24. devils must be driven out with devils

25. let one devil ding another

26. like cures like

27. like for like

28. a mad parish must have a mad priest

29. one poison drives out another

30. a peg is driven out by a peg, a nail by a nail

汉语成语：

1. 以眼还眼，以牙还牙 2. 针锋相对 3. 以血洗血 4. 睚眦必报 5. 请君入瓮 6. 以毒攻毒

英语成语例解：

（1）成语 pay someone in their own coin 亦作 pay someone

back in the same coin，意思是给某人以同样的回敬，即以其人之道还治其人之身。这句成语最早出现在古罗马喜剧作家普劳图斯（Plautus）的作品中，喻指用对方所使的手段回击对方。

例：I was glad that he had given her a sop of the same sauce, and paid her his debt in her own coin.

很高兴他以同样的方法回敬了她，真可谓以其人之道还治其人之身。

（2）成语 give someone a dose of their own medicine 亦作 treat someone with a dose of their own medicine 以及 get a dose of one's own medicine，原意为"给某人吃他自己配制的药"。这一口头用语始用于 1890 年左右。药一般都不太好吃，因此这一成语除了有"让某人也尝尝苦味"的含义，还有"对他进行报复"的意思。

例：To snub Peter, she only gave him a dose of his own medicine.

她给彼得一个钉子碰，只是以其人之道，还治其人之身罢了。

（3）Dose a man with his own physique. 是一句谚语，即是以其人之道，还治其人之身之意。

（4）成语 an eye for an eye and a tooth for a tooth 意为"以眼还眼，以牙还牙"，即一报还一报之意。语出《圣经·旧约·出埃及记》：But if there is harm, then you shall pay life for life, eye for eye, tooth for tooth, hard for hard, foot for foot, burn for burn, wound for wound, stripe for stripe.（若有伤害，就要以命偿

命,以眼还眼,以牙还牙,以手还手,以脚还脚,以烙还烙,以伤还伤,以打还打。)

这是上帝令摩西订立的对待奴仆的律法,告诫做主人的不可伤害或虐待奴仆或婢女,否则,就应照对等的原则报复,以其人之道还治其人之身。这条成语应用得很广泛,可以用来形容任何针锋相对的事情。

例:Ye have heard that it has been said, an eye for an eye and a tooth for a tooth; but I say unto you, that ye resist no evil, but whosoever shall smite thee on thy right check, turn to him the other also. (Bible, Matthew 5:38-39)

你们听说过以眼还眼,以牙还牙;但是我要告诉你们,不要和邪恶抗争,不管谁打你的右脸颊,你把左脸颊也朝他转过去。(《圣经·新约·马太福音》第5章第38—39节)

(5) 成语 return(或 requite)like for like 的意思是以同样的手段回报,以眼还眼,以牙还牙,以某人之道还治其人之身,有时减缩为 like for like(以命抵命)。

(6) 成语 serve one with the same sauce 亦作 serve the same to someone,意思为用同样的调味汁招待某人,意即以眼还眼,以牙还牙,以其人之道还治其人之身。

例:"I can't possibly take a holiday until I've paid back the money I owe him." — "What nonsense! Look how long he kept you waiting before he paid his debt to you. You take my advice, and serve him with the same sauce!"

"我欠他的钱没有还清,我就不可能休假。"——"多蠢的废话，想想他欠你的钱，让你等了多久他才还？听我的劝告吧，他怎么待你，你也怎么待他。"

（7）成语 go toe to toe 的本意是脚尖对脚尖，意即针锋相对，互不相让。

例：Men in the courtroom can go toe to toe and then go off patting each other on the back.

人们很可能在法庭上针锋相对，退庭后又拍拍打打亲亲热热。

（8）成语 answer a fool according to his folly 的本义是"要照愚昧人的愚妄话回答他"，其意与"以其人之道还治其人之身"相近。典出《圣经·旧约·箴言》：Answer not a fool according to his folly, lest you be like him yourself. Answer a fool according to his folly, lest he be wise in his own eyes. （不要照愚昧人的愚妄话回答他，恐怕你与他一样。要照愚人的愚妄话回答他，免得他自以为有智慧。）

（9）成语 cast out devils through the prince of the devils 语出《圣经·新约·马太福音》第9章第32—34节。耶稣在故乡加利利传道、驱鬼、治病，名声越来越大。一天，有人将一个鬼附着的哑巴带到耶稣面前。耶稣将哑巴身上的鬼赶了出去，那哑巴就开口说起话来。许多人都说这是从未见过的奇迹。法利赛人不相信耶稣是靠上帝的力量驱鬼，而是"靠着鬼王赶鬼"。"靠鬼王赶鬼"一语后来成为表示"以恶除恶""以毒攻毒"的成语。

（10）成语 Happy shall he be, that rewardeth thee as thou hast

served us. 典出《圣经·旧约·诗篇》第 137 篇（巴比伦囚虏的哀歌）："我们曾在巴比伦的河边坐下，一追想锡安就哭了。我们把琴挂在那里的柳树上，因为在那里，掳掠我们的要我们唱歌，抢夺我们的要我们作乐，说：'给我们唱一首锡安歌吧！'我们怎能在外邦唱耶和华的歌呢？耶路撒冷啊，我若忘记你，情愿我的右手忘记技巧；我若不纪念你，若不看耶路撒冷过于我最喜乐的，情愿我的舌头贴于上膛。耶路撒冷遭难的日子，以东人说：'拆毁，拆毁，直拆到根基！'耶和华啊，求你记念这仇。将要被灭的巴比伦城啊，报复你，像你待我们的，那人便为有福。拿你的婴孩摔在磐石上的，那人便为有福。"后来，"报复你，像你待我们的，那人便为有福。"便成为常被引用的一句成语，意为"以眼还眼，以牙还牙""以怨报怨"。

（11）成语 fight fire with fire 最早出现在美国。从前在美国西部，大草原或森林发生大火时，移居者往往把其中一块预先纵火烧光以阻止野火蔓延。人们称此火为 backfire（迎火）。这种以火攻火的做法有一定的危险性，因为迎火很可能失控。Fight fire with fire 一语即源于此，本义是"以火攻火"，喻义则是"以其人之道还治其人之身"。

例：Spain, clearly fearing Ireland's physical strength, have decided to fight fire with fire in this match.

西班牙队显然很害怕爱尔兰队的体力，决定在这场比赛中以其人之道还治其人之身。

（12）成语 measure for measure 出自英国戏剧家威廉·莎士比亚的喜剧剧名，意思是"一报还一报"，该剧上演于 1604 年到1605年。剧中描写维也纳公爵假托出国，留在城内化装私访，发现以"执法如山"著称的安哲鲁是个道貌岸然的伪君子。他及时干预了安哲鲁以崇高的名义干坏事的卑劣行径。此语后来常常被人引用，意同汉语成语"以眼还眼，以牙还牙"。

例：Haste still pays haste, and leisure answers leisure; like doth quit like, and measure still for measure. (William Shakespeare, *Measure for Measure*)

一个死得快，一个也不能容他缓死；用同样的处罚抵消同样的罪，这才叫报应循环！（威廉·莎士比亚，《一报还一报》）

（13）成语 hair of the dog 的字面意思是"狗毛"，其喻义是"以毒攻毒""用不良事物本身的特点来反对不良事物的补救办法"。这句成语源自古代人们相信人被疯狗咬伤以后，可以用该狗尾巴的毛烧成的灰来敷治。

例：At the first signs of an economic hangover from past inflation, the hair of the dog will be urged on the present Administration.

从过去通货膨胀在经济上遗留的种种初步迹象看来，现在的行政当局一定要竭力采取以毒攻毒的补救办法。

（14）成语 a Roland for an Oliver 的意思是"势均力敌""旗鼓相当"。传说罗兰（Roland）和奥利弗（Oliver）是中世纪法兰克王国查理大帝（Emperor Charlemagne）手下两名所向披靡的武士，几乎很难判断出谁更为骁勇。后来他俩在莱茵河的一个小岛上进行了五天五夜的激烈格斗，不分胜负，直至最后两人同归于尽。后来人们便用这条成语表示"旗鼓相当"或

"针锋相对"等意思。

例：We resolved to give him a Roland for his Oliver, if he attacked us.

如果他进攻我们，我们决心给他个以牙还牙。

（15）Dirt will remove dirt, reproach will overcome reproach 是一句谚语，意为用恶语消除恶语，用谴责战胜谴责，喻以毒攻毒，以牙还牙。

（16）Requite like for like 是一句谚语，意为一报还一报，喻以牙还牙，以眼还眼。

（17）Evil must be driven out by evil 是一句谚语，意为必须以邪恶赶走邪恶，喻以恶治恶，以毒攻毒。

（18）Fire drives out fire 是一句谚语，意为用火灭火，喻以毒攻毒。

（19）成语 get some（或 a taste）of one's own medicine 的意思是得到报复性的待遇（或打击），得到报应。

例：For a time the news delighted labour MPs and trade union stalwarts: the City, at last, was getting a taste of its own medicine.

这个消息使工党议员们和工会忠实分子们很高兴：伦敦金融界终于得到了报应。

（20）成语 give someone a taste（或 dose）of their own medicine 意为以其人之道还治其人之身。

例：He came an hour late for their date to give her a taste of her own medicine.

为了以其人之道还治其人之身，他在赴约时，故意迟到了一小时。

（21）成语 give someone a pig of their own sow 意为一报还一报，即以其人之道还治其人之身。

（22）Set a thief to catch a thief 是一句谚语，意为以贼捉贼，转义为以毒攻毒。

例：You have been all your life evading the laws…; do you think this has qualified you peculiarly for being a guardian of the laws? Sir Terence replied: "Yes, sure. Set a thief to catch a thief is no bad maxim."

你的一生都在逃避法网……；你是不是认为你因此就特别有资格成为法律的维护者？特勒恩斯爵回答："不错，俗语说得好：以贼捉贼。"

（23）成语 beat（或 fight challenge）somebody at（或 with）their own weapon（或 weapons）之意为使用某人的手段来对付他本人，以其人之道还治其人之身。

（24）Devils must be driven out with devils 是英语谚语，意思是魔鬼须用魔鬼来驱逐，喻以毒攻毒。

（25）Let one devil ding another 是英语谚语，意思是让一个魔鬼去打另一个魔鬼，喻以恶制恶，以毒攻毒。

（26）Like cures like 是英语谚语，意思是同物相医，喻以毒攻毒。

（27）Like for like 是英语谚语，其意思是以德报德，以怨报怨；以眼还眼，以牙还牙。

（28）A mad parish must have a mad priest 是英语谚语，意

思是疯狂的教民得疯狂的牧师来治理,喻以毒攻毒。

(29) One poison drives out another 是英语谚语,意思是一种毒药能驱走另一种毒药,喻以毒攻毒。

(30) A peg is driven out by a peg, a nail by a nail 是英语谚语,意为一个竹签打出另一个竹签,一个铁钉顶出另一个铁钉,喻针锋相对,或以毒攻毒。

汉语成语例解:

(1)"以眼还眼,以牙还牙"是从西方成语引进的,所以也就无须加以解释和举例了。

(2)"针锋相对"是指针尖对针尖,比喻双方的思考、言行等尖锐对立。

例:我以为应该对于那些批评,完全放开,而自己看书,自己作论,不必和那些批评针锋相对。(鲁迅,《鲁迅书信集·致徐懋庸》)

(3)成语"以血洗血"是说用仇敌的血来偿还血债,指杀敌报仇。语出《旧唐书·源休传》:"可汗使谓休曰:'我国人皆欲杀汝,唯我不然。汝国已杀突董等,吾又杀汝,犹以血洗血,污益甚尔。'",亦作"以血偿血"。

例:倘有敌人,我们早就该抽刃而起,要求"以血偿血"了。(鲁迅,《华盖集·忽然想到(十)》)

(4)成语"睚眦必报"语出《史记·范雎传》:"一饭之德必偿,睚眦之怨必报。"(纵然只给过一顿饭的小恩,也要报答;纵然只瞪过一眼的小怨,也要报复。)这就是两句成语

"一饭必偿"和"睚眦必报"的来源。

例：此狐快一朝之愤，反以陨身，亦足为睚眦必报者戒也。（清·纪昀，《阅微草堂笔记·滦阳续录》）

（5）"请君入瓮"语出《资治通鉴·唐则天皇后天授二年》："俊臣乃索大瓮，火围如兴法，因起谓兴曰：'有内状推兄，请兄入此瓮'"，比喻以其人之道还治其人之身。

例：鲸吞鱼，鱼食虾，蝼蚁之微生可悯。当掬西江之水，为尔湔肠；即烧东壁之床，请君入瓮。（清·蒲松龄，《聊斋志异·席方平》）

（6）"以毒攻毒"的意思是用毒药治疗毒疮、肿瘤等疾病，比喻用对方使用的厉害手段制服对方，也比喻利用恶人来制服恶人。

例：骨咄犀，蛇角也，其性至毒，而能解毒，盖以毒攻毒也。（元·陶宗仪，《南村辍耕录·卷二十九·骨咄犀》）

30 "ants in one's pants" 与 "如坐针毡"

英语成语：

1. ants in one's pants

2. sit upon hot cockles

3. like a cat on hot bricks

4. cat on a hot tin roof

5. fart in a colander

6. like a hen on a hot girdle

7. on pins and needles

8. on the anxious bench

9. on tenterhooks

10. give someone the jumps

11. on nettles

12. in a stew

13. sit on thorns

汉语成语：

1. 如坐针毡   2. 芒刺在背

英语成语例解：

（1）英语成语 ants in one's pants 的出处不大明确，但有一种说法比较合情入理。据说，从前到荒山野岭去探险的人们，为了防备猛兽的袭击，做好了各种各样的准备工作。他们带上防身的武器，以防不测。但是他们都没有料到，猛兽对他们的威胁不大。因为这些野兽对这些不速之客也怀有一种畏惧心理。早就逃之夭夭了。倒是草丛里的小昆虫、蚂蚁却毫无顾忌地钻进了他们的裤脚，在他们的身上乱爬，搞得这些探险家坐立不安，无所适从。逐渐的，ants in one's pants 便成了一条成语。

例：Tom has got a ticket to the football match, but his father ordered him to write the composition at home. He has ants in his pants.

汤姆得到了主场足球赛的票，但他父亲让他在家写作文，他急得像热锅上的蚂蚁，坐立不安。

（2）成语 sit upon hot cockles 之义是"如坐针毡"。Hot cockles 是旧日乡间儿童玩的一种游戏：一个孩子把眼睛蒙起来，其余的人在他的后面打他的屁股，让他猜是谁打的。Sit upon 可以指"等待"或"就座"，所以 sit upon hot cockles 可能指挨打前忐忑不安的焦躁心情,或指被游戏伙伴打过后坐下时屁股的不适之感。

例:He laughs and kicks like Chrysippus when he saw an ass eat figs; and sits upon hot cockles till it be blazed broad.

当他看见一头驴在吃无花果时,他像禁欲主义哲学家克里西波斯一样又笑又踢脚,坐立不安,非惊动大家不可。

(3)成语 like a cat on hot bricks 的字面意思是"像热砖头上的猫",相当于汉语熟语"像热锅上的蚂蚁",表示局促不安或如坐针毡。

例:Suddenly Sugar screwed up his face in pain and grabbing one foot in his hands, hopped around like a cat on hot bricks, "Can't we get a tram, Jack? Me feet is givin' me hell in these new shoes."

忽然间休格痛苦地皱起面孔,两手抓住一只脚,像热砖头上的猫一样,团团转地跳着。"杰克,难道我们不能坐电车吗?我脚上穿的是新鞋,简直要我的命。"

(4)成语 cat on a hot tin roof 的意思与句子结构极近上条 cat on hot bricks,"被晒热了的铁皮房顶上的猫"能是一种什么状态,不言而喻,是局促不安,如坐针毡。美国著名剧作家田纳西·威廉斯(Tennesse Williams)在1955年写的一个剧本就是以 *Cat on a Hot Tin Roof*(《被晒热了的铁皮房顶上的一只猫》)为剧名的。

(5)成语 fart in a colander 的意思是"坐立不安""焦虑不安""心神不定""六神无主"。这一成语的出现可追溯到1980

年前后，指的是滤锅中的气体四处乱窜找出气孔逸出。它的喻义是指人对某一问题应该采取什么解决办法拿不定主意。

（6）成语 like a hen on a hot girdle 的字面意思是"像热锅上的一只母鸡"，喻指"坐立不安""如坐针毡""有如热锅上的蚂蚁"。

例：The Bailie...had all this while shifted from one foot to another with great impatience "like a hot gridle".

郡长……在这段时间一直很不耐烦地交替移动着两脚，"活像热锅上的蚂蚁"。

（7）成语 on pins and needles 的意思是"如坐针毡""坐立不安"，原指麻木的手脚恢复知觉时的一种针刺似的感觉。一个心烦意乱、如坐针毡的人肉体上未必真正会有被针刺痛的感觉，但英语和汉语的成语中都运用这一比喻。

例：He was plainly on pins and needles, did not know whether to take or to refuse a cigar.

他显得十分不安，不知道究竟是接受雪茄好，还是不接受好。

（8）成语 on the anxious bench 原意为"坐在忏悔者的座位上"。出现于19世纪初，与复兴宗教信仰的大会，即忏悔大会的习俗有关。在这种会上，讲台近旁放有一张长凳，称为 anxious seat（忏悔者的座位）。那些信仰动摇、为自己灵魂的归宿感到不安，并急切希望忏悔使自己灵魂得到拯救的人就坐到这种座位上。这样，这一成语的引申意思就用来指"心情焦虑的人"。

例：Women pray and exhort in public, persons under excitement are called forward to the anxious benches to make confession.

妇女们当众祈祷和规劝，那些忐忑不安的人们被唤到前面忏悔者的座位上忏悔。

（9）成语 on tenterhooks 的意思是"提心吊胆""如坐针毡""坐立不安"。Tenter 原指"拉幅机"，即旧时纺织厂用来拉宽织物幅度的框架结构，而 tenterhooks 则指"拉幅钩"或"张布钩"，即拉幅机拉布用的钩子，以后 tenterhook 也一度指肉店挂肉用的钩子。在欧洲中世纪有一种拉肢刑架也叫 tenter，用以拉脱犯人的四肢关节。用钩子把犯人吊在刑架上拉就叫 stretch on the tenterhooks。后来，短语 on tenterhooks 转义表示"提心吊胆""如坐针毡"及"焦虑不安"等义。常与动词 keep 连用，作 keep someone on tenterhooks。此语始见于 16 世纪。

例：After the interview he was on tenterhooks, wondering if he'd got the job.

面试以后他坐立不安，不知道能不能获得那份工作。

（10）成语 give someone the jumps 的意思是使人忐忑不安、使人心惊肉跳。

例：Don't go, or come again soon. This place fairly gives me the jumps.

别走，要不就快点回来。这个地方真叫我心惊肉跳。

（11）成语 on nettles 意为忐忑不安、如坐针毡。

例：Some of them were on nettles till they learned your name

was Dickson.

他们中间有一部分人，在知道你的大名是迪克逊之前，一直坐立不安。

（12）成语 in a stew 的意思是因某事而焦急，转义为坐立不安。

例：I never was more glad to get rid of a book! I've been in a continual stew for fear of being overseen with it!（John Galsworthy, *The Silver Spoon*）

我从来没有对一本书像对本书那样，巴不得赶快把它读完丢开。我一直坐立不安，生怕有人看见我在读它。（约翰·高尔斯华绥，《银匙》）

（13）成语 sit（或 be）on thorns 的意思是坐在荆棘上，喻如坐针毡、坐卧不宁。

例：The reactionaries of various countries are sitting on thorns.

各国反动派惶惶不可终日。

汉语成语例解：

（1）"如坐针毡"，出于《晋书·杜锡传》："太子患之，后置针着锡常所坐处毡中，刺之流血。"成语由此概括而来，常用以形容心神极其不安，坐卧不宁，像针扎屁股一样。

（2）"芒刺在背"出自《汉书·霍光传》："宣帝始立，谒见高庙，大将军霍光从骖乘，上内严惮之，若有芒刺在背。"芒和刺都是指植物果实和枝叶上的细刺儿。此成语形容心情特别不安，或者处境不顺，感到不自在。

31 "kick when he is down" 与 "落井下石"

英语成语：

1. kick when he is down
2. fish in troubled waters
3. Don't pour water on a drowned mouse.
4. Don't pour water on a drowning dog.
5. hit a man when he's down
6. When a man is going down-hill, everyone will give him a push.

汉语成语：

1. 落井下石 2. 趁火打劫 3. 乘人之危

英语成语例解：

（1）成语 kick when he is down 的意思是当他倒下之后还踢

他，喻落井下石。

例：He had been quite ill for some time, and I could not tell him that he had lost his job—that would be kicking a man when he was down.

他已经病了一些日子，我不能把他被解雇的消息告诉他——那等于是给他雪上加霜。

（2）成语 fish in troubled waters 或 fish in the muddy waters，一般辞书认为语源不详，但它可以追溯到19世纪，很可能是从法语 pêcher en eau trouble 迻译而来的。有的辞书则认为它源出《伊索寓言》：一个渔夫在河里捕鱼，他把渔网撒在河道里，然后拿着系了石头的绳子不停地拍打水面，使河水混浊，鱼儿在慌乱中纷纷自投罗网，渔夫因此捕到了许多鱼。附近的人指责他："我们全靠这条河过日子，你把水弄成这样，叫我们上哪儿找清水喝呢？"渔夫却回答说："我如果不这么做，就非饿死不可。"

于是，人们就用 fish in troubled waters 来比喻"试图从混乱中获利""利用别人的灾难为自己谋私利"等义，并衍生出"浑水摸鱼""趁火打劫"两句尽人皆知的成语。

例：Frank is fishing in troubled waters by buying more shares in that firm. They are supposed to be in financial difficulties.

那家公司被认为陷入了财政困难。弗兰克趁火打劫，更多地收购该公司的股票。

（3）Don't pour water on a drowned mouse. 是一句谚语，意思是不要往淹死了的老鼠身上倒水，喻不要落井下石。

（4）Don't pour water on a drowning dog. 是一句谚语。意思是不要往快淹死的狗身上倒水，喻不要落井下石。

（5）成语 hit a man when he's down 的意思是当一个人倒地时还去打，喻落井下石、乘人之危。原指拳击比赛中，一方击倒对方时，须待他爬起来后，方能再次出拳。

例：To demand money from a person who has just lost his job is hitting a man when he's down.

向刚刚失业的人讨债简直是落井下石。

（6）When a man is going down-hill, everyone will give him a push. 是一句谚语，意思是人走下坡路时，人人都会推搡他，喻乘人之危，落井下石。

汉语成语例解：

（1）"落井下石"语见唐代韩愈《柳子厚墓志铭》："一旦临小利害，仅如毛发比，反眼若不相识，落陷阱，不一引手救，反挤之，又下石焉者，皆是也。"成语由此概括而来，比喻乘人之危加以陷害。

（2）"趁火打劫"谓趁别人有危难时去捞好处。

例：这一天见来的很是不少，黄通理更代为踌躇，怕的是越来越多，容不下去，而且难免有趁火打劫，顺手牵羊的事。（清·颐琐，《黄绣球》三回）

（3）"乘人之危"谓趁人危难之际，去要挟侵害。语出南朝宋范晔《后汉书·盖勋传》："谋事杀良，非忠也；乘人之危,非仁也。"

例:父亲向来正直不苟,何况这事颇有乘人之危的嫌疑,当然更加不肯容纳。(冯玉祥,《我的生活》第一章)

32 "between the devil and the deep sea" 与 "进退维谷"

英语成语：

1. between the devil and the deep sea

2. between Scylla and Charybdis

3. on the horns of a dilemma

4. up a gum tree

5. in a box

6. in a scrape

7. in chancery

8. in the cart

9. send to Dulcarnon

10. on thin ice

11. get into a jam

12. get into a mess

13. between the upper and nether millstones

14. stick in the mire

15. wind oneself a bonny pirn
16. be put to the push
17. like a rat in a hole
18. in the shit
19. in the soup
20. pretty state of affairs
21. up against it
22. at the end of one´s rope
23. behind the eight ball
24. shoot one´s bolt

汉语成语：

1. 进退两难 2. 进退维谷 3. 腹背受敌 4. 骑虎难下
5. 四面楚歌

英语成语例解：

（1）成语 between the devil and the deep (blue) sea 一般被认为是航海用语。据1612年关于此语用法的最早记载，语中的 devil 并不是指魔鬼，而是指木船舱面厚板之间的接缝，尤指最靠两舷的长缝。海员在波涛汹涌的海面上踩到这种船缝常有掉到深海里的危险，故称此缝为 devil。由此产生了 between the devil and the deep (blue) sea 一语，后来转义为"进退两难"或

"进退维谷",现一般用于口语。

例:The pirates had to fight and be killed or gave up and be hanged: they were between the devil and the deep blue sea.

海盗们要么战死,要么投降被绞死:他们陷入进退两难的境地。

(2)成语 between Scylla and Charybdis 源出希腊神话。斯库拉(Scylla)和卡律布狄斯(Charybdis)系荷马史诗《奥德赛》中的两个女妖,分别居住于梅西纳(Messina)海峡两岸。Scylla 原是一美貌少女,为海神格劳科斯(Glaucus)所爱,后遭她的情敌女巫喀耳刻(Circe)妒忌,被变成一个面目狰狞的妖怪:十二只脚六个头,每张嘴里长有三排利齿,脖颈长如蛇,鸣声似恶犬。斯库拉住在墨西拿海峡意大利一侧的岩洞中,若有船只靠近,一下可以吞掉六个人,奥德修斯的六个伙伴就是被其吞食的。在对岸靠西西里岛的一株无花果树下伺伏着女妖卡律布狄斯,她每天吞吐海水三次,形成巨大的漩涡,过往船只无不遭殃。根据上述神话传说,后人便将墨西拿海峡上的大岩礁命名为斯库拉,而将其对岸的大漩涡命名为卡律布狄斯。来往船只要想绕过岩礁,就可能陷进漩涡,如要避开漩涡,又有触礁的危险。据此,between Scylla and Charybdis 一语常用来比喻"腹背受敌"或"进退两难"之意,多在文学作品中使用。

例:He would have preferred to be on good terms with both his wife and his mother, but the effort of pleasing one without offending the other was like steering between Scylla and Charybdis.

他本想和妻子、母亲都搞好关系,但要做到取悦一个而又不得罪另一个,叫他实在左右为难。

(3) 成语 on the horns of a dilemma 的意思是"处于左右为难的境地""进退维谷"。Dilemma 一词源于希腊语,由 di-(二)和 lemma(前提,命题)两部分构成,在逻辑学或修辞学上指"二难推理"。在二难推理中要在两个同样的不确定或不能接受的前提之间作出抉择确实令人左右为难,因为两者中的任何一个必然会引向一个不受欢迎的结论。中世纪哲学家用公牛的每一只角来比喻一个前提(lemma),用两只角(horns)来比喻二难推理,因为你不是被这只角挑着就是被那只角挑着,都同样使你不好受。哲学家还造了一个拉丁短语 argumentum cornutum,相当于英语 a horned argument(有角的论证)。On the horns of a dilemma 这一成语即由此而来。

例:He was on the horns of a dilemma, precisely the same dilemma which had always worried him.

他处于进退两难的境地,一直使他担心的那种境地。

(4) 成语 up a gum tree 的意思是"处于困境""进退两难"。Gum tree 是产树胶的树,即"树胶树"。一只被追猎的野兽在拼命逃生时,急忙爬上这样一种能分泌胶黏物质的树,其处境可想而知。负鼠(possum)在猎犬的追逐下常常被逼爬上这种树,只能等着猎人来捕获它。Up a gum tree 按字面意思是"上了树胶树",但它通常只用于喻义,表示"处境困难""进退两难"或"一筹莫展",一般用于口语,并带有幽默情趣。

例:What do we do now? We've missed the last train back.

We're really up a gum tree!

我们错过了末班返程火车,该怎么办呢?真是进退两难!

(5) 成语 in a box 的意思是"处于困境""进退维谷"。通常认为这句成语源于棒球运动,但实际上它早在 18 世纪就出现了,当时还没有棒球运动。曼森·威姆斯(Mason Weems)在《醉鬼的镜子》(*The Drunkard's Looking Glass*)一书中用过这个成语:You are now in a bad box, for if you take no notice of him at all, he is sure to turn mad. (你现在真是左右为难了,因为你要不理睬他,他肯定会发疯的。)

在棒球赛中,跑垒员不得不在两垒之间来回奔跑,避免在守队队员来夹攻之下触杀出局。这时他就"处在困境之中"(in a box 或 in a pickle),这种处境也可称为 hot-box。相关的成语是 in the same box (处在同样的困境中)。亦作 in a bind。

例:Sam is in a bind because if he carries home his aunt's groceries, his teacher will be angry because he is late, and if he doesn't his aunt will complain.

萨姆处于进退两难的困境,这是因为如果他把姨妈的杂货送回家去,他的老师就要对他的迟到发怒,如果他不送回家,姨妈就要抱怨他。

(6) 成语 in a scrape 的意思是"处于困境"。这句成语始用于 18 世纪初,其出处说法不一。有人认为 scrape 是某些季节中鹿在地上挖的洞穴;也有人认为 scrape 是指高尔夫球场上导致球手击球失误的坑洼,苏格兰人称为"野兔穴"。然而,《牛津英语词典》却认为 scrape 是源自动词 scrape (穿过狭窄的通道时擦伤了)。这种解释比较可信,因为擦伤皮肤比受重伤容易治疗得多。因此,scrape 是指"可以摆脱的困境"。此成语亦作 get into scrapes(或 a scrape)。

例:I was generally the leader of the boys and sometimes led them into scrapes.

通常我是那些男孩子们的领导,但有时也会把他们领进困境。

(7)成语 in chancery 原意为"在大法官法院诉讼中"。大法官法院(Court of Chancery)指英国 15 世纪开始建立的隶属大法官的衡平法法院,用以向当事人提供某些不能从普通法院获得的法律救济,现在它已成为高等法院的大法官庭。大法官法院以作风拖拉出名,审理案件旷日持久,使当事人不堪拖累。由此成语 in chancery 引申出"处于进退两难""骑马难下"的含义,并成为一个摔跤用语,指的是头被夹在对手左腋下,难以动弹。它常出现在短语 one's head in chancery 中。

例:He'll not put his head in chancery, that's clear.

很明显,他不会作茧自缚。

(8)成语 in the cart 的意思是"处于困境""身陷绝境"。这是一句英国俚语。原意可能指将死囚置于囚车内,解赴泰伯恩绞刑场(Tyburn)处死;也可能指绞死犯人的一种具体方法:将犯人置于车中,推到绞刑架下,将绞索套上脖子,然后将车子推开,犯人便悬空吊在绞架上。

例:We were simply all over 'em and had 'em in the cart...

我们都围着他们献殷勤,使他们很为难……

(9) 成语 send to Dulcarnon 原意为"把某物挂在角上"。喻指处境困难，进退两难。Dulcarnon 一词来自阿拉伯语，意为"长着两只角的动物"。14 世纪乔叟在《特罗伊拉斯和克莱西德》(*Troilus and Criseyde*) 中使用了这一成语：I am, til God me bettere mynde sende, at Dulcarnon, right at my wittes ende.（直到上帝赐给我智慧，我才完全摆脱茫然不知所措的困境。）此成语亦作 be in Dulcarnon.

(10) 成语 on thin ice 的意思是在薄冰上，喻处境困难。

例①：Without some facts to support you, you're on thin ice with that argument.

如果没有一些事实作为根据，你的论点是站不住脚的。

例②："Your brother? Ah!" It was just as if he had said to himself out loud: "This young woman wants something out of me." Dinny felt suddenly that she was on very thin ice.

"啊！你的哥哥吗？"他那口气好像就在高声地自言自语道："这位年轻的女人一定是想从我身上捞到点什么。"狄妮突然感到自己处境不妙。

(11) 成语 get into a jam 意为陷入困境。

例：If you continue to disregard those "no parking" signs, you'll certainly get into a jam with the police.

要是你还是不管那些"禁止停车"的牌示，随处停车，警察肯定会来找你的麻烦的。

(12) 成语 get into a mess（或 scrape）意为陷入困境，遇到麻烦。

例：He got into a mess driving without a license.

他因无执照开车，碰到了麻烦。

（13）成语 between the upper and nether millstones 的意思是在上下两片磨盘之间，喻陷入困境。

例：He was caught between the upper and nether millstones.

他被上下夹攻，受到无法抗拒的压力。

（14）成语 stick（或 be/find oneself）in the mire 的意思是陷在泥淖里，喻陷入困境。

例：The Foreign Legion will find itself in the mire in Africa.

外籍兵团早晚会发现自己陷在非洲的泥淖里。

（15）成语 wind oneself a bonny pirn 的意思是遇到困难，陷入困境。

（16）成语 be put to the push 的意思是陷入困境。

（17）成语 like a rat in a hole 意为陷入困境，无路可逃。

（18）成语 in the shit 意为陷入困境，一筹莫展。

（19）成语 in the soup 的意思是在汤里，转义为处境困难。

例："No good crying before we're hurt," he said: "the pound's still high. We're good stayers." "In the soup, I'm afraid." (John Galsworthy, *The White Monkey*)

"在我们元气未损之前就哭起来是没有好处的，"他说，"英镑的价值还是高的。我们是很有持久力的。""困难吧，我恐怕。"（约翰·高尔斯华绥，《白猿》）

（20）成语 pretty state of affairs 的意思是处于困境。

例：He hasn't got a penny, his wife's ill. It is a pretty state of affairs.

他身无分文，而老婆又病了，处境十分困难。

（21）成语 up against it 的意思是处境十分困难。

例：We're up against it at the moment. We have a lot of work and half the staff are away ill.

我们现在困难重重，我们有许多事要做，而半数的职员却生病没上班。

（22）成语 at the end of one's rope（或 tether）中的 rope 或 tether 原指系牲畜的绳子。被系在拴绳上的牲畜只能在拴绳长度所及的范围内活动。据此人们以 rope 或 tether 喻指行动、能力、办法等的限度，以 the end of one's rope（或 tether）（拴绳的末端）喻指"山穷水尽""智穷才尽""一筹莫展""黔驴技穷"等义。在成语前通常用介词 at 与之搭配，有时用动词 reach，有时也用 come to 或 get to。这条成语始见于 1686 年一部法国作品的英文译本。

例①：By 6 o'clock after a busy day, I'm at the end of my tether.

忙碌了一天，到六点钟我已是筋疲力尽了。

例②：I'm at the end of my rope! I just can't go on this way!

我已到了山穷水尽的境地！我简直无法再这样坚持下去了！

（23）behind the eight ball 的字面意思是"藏在八号球后面"，喻指一个人处于困难的境地，走投无路，这种说法出自一种台球游戏。这种台球游戏共有 15 个编了号的台球和一个主球。玩球的人用球杆击打主球，用它去撞击其他编号的球，目的是将这些编号的球一个个打进台球桌边上的六个落袋里。玩球的人要设法将其他编号的球都打进袋子,最后打八号球进袋,如果还有别的球没有打进却把八号球不小心打进去了,那他就算输了。所以,要是主球位于八号球的后面,你的处境就不妙了,也就是说局面相当困难。

例①:Mr. Thompson is an older man, and when he lost his job, he found he was behind the eight ball.

汤姆逊已经上了年纪,当他失业时,他发现他已经走投无路了。

例②:Bill can't dance and has no car, so he is behind the eight ball with the girls.

比尔既不会跳舞,也没有汽车,所以在女孩子们面前吃不开。

(24)成语 shoot one's bolt 源自 13 世纪的一句古老的谚语,后来曾出现在约翰·海伍德的《谚语集》和莎士比亚的剧本《亨利五世》中:A fool's bolt is soon shot.(蠢人的箭很快就射完了。)喻蠢人容易智穷力竭。语中的 bolt 是指古代弩弓射出的箭。射出一支箭后,弩弓手需花时间弯弓发射下一支箭。这时,他实际上毫无防御之力。因此弩弓手每发一支箭都须尽力射中,并冒着一箭不中受敌攻击的危险。这一成语虽可用于各种场合,但最常见于体育新闻报道。

例①:The home players had shot their bolt, and in thirty minutes the Birmingham team added two goals.

本地队队员已黔驴技穷,30 分钟内,伯明翰队连进两球。

例②:"Well?" said he. But I had shot my bolt and sat speechless.

"怎么样?"他问道。但我已无话可说,坐着一言不发。

汉语成语例解:

(1)"进退两难"的意思是前进和后退都感到为难,形容处境很困难。

例①:王伦当初苦苦相留,俺却不曾落草,如今脸上又添了金印,却去投奔他时,好没志气。因此踌躇未决,进退两难。(明·施耐庵,《水浒全传》第十七回)

例②:那时安公子正在窗外进退两难。(清·文康,《儿女英雄传》第十四回)

(2)"进退维谷"出自《诗经·大雅·桑柔》:"人亦有言,进退维谷",意为无论是进还是退都陷于困难的境地。

例①:心同穷猿之木,官比沐猴之冠,进退维谷,实可哀怜。(明·袁宏道,《去吴七牍·乞归稿一》)

例②:这时也实在使我有些"进退维谷",因为柏拉图式的恋爱论,我能看,能言,而不能行的。(鲁迅,《我的种痘》)

(3)"腹背受敌"出自北齐·魏收《魏书·崔浩传》:"裕西入函谷,则进退路穷,腹背受敌。"腹,肚子,指前面;背,脊背,指后面。谓前后都受到敌人的攻击,一般用于形容在军事上受困,处于被动不利的局面。

例①:而又知左车奇兵实已断后,欲使吾腹背受敌,始可全胜。(宋·陈亮,《酌古论·韩信》)

例②：如果湘军一定要与直军较量高低，则广东北阀军乘机而入，湖南就会处于腹背受敌的地位。(陶菊隐，《北洋军阀统治时期史话》)

(4)"骑虎难下"出自南朝宋何法盛《晋中兴书》："今日之事，义无旋踵，骑虎之势，可得下乎！"成语由此概括而来，比喻事情虽然中途遇到困难，但形势所逼，无法终止。

例①：这件事都是仲英闹出来的，此刻骑虎难下。(清·吴趼人，《近十年之怪现状》第三回)

例②：本月三日抛出的一百万公债，都成了骑虎难下之势，我们只有硬着头皮干到哪里是哪里了！(茅盾，《子夜》)

(5)"四面楚歌"出自司马迁《史记·项羽本纪》："夜闻汉军四面皆楚歌，项王乃大惊。"原指从四面八方传来楚地的歌声，后常用来比喻处于孤立无援、四面受敌的困难境地。

33 "hammer and tongs" 与 "全力以赴"

英语成语:

1. hammer and tongs

2. flat out

3. go great guns

4. lean over backwards

5. leave no stone unturned

6. like billio

7. tooth and nail

8. bust a gut

9. do up brown

10. full tilt

11. go baldheaded for

12. put in one's best licks

13. put one's shoulder to the wheel

14. by hook or by crook

15. put one's best foot forward

16. move heaven and earth

17. put one's heart into

18. go the whole hog

19. go any length

20. do one's level best

21. for dear life

22. for one's life

23. with might and main

24. strain every nerve

25. all out

26. do one's possible

27. do all in one's power

28. at full steam

29. pull out all the stops

30. at full stretch

31. pull every string

32. with teeth and all

33. to the uttermost of one's power

34. to the hilt

35. bend over backward

36. at full throttle

汉语成语：

1. 全力以赴 2. 不遗余力 3. 千方百计

英语成语例解：

（1）成语 hammer and tongs 表示"竭尽全力""全力以赴"之义。Hammer 和 tongs 都是旧时铁匠所用的主要工具。铁匠用长把钳将烧红的铁块从锻炉中夹出，然后放在铁砧上用锤反复使劲敲打，在震耳的噪声中锤打出各种铁制品。据此，人们就用 hammer and tongs 一语来比喻"拼命""竭尽全力""全力以赴"等义。此成语始见于17世纪，多用于口语，常出现在 fight hammer and tongs, go at something hammer and tongs 等搭配中。

例①：The dogs were fighting each other hammer and tongs.
那些狗在拼命地厮打。

例②：In his usual energetic manner, Jones went after every new prospect hammer and tongs.
琼斯像往常一样劲头十足，对每位可能成为主顾的人都竭尽全力地去争取。

（2）成语 flat out 表示竭尽全力之意。当某人开汽车时使劲地踩油门踏板，一直踩到它与驾驶室的车底板一样平时，他就以他的行动表明了这句成语的含义，即全速、竭尽全力等义。这句成语也是这样开始通用起来的。

例①：The car does 100 mile per hour flat out.
此车全速每小时跑100英里。

例②：They work flat out to check blackmail and embezzlement.
他们竭尽全力地遏制敲诈勒索和挪用公款。

（3）成语 go great guns 的含义是"全力以赴或干得很成功"。Great guns 是重型大炮，它是与步枪、手枪之类的小武器相对而言的。所以这句成语的言外之意是认真和以不同寻常的努力去对待或做某件事,而这样做的结果常常是大获成功。

例:The team was going great guns in the second half of the game.

该队在下半场比赛中全力拼搏,打得很成功。

(4) 成语 lean over backwards 的意思是"竭尽全力"。18 世纪英国实行司法改革之后任命了许多新法官,他们对被告的公民权很敏感,而老法官则拥护王权或向王权倾斜,两者形成了鲜明的对照。人们便说这些新法官在审理案件时"身子向后倾斜"(lean over backwards),意即向被告而不向王权或原告倾斜。为了显示自己是诚实、公正和无私的,他们往往超越常规,使人感到意外,尽管他们和政府有着种种联系。后来 lean over backwards 一语在口语中常被用来表示"竭尽全力"之义。有时亦作 bend(fall)over backwards。

例①:I bend over backwards to help him, but I never get any thanks for it.

我竭尽全力帮他忙,却从未得到任何感谢。

例②:Banks are bending over backwards to help those in difficulties.

银行竭尽全力帮助那些处于困难之中的人。

(5) 成语 leave no stone unturned 是"千方百计""想方设法""竭尽全力"之义。公元前 499 年古希腊各城邦掀起了反抗波斯帝国统治的战争,史称希波战争。公元前 480 年希腊人在萨拉米斯(Salamis)海战大败波斯舰队,翌年又在普拉塔亚

(Plataea)战役中一举击溃波斯的优势兵力。波斯军队被迫撤离希腊后,盛传波斯大将马多尼奥斯(Mardoius)溃逃之前,曾在普拉塔亚丢下了大批珍宝。底比斯(Thebes)大将波利克拉提斯(Polycrates)久觅无着,便前往特尔斐(Delphi)阿波罗神殿询求神谕。神谕指示他把普拉塔亚战场的石头一块不漏地翻转过来。他遵此行事,终于在那位波斯败将的帐篷底下掘出了埋藏的财宝。英语成语 leave no stone unturned 便是从这一神谕直译过来的。1550年这一成语始见于英国文学作品中,但其原始词义已全然丧失,仅用喻义,表示"千方百计""想方设法""竭尽全力"。由于此成语用得非常广泛,成为人们熟知的一句成语,所以后来当美国幽默诗人纳什(Ogden Nash, 1902—1971)写道:When I throw rocks at seabirds, I leave no tern unstoned. (我向海鸟扔石块,把所有海鸟无一遗漏地都砸死了。)人们很容易就理解了基于这句成语创造出的 leave no tern unstoned 一语的双关含义。

例①:He left no stone unturned in his search for his natural mother.

为了寻找生身母亲,他想尽了办法。

例②:Both organizations have vowed to leave no stone unturned in the search for peace.

两个组织都发誓要不遗余力地寻求和平。

(6)成语 like billio(或 billyo)之义为"竭尽全力","猛烈地"。关于此语的来源说法有三。其一,源自17世纪一位名叫约瑟夫·比利奥(Joseph Billio)的清教主义牧师的大名。他因脱离英国国教圣公会而被解除教区长的职务。1682 年他在埃塞克斯郡（Essex）马尔登（Maldon）创立独立教会（the Independent Congregation）。有人认为，此说不太可能。首先，人们通常不会将这种短语和一个清教主义牧师相联系，不论他是多么精力充沛。其次，时间不一致。此语似乎最早出现于 19 世纪。其二，源自意大利民族解放运动领袖加里波第（Garibaldi, 1807—1882）手下一位名叫尼诺·比利奥（Nino Biglio）的陆军中尉。他带兵去打仗时常爱吹嘘说："Follow me, and fight like Biglio!"（跟着我，像 Biglio 一样进行搏斗！）其三，源自发明铁路机车的 19 世纪英国发明家斯蒂芬森（George Stephenson, 1781—1848）命名为普芬比利蒸汽火车（Puffing Billy Railway）的机车。Like billio（或 billyo）一语已普遍用于英语口语中，表示"竭尽全力"或"猛烈地"。

例①：They're fighting like billyo.
他们在拼命地搏斗。

例②：The home-made jam and cakes and sweets sell like billyo.
家庭做的果酱、糕饼和糖果销路很好。

（7）成语 tooth and nail 的意思是"竭尽全力""拼命地""猛烈地"，原作 with tooth and nail。动物在搏斗时，总是用牙咬和用爪抓。人，特别是女人，在拼命时也总是牙齿和指甲并用。这一形象的短语常用于喻义，表示"拼命地""竭尽全力"，常出现在 fight tooth and nail, go to it tooth and nail 等搭配之中。这句成语始见于 16 世纪初。

例①：Having been struck twice by the man, the boy went for him tooth and nail and bit and scratched with all his might.

男孩被那男人打了两下，就猛力地向他扑去，拼命地又咬又抓。

例②：Instantly the fiddler grins and goes at it tooth and nail. (Charles Dickens, *American Notes*)

那提琴手立即笑了一下，使劲地拉起琴来。（查尔斯·狄更斯，《美国游记》）

(8) 成语 bust a gut 原意为"用力过度，引起小肠串气"，喻指人在体力上或脑力上尽其所能或过度劳累。

例：She has been staying up at nights busting a gut over the work she has to do.

她连续几晚熬夜，竭尽全力完成她应做的工作。

(9) 成语 do up brown 的意思是"竭尽全力""尽力而为"。据《牛津英语词典》载，do brown 原来可能是一个烤肉用语，即把肉烤透呈棕色。Do up brown 即由 do brown 演化而来，意即"竭尽全力""把事情做得尽善尽美"。

例：We are all of us done so uncommonly brown!

我们每个人都尽了全力。

(10) 成语 full tilt 的意思是"全速地""全力地""拼命地"。其中 tilt 指骑马持矛冲刺。据说此成语来源于古代骑士比武时跃马持矛全速向对手冲去。它的使用可以追溯到 1600 年左右，曾出现在格雷顿（Frederic E. Gretton）所著《半个世纪的追忆》(*Memory's Harkback through Half-A-Century*, 1808 to 1858)

一书中：The Earl rode full tilt at him as though he would have unhorsed him.（伯爵跃马持矛全速向他冲去，似乎要刺得他翻身落马。）

例：The animal had somehow managed to get out after all and was pursuing him full tilt down the pathway.

不知怎么的，那动物终究跑了出来，正沿着小径拼命地追赶着。

（11）成语 go baldheaded for 的意思是"全力以赴"。此语源出1760年瓦尔堡战役（Battle of Warburg）中的一段逸事。当时克兰比勋爵（Lord Granby）率领着英国王家禁卫军（the British Life Guards）参战，当他快马加鞭地驰入战场时，他的帽子和假发全掉了下来，露出了秃头。亦作 go for（或 into）something bald-headed。

例：It ain't my principles nor men my prudent course is steadied, I scent which pays the best and then go into it bald-headed.

决定我办事方针的，既非道义，亦非人事，我觉察出什么事情最有利，就不顾一切地追求它。

（12）成语 put in one's best licks 的意思是"尽最大努力""竭尽全力""拼命地"。在美国英语中，lick 是"力量或干劲的发挥"，以后又扩展为"努力的机会"。在棒球赛中，last licks 是指在最后一局（即第九局）下半场中进攻队取胜的机会。所以 put in one's best licks 是指"努力取胜的机会"。此语自18世纪沿用至今，其变体有 put in big licks 和 put in solid licks。

例：I saw coming my grey mule, putting in her best licks, and a few yards behind her was a grizzly.

我看见我的那只灰骡子拼命地向我跑来，原来在她后面几码远的地方有一只灰熊。

（13）成语 put one's shoulder to the wheel 的意思是"竭尽全力"。这句成语可能出自一则寓言故事：一位车夫在车轮深陷泥中动弹不得时，请求大力海格立斯（Hercules）帮忙。赫拉克勒斯来到现场，责怪车夫自己不肯花力气而求助神力。接着海格立斯"用肩膀将车子推出了泥潭"。

例①：The effort to get a new high school succeeded because everyone put his shoulder to the wheel.

由于每个人都出了大力气，一所新中学办成了。

例②：This has been made a test case, all who would prosper in the future must put a shoulder to the wheel.

这已成为一种通例，凡是想有所成就的人都必须竭尽全力工作。

（14）成语 by hook or by crook 的意思是"用种种方法""千方百计地""想方设法""竭尽全力地"，为最古老的英语成语之一。1380 年在英格兰神学家、《圣经》的英译者威克里夫（John Wycliffe，1330—1384）的著作中即已使用。关于其由来，说法不下十种，被广为接受的有以下两种。

其一，在中世纪的英国封建社会，森林归国王或领主所有，禁止平民随意进去。农民需要烧柴，只许在林中拾取地上的枯枝，或砍折生于低处的树枝。Hook 指"弯刀""镰刀"，crook 指"牧羊人用的曲柄杖"，by hook or by crook 一语照字面含义讲即"用弯刀或用曲柄杖"。凡用弯刀或用曲柄杖所能及的树枝皆允许砍折。此语后转义为"用种种方法""千方百计"。需要指出的是，by hook 往往暗含"用正当手段"，而 by crook 则往往暗含"用不正当手段"之义。

其二，1100 年，一位名叫普尔基斯（Purkiss）的烧炭者发现英格兰国王鲁弗斯（William Rufus）被一个弓箭手射死在汉普郡新林区（Hampshire's New Forest）。珀基斯用大车将国王的尸体运送到温切斯特（Winchester）。作为奖赏，他被允许在那个林区内采集他炭炉所需的木材，只要他砍折的是用弯刀或曲杖够得到的。900 多年过去了，珀基斯家族的人仍然居住在新林区。由于当时的那个保护法，如今那里有英格兰最大的中世纪森林。

例①：Ed determined to get an A on the exam by hook or by crook.

埃德决心无论如何要在这次考试中拿个优。

例②：I'll find out where she lives by hook or by crook.

我会想方设法打听到她的住处。

（15）成语 put one's best foot forward 的意思是"尽快""全力以赴""尽量给人以好的印象"。语中的 best foot 指"右脚"（right foot）。自古以来人们不管动身去旅行还是跨进门槛往往先迈右脚，因为先迈左脚被认为是不吉利的。据说在古罗马时，官邸门口经常站有一个小孩，提醒进门的人先迈右脚。直到今天，许多英国新娘在进教堂时仍坚持这一传统习俗。古希腊哲学家和数学家毕达哥拉斯（Pythagoras，约公元前580—约前500）甚至认为每天早穿鞋也应该先穿右脚的鞋。如今虽然一般人已不再有这种迷信，但 put one's best foot forward 一语却保留了下来。它已丧失"先迈右脚"这一本义，现表示"尽快""全力以赴""尽量给人以好的印象"等义，通常用于口语。亦作 put one's best leg forward。

例①：Don't worry too much about the examination. Just put your best foot forward and do what you can!

不要为考试过于担忧。只要全力以赴，尽力而为就行了。

例②：Right, if we're going to get this job done, we'll have to put our best foot forward.

说得对，如果我们打算完成这项工作，我就得全力以赴。

(16) 成语 move heaven and earth 的意思是"想尽一切办法""竭尽全力""千方百计"。

例①：I am already in debt again, and moving heaven and earth to save myself from exposure and destruction.

我又负了很多的债，正在想方设法不露马脚，免遭毁灭。

例②：I moved heaven and earth to get him out of town and did not succeed。

我千方百计使他离开市镇，可是没有成功。

(17) 成语 put one's (whole) heart (and soul) into 的意思把全部心思放进什么里，喻全力以赴。

例①：He puts his heart into all he does.

他不管做什么事，都是全力以赴。

例②：If each one of us puts his whole heart and soul into this next content, nothing can stop us.

要是我们每一个人在下次比赛都全力以赴，就没有什么东西能够阻挡我们获胜。

(18) 成语 go the whole hog（亦作 go whole hog）意为干到底，全力以赴。

例①：Once he had made up his mind, he went the whole hog.

他一旦下定决心就干到底。

例②：We went the whole hog and took a cruise around the world.

我们一不做二不休，干脆做了一次环球航行。

(19) 成语 go (to) any length（或 lengths）（亦作 go all lengths; go to all lengths; go to great lengths 或 go the whole lengths）之意为竭尽全力，全力以赴。

例①：I was conscious that a moment's mutiny had already rendered me liable to strange penalties, and like any other rebel slave, I felt resolved, in my desperation, to go all lengths. (Charlotte Brontë, *Jane Eyre*)

我明白，小小的反抗，已使我受到意想不到的惩罚。于是，像其他反叛的奴隶一样，在绝望中我决心反抗到底。（夏洛蒂·勃朗特，《简·爱》）

例②：If your father hadn't been against me they wouldn't

have gone to any such length in making me the victim. (Theodore Dreiser, *The Financier*)

要不是你父亲反对我的话,他们就不敢这样极力地陷害我了。(西奥多·德莱塞,《金融家》)

(20) 成语 do one's level best 意为尽最大的努力,全力以赴。

例:"It's silly of you to worry about this exam. After all, you've got three months still before it comes off, and if you make up your mind to do your level best during that time, you'll find that you'll pass easily."

"你为这场考试烦恼,真是可笑。现在离考试毕竟还有三个月,在这期间要是你下决心全力以赴的话,就会轻而易举地考试及格。"

(21) 成语 for dear life 之意为拼命地、全力以赴地。

例①:He fights for dear life.

他作殊死搏斗。

例②:Jack rode fast for dear life.

杰克拼命地骑马奔跑。

(22) 成语 for one's life 的意思也是拼命地、全力以赴地。

例:Mr. Swiveller and Sampson Brass rushed out into the street—darting along in the middle of the road, and dashing aside all obstructions, as though they were running for their lives. (Charles Dickens, *Old Curiosity Shop*)

斯威夫勒先生和桑普森·布拉斯冲到大街上,在马路中间

狂奔,突破一切障碍,好像逃命似的奔跑。(查尔斯·狄更斯,《老古玩店》)

(23) 成语 with(或 by)might and main 意为全力以赴、竭尽全力。

例①: Such people there are living and flourishing in the world—faithless, hopeless, charityless; let us have at them, dear friends, with might and main. (William Makepeace Thackeray, *Vanity Fair*)

这等人无情无义,背弃了信仰和希望,在这个世界上却一帆风顺,亲爱的朋友们,咱们应该全力和他们斗争。(威廉·梅克比斯·萨克雷,《名利场》)

例②: In the smaller public-houses fiddles with all their might and main were squeaking out the tune to staggering feet. (Charles Dickens, *The Old Curiosity Shop*)

在较小的酒店里,小提琴配合着人们的蹒跚的脚步,拼命地拉吱吱刺耳的调子。(查尔斯·狄更斯,《老古玩店》)

(24) 成语 strain every nerve 意为全力以赴、竭尽全力。

例①: We strained every nerve to make the performance a success.

我们竭尽全力使演出成功。

例②: It was only by straining every nerve that the sailors were able to keep the ship off the rocks.

全靠船员们拼命努力,船只才免于触礁。

(25) 成语 all out 意为竭尽全力、开足马力。

例：My car does 80 miles an hour when it's going all out.

我的汽车全速行驶时每小时能跑 80 英里。

（26）成语 do one's possible 的意思是竭尽所能、全力以赴。来自法语 faire son possible。

例：I had done my possible to gratify you.

我已经尽了最大的努力来满足你。

（27）成语 do all in one's power 的意思是尽力、竭尽全力、全力以赴。

例：He'll do all in his power to help you.

他将尽一切力量帮助你。

（28）成语 at full steam 原义为开足马力，转义为全力以赴。

例：The ship was sailing for Shanghai at her full steam.

那条轮船开足马力驶向上海。

（29）成语 pull out all the stops（亦作 pull all the stops out）的原义是拉出风琴所有的音栓，转义为全力以赴、千方百计。

例①：He pulled all the stops out to complete the work in time.

他竭尽全力按时完成了工作。

例②：The government pulled out all the stops to get the Industrial Relation Bill through Parliament in a single session.

政府想方设法使议会在一次会议中就通过《工业关系法案》。

（30）成语 at full stretch 的意思是极其紧张、全力以赴。

例①：The factory is working at full stretch.

整个工厂都在紧张地生产。

例②: They had to work at full stretch in order to get the job finished before the end of the week.

我们为了要在周末以前完成工作,不得不全力以赴。

(31) 成语 pull every string 的意思是拉紧每一根绳。转义为想尽办法、千方百计、全力以赴。

例: He pulls every string to attain the end.

他想尽一切办法以达到目的。

(32) 成语 with teeth and all 意为全力以赴、竭尽全力。

(33) 成语 to the uttermost of one's power 之意为不遗余力、竭尽全力、全力以赴。

(34) 成语 to the hilt 之意为毫无保留,全力以赴。

例: If you like a candidate, back him to the hilt.

要是你喜欢一个候选人,你就应该全力支持他。

(35) 成语 bend over backward 的意思是竭尽全力。

例: The government is bending over backward to attract foreign investors.

政府正想办法吸引外国投资者。

(36) 成语 at full throttle 意为全力进行,全力以赴。

例: If Croatia enters the war at full throttle, the Balkan equation will change entirely.

如果克罗地亚全力参战,巴尔干的均势将完全改观。

汉语成语例解:

(1) "全力以赴" 意为把全部力量或精力投进去。

例：①他们缺乏一种主动的积极的高兴的欢迎的全力以赴的精神。(毛泽东,《中国农村的社会主义高潮》序言)

(2) 成语"不遗余力"之意为毫无保留地用出全部力量。语出《战国策》："王曰：秦之攻我也，不遗余力矣，必以倦而归也。"

例：二子能养矣，孺人犹自劳苦，不遗余力。(明·归有光,《沈引仁妻周氏墓志铭》)

(3) 成语"千方百计"意为想尽一切办法。语出宋代朱熹《朱子语类·论语·一七》："譬如捉贼相似，须是著起气力精神，千方百计去赶捉他。"

例①：那些庸医千方百计，骗了好些银两，可不是他造化。(明·冯梦龙,《醒世恒言》卷二八)

例②：我好容易千方百计的凑了这些银子来践你的前约。(清·刘鹗,《老残游记续集》第四回)

34 "at sixes and sevens" 与 "乱七八糟"

英语成语：

1. at sixes and sevens
2. kettle of fish
3. make a hash of
4. make hay of
5. in a mess
6. make a mess of
7. play the mischief with
8. make a muck of something
9. make a muddle of
10. make a mull of something
11. make a mush of
12. in a pickle

汉语成语：

1. 一塌糊涂　2. 乱七八糟　3. 七零八落　4. 七颠八倒
5. 杂乱无章

英语成语例解：

（1）成语 at sixes and sevens 在 14 世纪时便已出现。关于它的起源有很多说法，但其中最有可能的，是一种来自掷骰子的赌博游戏 hazard。此种游戏的规则，基本上是将赌本压在骰子最有可能出现的点数上，但另外还有许多混乱多变且复杂的规则，因此想要获胜相当困难。

而用数字中的六和七来表达，被认为是起源于法语的 to set on cinque and sice。Cinque 和 sice 分别是指数字五和六，是两个在此骰子游戏中被认为风险最大的数字，选择的人还会被认为相当粗心，不依照几率估算可能的点数。而到了后来，数字五演变成七，是因为一个骰子上不可能有七点，借以讽刺不在乎输赢或规则，随便压号码的人。现代英语中，at sixes and sevens 用以表示乱七八糟，但并非正式用语。

例：We had a party last night to celebrate Judy's birthday and the house was at sixes and sevens this morning.

我们昨晚聚会庆祝茱蒂的生日，今天早晨房间里乱七八糟的。

（2）成语 kettle of fish 的意思是"乱七八糟""一塌糊涂"，为英国人口头用语，原指在河边野餐时所煮的"一锅鱼"，后来引申为"野餐"本身。纽特（Thomas Newte）在《1785年英格兰与苏格兰游记》（*A Tour in England and Scotland in* 1785）中有如下描述：在特威德河（Tweed River）一带的绅士常举行 Fete Champetre（野外欢宴）来款待邻居和朋友。他们支起帐篷，生起篝火，将鲜活的大马哈鱼丢进沸腾的锅中煮，称这种野餐为 a kettle of fish。也有人认为 kettle 是 kiddle（沉在河中捕鱼的网）的讹用，但"一网鱼"似乎并不能解释这成语的比喻用法。Fine, pretty, nice, rare 等形容词常和 kettle of fish 连用。

例：When she had gone Soames reached for the letter. "A pretty kettle of fish," he muttered. "Where it'll end, I can't tell" (John Galsworthy, *The White Monkey*)

等她走了之后，索米斯伸手拿这封信。"这真是糟糕透顶！"他咕噜道，"将来结局如何，连我也不知道"。（约翰·高尔斯华绥，《白猿》）

（3）成语 make a hash of 原指将肉食和蔬菜切碎后烧煮在一起的乱炖杂烩，比喻任何不协调的混合物，自18世纪初，此成语喻指把事情搞得乱七八糟、一塌糊涂。

例：He spent some time in the army but made a hash of his chances of becoming an officer by arguing with the captain.

他在军队里服役过一段时间，由于和上尉发生争执，把提升为军官的机会给葬送了。

（4）成语 make hay of 的意思是"将事情搞乱""使之乱七

八糟",农民将割好的青草,摊在地上晒干,为了晒透还需要用叉子翻动,翻抖的结果是草变得乱蓬蓬的,这就是这句成语的由来,现在多用于表示"零乱不堪""乱七八糟"。

例:When they woke up, the children began to play roughly; they made hay of the bed-clothes.

孩子们醒来后在床上胡闹,把被褥搞得乱七八糟。

(5) 成语 in a mess 意为零乱、乱七八糟。

例:The children left the whole room in a mess.

孩子们把整个房间弄得乱七八糟。

(6) 成语 make a mess of 的意思是把什么弄得一团糟,把什么搞得一塌糊涂。

例:I must say you've, certainly, made a mess of things.

老实说,你的确把事情弄得一塌糊涂。

(7) 成语 play the mischief with 的意思是把什么弄得乱七八糟。

例:The wind has played the mischief with my papers.

风把我的文件吹得乱七八糟。

(8) 成语 make a muck of something 的意思是把某事弄得一团糟。

例:I've made a muck of it. What the hell can I do now?

我已经把事情弄得一塌糊涂,现在该怎么办?

(9) 成语 make a muddle of 的意思是事情弄得一团糟。

例:Don't make a muddle of the whole business.

不要把事情弄得一塌糊涂。

(10) 成语 make a mull of something 的意思是把事情弄糟了。

例:"I always make a mull of it." he said to himself when the girls went up to get their hats.

"我总是把事情搞糟。"当姑娘们上楼去取帽子时,他对自己说。

(11) 成语 make a mush of 的意思是把什么弄得一团糟,搞得一塌糊涂。

例:The storm made a mush of our seed-plots.

暴风雨把我们的苗床弄得一塌糊涂。

(12) 成语 in a (sad, sorry 等) pickle 的意思是乱七八糟、十分混乱。

例:The house was in such a pickle that one could scarcely believe anyone was living in it.

屋里乱糟糟的,简直令人难以相信有人住在里面。

汉语成语例解:

(1) "一塌糊涂"用来形容乱到极点、糟到极点。

例:"与其顾惜场面,硬充好汉,到临了弄的一塌糊涂,还不如一老一实,揭破真情,自寻生路。(清·曾朴,《孽海花》三〇回)

(2) "乱七八糟"形容混乱之极,毫无条理、秩序。

例:你看屋里的图书字画,家具器皿,布置得清雅整洁,不像公坊以前乱七八糟的样子,这是霞郎的成绩。(清·曾朴,

《孽海花》第五回)

(3)"七零八落"形容零散琐碎,很不完整。语出宋代惟白《建中靖国续灯录》卷六:"无味之谈,七零八落。"

例:因为清醒一点的青年画家,已经被人弄得七零八落,有的是在做苦工,有的是走开了,所以抓不着一点线索。

(4)"七颠八倒"形容异常纷乱。语出宋代释道原《景德传灯录》卷二十一:"问:'如何是佛法大意?'师曰:'七颠八倒。'"

例:如今不幸他殁了,已得三年,家里的事,都七颠八倒。(元·施耐庵,《水浒全传》第二十四回)

(5)"杂乱无章"意为庞杂零乱,没有条理,语出唐代韩愈《送孟东野序》:"其为言也,乱杂而无章。"

例:救火车开不进狭窄的弄,水桶拿不出许多,往来取水只是杂乱无章的一阵胡闹。(叶圣陶,《一桶水》)

35 "all one's geese are swans" 与 "敝帚千金"

英语成语：

1. all one's geese are swans
2. Everybody thinks of his copper as gold.
3. Each bird loves to hear himself sing.
4. Every man thinks his own things best.
5. Every mother thinks her child beautiful.
6. Every peddler praises his own needles.
7. Every peddler thinks well of his pack.
8. Every cook praises his own broth.
9. Every potter praises his own pot.
10. Every salesman boasts of his own wares.
11. There is nothing like leather.

汉语成语：

1. 敝帚千金

英语成语例解：

（1）All one's geese are swans 原意为"自己的鹅都是天鹅"。这是一条谚语，鹅并不漂亮，与珍稀高贵的天鹅无法相比。所以，把自己的鹅都看成是天鹅，是美化了实际，歪曲了事实，大有中国成语"敝帚千金"之意。这条谚语可以追溯到17世纪初，如今已少用。1621年，英国传教士、哲学家兼作家罗伯特·伯顿（Robert Burton）在他所著的《忧郁的解剖》（*The Anatomy of Menlancholy*）一书中最先使用了这一成语。

例："Yes," said Soames, "I daresay; you think all your geese are swans—never met a painter who didn't."(John Galsworthy, *Swan Song*)

"是的，"索米斯说，"也许是吧；你一定以为你的鹅群都是天鹅吧？——从来没遇到过一个画家不是这样想的。"（约翰·高尔斯华绥，《天鹅之歌》）

（2）Everybody thinks of his copper as gold. 是一句谚语，意为人人都把自己的铜看作金子，喻敝帚千金。

（3）Each bird loves to hear himself sing. 是一句谚语，意思是每只鸟儿都爱听自己唱，喻人皆欣赏自己，有敝帚自珍之意。

（4）Every man thinks his own things best. 是一句谚语，意思是人都认为自己的东西最好，喻敝帚自珍。

（5）Every mother thinks her child beautiful. 是一句谚语，意思是做娘的总觉得自己的孩子漂亮，喻敝帚千金。

（6）Every peddler praises his own needles. 是一句谚语，意为卖针的都夸自己的针好，喻王婆卖瓜，自卖自夸。

(7) Every pedder thinks well of his pack. 是一句谚语，意为商人都认为自己的货好，亦是王婆卖瓜，自卖自夸之意。

(8) Every cook praises his own broth. 是一句谚语，意思是每个厨子都夸自己做的汤，喻王婆卖瓜，自卖自夸。

(9) Every potter praises his own pot. 是一句谚语，意思是每个陶工都夸自己做的罐子好，喻王婆卖瓜，自卖自夸。

(10) Every salesman boasts of his own wares. 是一句谚语，意思是商人都吹嘘自己的商品好，喻王婆卖瓜，自卖自夸。

(11) There is nothing like leather. 是一句谚语，意思是世上唯有皮革好，源出一古老传说：有一城池被围，于是大家开会商讨对策，泥瓦匠提议修筑坚固的城墙；造船工人建议造"木墙"（战船）。等大家都说完了以后，制革匠站起来说："There's nothing like leather."（什么东西也没有皮革牢靠。）喻敝帚自珍，王婆卖瓜，自卖自夸。

汉语成语例解：

(1)"敝帚千金"的意思是家里有一把破扫帚，看作价值千金。比喻自己的东西即使不好，也看得非常珍贵，有时也比喻有缺点看不见，反把缺点当长处。

东汉官修本朝纪传体史书《东观汉记·光武帝纪》载，汉光武帝曾在一次诏令中说："城降，孩儿老母口万数，一旦放火纵兵，可谓鼻酸。家有敝帚，享之千金。"意思是说，攻下一个城池的时候，城里小的老的上万人口，若是放纵部队，任其烧杀抢劫，那真叫伤心难忍。须知老百姓家里，哪怕一把破扫帚，都当作价值千金的宝贝一般爱惜的啊！

此成语亦作"敝帚自珍"，出自南宋诗人陆游诗句："遗簪见取终安用，敝帚虽微亦自珍。"

36 "kill two birds with one stone" 与 "一箭双雕"

英语成语：

1. kill two birds with one stone
2. catch two pigeons with one bean
3. He fells two dogs with one stone.
4. Stop two gaps with one bush.
5. Kill two flies with one flap.
6. One journey and two errands.

汉语成语：

一举两得

英语成语例解：

（1）成语 kill two birds with one stone （一石二鸟）1656 年

曾被英国哲学家托马斯·霍布斯（Thomas Hobbes，1588—1679）当作比喻使用，但第一次是1611年在科特格雷夫（R. Cotgrave）所编的《英法词典》中出现的，法语译为"d'une Pierre faire deux coups"。

例：My sister lives just outside London. When I visited my brother in London, I decided to kill two birds with one stone and go see her as well.

我姐姐恰好住在伦敦城外，当我拜访住在伦敦的哥哥时，我决定一举两得，同时也去看看她。

（2）成语 catch two pigeons with one bean 的意思是用一粒豆子抓获两只鸽子，其字面含义与引申意义都是一清二楚的，与汉语成语"一箭双雕"和"一举两得"几乎完全相同。

例：If you walk to work, you will get some exercise as well as saving money, so you'll be catching two pigeons with one bean.

如果你步行上班，既省钱又能锻炼身体，这样你将一举两得。

（3）He fells two dogs with one stone. 是英语谚语，意思是一块石头打倒两条狗，喻一举两得。

（4）Stop two gaps with one bush. 是英语谚语，意思是用一根灌木填塞两个墙缝，喻一举两得。

（5）Kill two flies with one flap. 是英语谚语，意思是一拍打死两只苍蝇，喻一举两得。

（6）One journey and two errands 是英语谚语，意为走一趟办好两件事，喻一举两得。

汉语成语例解：

"一举两得"比喻做一件事而达到两方面的目的或同时得到两方面的好处。

例①：壮年一箭落双雕，野饷如今撷药庙。（宋·陆游《遣兴》诗）

例②：胡统领上船之后，要茶要水，全是龙珠一人承值；龙珠偶然有事，便是凤珠替代。因为凤珠也是十六岁的人了，胡统领早存了个得陇望蜀的心思，想慢慢施展他一箭双雕的手段（清·李伯元《官场现形记》一二回）

（2）成语"一举两得"的典故出自《史记·张仪列传》，形容做一件事，同时得到两方面的好处。

例①：吾得临淄，即西安孤，必覆之矣。所谓一举两得者也。(《东观汉记·耿弇传》)

例②：伯牙讨这个差使，一来，是个大才，不辱君命，二来，就便省视乡里，一举两得。（明·冯梦龙，《警世通言》卷一)

37 "Alexander and the Robber" 与 "一丘之貉"

英语成语:

1. Alexander and the Robber
2. Tweedledum and Tweedledee
3. tarred with the same brush
4. birds of a feather
5. cut from the same cloth

汉语成语:

1. 一丘之貉 2. 一路货色

英语成语例解:

（1）英语成语 Alexander and the Robber（一丘之貉）出自

一个民间传说。海盗狄奥米达斯被捕获后押去见马其顿国王亚历山大。国王问他:"你为什么胆敢骚扰海面,威胁船只,伤害百姓呢?"海盗冷冷地答道:"这怎么说呢?我只是一艘单桅杆帆船的船主,被你们斥为强盗。可你们这些利用庞大舰队四处掠夺的人,却反而被尊为国王。"亚历山大感到其言有理,无话可对,就下令放了他。由这个传说产生了这句成语,比喻都不是好东西。

(2) 英语成语 Tweedledum and Tweedledee 为英国诗人约翰·拜伦(John Byron)于1725年所创,出现在他的诗作《汉德尔与博农奇尼》(*Handel and Bononcini*)之中。汉德尔和博农奇尼是18世纪上半叶代表两个流派的音乐家。他们两人争论不休,社会上流人士之间也展开了关于他们谁优谁劣的争论。这首诗对此进行了讽刺。诗人用了两个带有tweedle的词,表示乐器奏出的尖声:

> Some say, compared to Bononcini
> That mynheer Handel's but a ninny;
> Others aver, that he to Handel
> Is scarcely fit to hold a Candle.
> Strange all this difference should be
> Twixt Tweedledum and Tweedledee.

有人说同博农奇尼相比
汉德尔先生真是愚不可及;
可别人却说博农奇尼

简直不配和汉德尔相比。
这些争论可真是稀奇,
他俩无非一路货色而已。

由讽刺诗产生的这条成语,后来被刘易斯·卡罗尔(Lewis Carroll)用在他的儿童文学作品《镜中世界》(*Through the Looking Glass*)中,使这句成语作为一对宝贝的名字,广泛流传开来。

例:The ass or scoundrel Robinson is no great than or not as great an as and scoundrel as that ass and scoundrel Jones. Tweedledee and tweedledum!(Theodore Dreiser, *Tragic America*)

罗宾逊的愚蠢和无赖既不超过琼斯,也不亚于琼斯。一对半斤八两的活宝。(西奥多·德莱塞,《美国的悲剧》)

(3)关于成语 tarred with the same brush(或 stick)的起源,有些学者认为,早期的牧民为了医治羊的溃疡,便会将焦油(tar)用刷子涂在羊身上,若是有多只羊都有溃疡,牧民就会用同一把刷子来为它们涂抹。

另外的一种说法是,早期有一种惩罚坏人的方法,称作 tar and feather,也就是将坏人的衣服脱光,涂上温热的焦油,之后再将他的全身粘满羽毛,并让他游街示众。因此,只要被涂上焦油的,不用问都不是好人,是一丘之貉。

从这两种起源来看,"用同一把刷子涂上焦油"的对象,不论是一群羊还是人,都是相同的货色,拥有一样的缺点或做了同样的坏事,这句成语也因而带有贬义。

例①：I dislike politicians of all parties, as far as I'm concerned they're all tarred with the same brush—they simply will not tell the public the truth.

我讨厌各党的政客，我认为他们都是一路货色——都不愿对公众说真话。

例②：Stephanie feels she is tarred with the same brush because everyone knows her sister is very arrogant.

史黛芬妮觉得，因为大家知道她的妹妹很自大傲慢，自己也被认定为这样的人。

（4）成语 birds of a feather 是谚语 birds of a feather flock together（物以类聚，人以群分）的一部分，表示同类的人或一丘之貉。

例①：He has conspired against me like the rest, and they are but birds of one feather. (Charles Dickens, *Martin Chuzzlewit*)

他和其余的人一样阴谋同我作对，他们不过是一丘之貉。（查尔斯·狄更斯，《马丁·朱述尔维特》）

例②：His expenses were two pence a day for food and four pence for his bed in a cafe full of other birds of his feather. (John Galsworthy, *Caravan*)

他的开支是每天伙食费两个便士，另外再花四个便士在一家小咖啡店寄宿，那家小咖啡店里聚集了大批和他一类的人。（约翰·高尔斯华绥，《商队》）

（5）成语 cut from（或 out of）the same cloth 的本义是从同一块布上剪下来的料子，转义为如出一辙，一路货色，近乎一丘之貉。

例：Modern revisionism is cut from same cloth as Kautskyism. 现代修正主义和考茨基主义是一路货色。

汉语成语例解：

(1)"一丘之貉"典出《汉书·杨恽传》：

西汉汉宣帝时，司马迁的外孙杨恽，很有才干，而且结交广泛。其父亲也是朝中大官，甚至代理过丞相一职。杨恽自己也因告发霍光谋反有功，被封为平通侯。

但是杨恽生性傲慢，说话刻薄，觉得自己受皇帝器重，自命不凡，不把朝中大臣放在眼里，因此遭到一些人记恨。太仆戴长乐因被人告发而入狱，他怀疑是杨恽所为。于是在狱中写了一封信，向皇帝告状，说杨恽诽谤朝廷。信中指责杨恽四处宣扬不当言论，如下：

"得不肖君，大臣为画善计不用，自令身无处所，若秦时但人笑臣，诛杀忠良，竟以灭亡；令亲任大臣，即至今耳。古与今如一丘之貉。"

意思是说，遇到昏君，无论大臣们给他出多少好主意都不够，到头来只会落得死无葬身之地。就像秦朝那样，任用小人，滥杀忠良，最后自取灭亡。如果当时能任用贤臣，江山一定会传到现在。古往今来，道理是一样的，就像一个山上的貉。

皇上看到信，十分生气。将他停职，贬为庶民，不过没有杀掉他。但是后来一直有人在皇帝面前攻击他，同时他写给朋友的一封满是牢骚的信又被传到了皇上那里，最后杨恽终被处死。

貉是栖息在山林中的一种小兽,猎食鱼虾、鼠兔等,皮毛较为珍贵。人们用"一丘之貉"比喻彼此都是坏家伙,没有什么差别,总是用于贬意。

例:增加混乱的倒是有些悲观论者,不施考察,不加批评,但用"彼亦一是非,此亦一是非"的论调,将一切作者,诋为"一丘之貉"。(鲁迅,《准风月谈·中国文坛的悲观》)

(2)成语"一路货色"比喻同是一类丑货。"一路"意为同一类,货色意为货物。

前述五句英语成语,虽然有的来源于民间传说,有的来源于故事,有的来源于比喻,但它们要表达的意思都是"不相上下""伯仲之间""半斤八两""相差无几",而且它们有一个共同的特点,那就是贬义。

在汉语中,表示不相上下的成语虽然很多,但真正表示贬义的,也只有"一丘之貉"和"一路货色"两句。

正是由于这种原因,我们才把它们选来进行比较例解的。

38 "pinch penny" 与 "一毛不拔"

英语成语：

1. pinch penny
2. tight as the bark on a tree
3. close as a clam
4. cramp in the hand
5. long pocket and short arms
6. tight as Kelsey's nuts, tight as O'Reilly's balls, tight as Reilly's balls
7. skin a flea for its hide
8. cheese paring
9. as tight as a new girdle
10. squeeze the eagle
11. close as a vice
12. skin a flint
13. too near the wind

14. near the bone

15. Misers put their back and their belly into their pockets.

16. close as wax

17. He wouldn't give you the parting of his nails.

汉语成语：

1. 一毛不拔   2. 缺口镊子

英语成语例解：

（1）成语 tight as the bark on a tree 的意思是"小气""吝啬"。这句成语原为美国口语，描述了早期定居美国的拓荒者所经历的困难，他们过着很艰苦的日子，就像"树皮紧绷在树干上"一样，形容日子过得有多么紧，由此产生了这个短语的转义。此成语亦作 near as the bark on a tree。

例：If you wasn't tighter than the bark on a tree, your wife wouldn't have to do her own washing.

如果你不这么吝啬，你妻子就不必亲自动手洗衣服了。

（2）成语 close as a clam 的字面意思是"紧得像一个蛤蜊"。蛤蜊的壳闭合紧密，掰开它很不容易。人们用它来指某人积聚的财物收藏严密，或喻指人小气吝啬，一毛不拔。

（3）成语 cramp in the hand 形容人之小气吝啬，就像铁钳子夹东西一样把它攥在手里。

(4) 成语 long pocket and short arms 形容人的小气吝啬，既形象又生动，而且直白易懂，衣服口袋缝得太深，两只胳膊伸进去都够不到底，掏出东西很困难，财物保管得自然很牢靠。

(5) tight as Kelsey's nuts, tight as O'Reilly's balls, tight as Reilly's balls 三个成语皆为吝啬、一毛不拔之义。三个成语都有人的名字，看来似乎可能与一个故事有关，只是由于形成年代久远，我们现在只知其用意和用法，而不知其出处了。

(6) 成语 skin a flea for its hide 亦作 skin a louse for the sake of its skin，二者都表示小气吝啬，贪婪无度，前者是说"要剩下一个跳蚤的皮"，后者是说"要剩下一只虱子的皮"，两者皆言吝啬之至，一毛不拔。

例："Generous!" I exclaimed: "Why, he's the meanest little hunks that ever skinned a flea for its hide."

"好大方！"我叫了起来，"哎呀，他是个自私贪婪的守财奴，从来一毛不拔。"

(7) 成语 pinch penny 的本义是"一个大钱捏出水来的人"，转喻吝啬鬼，铁公鸡一毛不拔。Pinch penny 一语早在 1412 年便已出现，既可作名词，指"小气鬼"，又可用作动词，表示"节俭"或"吝啬"。

例①：I'll have to pinch pennies if I am going to get through school.

我若想念完这书就得节省每一个铜板。

例②：They didn't pinch pennies on the new opera house.

他们在兴这建这座新剧院上花钱可没有斤斤计较。

(8) 成语 cheese paring 的原始意义为"干酪的碎皮屑""干酪屑",即"毫无价值的东西"。1813 年引申出"节省干酪屑""极度节俭"之义,用作名词。1857 年以后又开始用作形容词,表示"小气""吝啬"之义。类似的说法还有 candle paring(蜡烛屑,"蜡烛泪"),转义"小气""吝啬"。

例:They won't adopt the cheese paring policy.
他们不会采取一毛不拔的政策。

(9) 成语 as tight as a new girdle 和 as tight as the paper on the wall 都表示过分节俭乃至到了吝啬的程度。前者是勒紧裤带,后者是像贴在壁上的纸一样,一缝不漏。

(10) 成语 squeeze the eagle 本义为"把一块鹰洋捏出水",转义为小气、节省,乃至吝啬。这句成语是在传统说法 pinch penny 的基础上发展起来的。The eagle 是指大面额的硬币,美国的大额硬币或金币上都铸有鹰的图案。现在或许是由于通货膨胀,penny 的价值实在是微不足道,故有此新说。

(11) 成语 close as a vice 和 close as wax 都是形容小气和吝啬的成语。前者说人把钱守得像老虎钳一样紧;后者说人把钱守得像封了蜡一样密。两成语都是形容人一毛不拔的委婉语。

例:Don't ask him. That man was as close as wax.
不要求他,他是个一毛不拔的人。

(12) 成语 skin a flint 和 flay a flint 都是表示人爱钱如命,十分吝啬的成语。形容就是一块石头也要从它身上剥一层皮。

例:The miser would skin a flint if you could.
这个守财奴吝啬到了极点。

（13）成语 too near the wind 也是一句表示人十分吝啬、一毛不拔的成语。

（14）成语 near（或 close to）the bone 除了作"贫困"和"近乎下流"解之外，亦表示"十分吝啬""一毛不拔"之义。

（15）Misers put their back and their belly into their pockets. 是一句谚语，字面的意思是：守财奴把他们后背和肚子都装进了钱包，就是说守财奴宁可不穿衣、不吃饭，也舍不得掏腰包。喻铁公鸡——一毛不拔。

（16）成语 close as wax 的意思是吝啬、一毛不拔。

（17）He wouldn't give you the parting of his nails. 是英语谚语，意思是说有的人连剪下来的指甲都不肯送人，喻极其吝啬、一毛不拔。

汉语成语例解：

（1）"一毛不拔"语出《孟子·尽心上》：孟子曰："杨子取为我，拔一毛而利天下，不为也。"后概括为成语"一毛不拔"，形容为人极其吝啬自私。

例：差人道："我们管山吃山，管水吃水，都像你这一毛不拔，我们喝西北风！"（清·吴敬梓，《儒林外史》第四十一回）

（2）从"一毛不拔"这句成语，又产生了一句俗语"缺口镊子"。镊子是用来拔除细毛的一种工具，缺了口的镊子，当然难于拔下一毛了。宋朝苏东坡在给他朋友陈季常的一封信里，用过这句俗语，他写道："乡谚有云'缺口镊子'，君知之乎？"接着并加注释："缺口镊子者，取一毛不拔，恐未尝闻，故及。"

39 "hoist with one's own petard" 与 "作法自毙"

英语成语：

1. hoist with one's own petard
2. put one's head in the lion's mouth
3. make a rod for one's own back
4. have made one's bed and have to lie in it
5. stew in one's own juice
6. cut one's own throat
7. sign one's own death warrant
8. dig one's own grave
9. eat the fruit of one's own doings
10. reap what one has sown
11. ride for a fall
12. stir up a hornet's nest
13. pay the piper
14. get a taste of one's own medicine

15. serve somebody right

16. stick one's neck out

17. ask for it

18. get one's lumps

19. be a fool for one's pains

20. monkey with the buzz-saw

21. burn one's fingers

22. ask for trouble

23. borrow trouble

24. the joke is on someone

25. bite a file

26. cut one's nails on Sunday

27. He that mischief hatches, mischief catches.

28. He has made a halter to hang himself.

29. He that blows in the dust fills his own eyes.

30. He who dig a pit for others falls into it himself.

31. Self do, self have.

32. He has brought up a bird to pick out his own eyes.

33. I have brought an ill comb to my own head.

34. It is not good to wake a sleeping lion.

35. Let his own wand ding him.

36. Suffer the consequences of your deeds.

37. He who cooks a bad thing, eats of it.

38. Bear patiently that which you suffer by your own fault.

39. He who plays with fire gets burned.

40. lay up for oneself

41. put one's neck in the noose

42. recoil on

43. get into scrapes

44. meet trouble halfway

45. Never trouble trouble until trouble troubles you.

46. wake a sleeping wolf

47. what goes around comes around

48. lie in the bed one has made

49. As you bake so shall you eat.

50. He who throws stones on another gets them back on his own bones.

51. If you stir up the mire you must bear the smell.

52. He has made a balter to hang himself.

53. He is well worth sorrow that buys it with his silver.

54. Make ado and have ado.

汉语成语：

1. 作法自毙 2. 飞蛾扑火 3. 自投罗网 4. 自讨苦吃
5. 自取其咎 6. 自食其果 7. 自掘坟墓 8. 作茧自缚
9. 自作自受 10. 玩火自焚 11. 自作孽，不可活

英语成语例解：

（1）成语 hoist with one's own petard 的原意是"被自己的炸弹炸上了天"。语出莎士比亚悲剧《哈姆莱特》第三幕：哈姆

莱特与母亲在王后寝宫单独会面时,发现帷幕后藏着人,他以为是谋杀父王的新国王,便拔剑刺去,躲在帷幕后面的御前大臣波洛涅斯当场丧命。哈姆莱特将弑君的凶手与自己的父亲作对比,以此揭示王后灵魂深处的污点。他恳求王后当着上天承认自己过去的罪过,不要上新王的床,不要对新王泄露刚才他所说的一切以及所发生的事。接着他向王后告别,因为新王派他和两个不可信任的人一起到英国追索物质。他说:"对这两个家伙我要像对待两条咬人的毒蛇一样随时提防;他们要做我的先驱,引导我钻进什么圈套里去。我倒要瞧瞧他们的能耐。炮火要是被炮轰上天,也是一件好玩的事"(For' tis the sport to have the engineer hoist with his own petard),petard 是古时候用来炸开城门的爆炸装置或炸弹,点火起爆的人有被炸得血肉横飞的危险。这句成语用来形容害人反害己,作法自毙。

例:The criminal was hoist with his own petard when he tried to kill his wife, because he accidentally drank the poison that he intended to give to her. (*Longman Dictionary of English Idioms*)

该罪犯想毒死自己的妻子,结果想害人反而害了自己,因为他误喝了本想让妻子喝的毒药。(《朗文英语成语辞典》)

(2) 成语 put one's head in the lion's mouth 原意是"把脑袋伸进狮子的嘴里"。这个典故出自《伊索寓言》:一只鹤上了诡计多端的狼的当,把头伸到狼的嘴里去取一块被卡住了的骨头。骨头被取出来了,解除了狼的痛苦,可鹤却冒了被狼咬掉脑袋的风险。这句成语原来是 put one's head in the wolf's mouth,后来 wolf 变成 lion,可能是因为与另一个成语 beard the lion in his

den（到狮子洞里去捋狮子的胡须）混淆起来，也可能是因为狮子比狼更大更凶猛，因而也更能说明冒险者的鲁莽程度。这句成语用来形容自取灭亡，自找不幸。

例："The project is a perfectly mad one," Grassini exclaimed. "It is simply pulling one's head into the lion's mouth out of sheer wantonness. (Ethel Voynich, *The Gadfly*)

"这种计划荒唐极了，"格拉西尼叫喊起来，"这简直是鲁莽的行动，是拿自己的脑袋往狮子嘴里送。"（艾捷尔·伏尼契，《牛虻》）

(3) 成语 make a rod for one's own back 的字面意思是为自己将来后背被抽打而制作了一根枝条，这岂不是自我麻烦，自讨苦吃吗？此成语亦作 prepare a rod for one's own back。

例：Very well, spoil the child as much as you wish. I say no more, except that you are making a rod for your own back.

好吧，你要惯孩子就惯吧。我也不说什么了，不过你这是在为将来找麻烦。

(4) 成语 have made one's bed and have to lie in（或 on）it 的意思是"给自己铺好了床，就得自己躺上睡"，言外之意是自作自受，自食其果。此成语亦作 lie in（或 on）the bed one has made。二成语皆由谚语 As you made your bed, so you must lie on it. 演变而来。

例：I warned him not to change his job but now he is forced to work for a company that is losing money. He has made his own bed and now he must lie in it.

我曾劝他不要更换工作，但他不听，现在他只得任职于一家亏本的公司，真是自作自受。

（5）成语 stew in one's own juice 的字面意思是"在自己榨的汁中煎熬吧"，言外之意是由于自己处事不当而自食其果，自作自受。这句成语常与动词 let 或 leave 连用。

例：The last time I lent her money after she had spent all her own, she just wasted it, so this time I let her stew in her own juice.

上次她分文不剩时我借钱给她，可她拿去又乱花一气，这回我让她自作自受。

（6）成语 cut（或 slit）one's own throat 的字面意思是"割自己的喉咙"，这岂不是找死吗？这句成语多用于人由于狂妄自大或激愤暴怒而自己戕害自己，即自作自受之意。

例：Mrs. Warren: Can't you see that you're cutting your own throat as well as breaking my heart in turning your back on me? (George Bernard Shaw, *Mrs. Warren's Profession*)

华伦夫人：难道你看不出，现在你掉过头去不理我，固然叫我痛心，不也是让你自寻末路吗？（萧伯纳，《华伦夫人的职业》）

（7）成语 sign one's own death warrant 的字面意思是"签署自己的死刑执行令"，这就是自己宣布自己的死亡，这不正是自取灭亡的意思吗？

例：That company is losing a lot of money. If you accepted a job with them now, you'd be signing your own death warrant.

那个公司正在大亏其本，你要是现在接受他们的职务，无异于自我毁灭。

（8）成语 dig one's own grave 顾名思义就是自取灭亡之意，否则怎么会说是自掘坟墓呢？

例：I feel so sorry for Mike, he's in trouble with the police for stealing a car. —Well, he has dug his own grave, hasn't he? He shouldn't have stolen it.

我真为迈克难过，他偷了辆汽车，警察找上他了。——唉，他这不是自食其果吗？他不该偷东西呀。

（9）成语 eat the fruit of one's own doings 出自《圣经·旧约·以赛亚书》：

> Tell the righteous that it shall be well with them,
> for they shall eat the fruit of their doings.
> Woe to the wicked! It shall be ill with him,
> For what his hands have dealt out shall be done to him.
> 告诉正义的人，幸福将与他们共存，
> 他们将会吃到自己行为所结的果子。
> 作恶的人都要遭殃！不幸在等待着他，
> 他要为自己所作所为承担后果。

这句成语原意为"善有善报"，后来则常用于贬义，意指"自食其果"或"自作自受"。

（10）成语 reap what one has sown 典出《圣经·新约·加拉太书》，意为"自食其果"：

Do not be deceived: God is not mocked, for whatever one sows, that will he also reap.

不要自欺：神是嘲笑不了的，人种的是什么，收获的也是什么。

例：Each deadly sin is a deadly knife, for he shall reap what he sows.

每一次致命的罪行都是一把致命的刀，因为人种了什么，就会收获什么。

（11）成语 ride for a fall 原意为"故意从马上摔下来"。这一成语可能来自赛马。当赛马的职业骑马师想输掉一场比赛时，他就会故意让自己从马上摔下来。现在这句成语用来形容自惹危险或自找麻烦。

例：Mr. Smith has borrowed too much money on his home, He is riding for a fall. (*A Dictionary of American Idioms*)

史密斯先生为了房子借了很多钱，他这是自找麻烦。(《美国成语词典》)

（12）成语 stir up a hornet's nest 的字面意思是"捅了马蜂窝"，引申为"自找麻烦"或"自讨苦吃"。这句成语最早出现在塞缪尔·理查逊（Samuel Richardson, 1689—1761）的小说《帕米拉》（*Pamela*, 1739）中，现在已在英语中得到广泛使用。

例：Judges have stirred up a hornet's nest in the sacred territory of "the right to strike".

法官们侵犯了"罢工权"的神圣领域，因此就像捅了马蜂窝一样，自找了大麻烦。

（13）成语 pay the piper 的字面意思是"付报酬给吹笛的人"，后转义为由于自己的行为而引发的不良后果，即自作自受的意思。

1284 年，德国西北部的一个小镇患了鼠害，满街流窜的老鼠，弄得镇上鸡犬不宁，困扰人们的生活。

镇上来了一位吹笛子的人，他表示愿意为大家驱除鼠患，但要镇民们付出报酬。镇民们答应了。只见吹笛人笛声一响，全镇的老鼠便都乖乖地跟着他，自己往海里跳。然而，镇民们并没有照原先的约定，付给吹笛人任何酬劳。第二年，吹笛人再次来到镇上，并用笛声将全镇的孩子都带走了。这句成语就是这么来的。

例：Someday, Jeffrey will have to pay the piper all his lies.

总有一天，杰弗里会为他所有的谎言承担后果的。

（14）成语 get a taste of one's own medicine 的意思是说某人受到报复性的待遇或打击，亦即是自作自受之意。

例：For a time the news delighted Labour MPs and trade union stalwarts: the City, at last, was getting a taste of its own medicine.

这个消息使工党议员们和工会忠实分子们很高兴：伦敦金融界终于自作自受遭到了报应。

（15）成语 serve somebody right 是说某人应得的报应，某人活该，意即自作自受。

例：And as to confiscation of war profits, he was entirely in

favour of it, for he had none, and "serve the beggars right!" (John Galsworthy, *To Let*)

至于没收靠战争发来的财，他是完全赞成的，因为他自己没有这种财产，而且"那些家伙是自作自受，罪有应得!"（约翰·高尔斯华绥，《招租出让》）

(16) 成语 stick（或 put）one's neck out 的本义是"自己把脖子伸出去"，转义为"自找麻烦"或"自取其咎"。

例：A politician supporting an unpopular law is sticking his neck out: he may lose the next election.

一个政治家如果支持一项不得人心的立法，就等于是在冒险，在自取其咎，说不定下次选举时他就会落选。

(17) 成语 ask for it 除有"索求"之意外，还有"自找麻烦"和"自讨苦吃"的意思。

例：You're simply asking for it by coming in late when your father has told you to be early.

你父亲叫你早回家，你却迟回来，这是你自讨苦吃。

(18) 成语 get（或 take）one's（或 the）lumps 的本义是得到报应，即自作自受之意。

例：The school gets the lumps for it.

学校为这事吃了苦头。

(19) 成语 be a fool for one's pains 的意思是自找麻烦，自讨苦吃。

例：If you try to help the Smiths, you will be a fool for your pains.

要是你想帮助史密斯一家人的话，那你就将自讨苦吃。

（20）成语 monkey with the buzz-saw 的意思是介入危险之事，喻指自寻烦恼，自讨苦吃。

例：You can go see the president about it, but you'd be monkeying with the buzz-saw.

你当然可以找总统去说，但你这是在自讨苦吃。

（21）成语 burn one's fingers 之意为自寻烦恼，自讨苦吃，原指一个人在烧饭或煽火时不小心而烧伤手指，故亦作 get one's fingers burned。源出谚语 Never burn your fingers to snuff another man's candle（别剪别人的蜡烛而烧伤自己的手指）。

例：If you get involved in the controversy, you may burn your fingers.

要是你卷入这场争吵的话，你会自讨苦吃的。

（22）成语 ask for（或 look for, seek）trouble 的意思是自讨苦吃，自找麻烦。

例：You'd better not touch the apples in that orchard, if you do you're just asking for trouble.

你最好别碰那果园里的苹果，否则你将自找麻烦。

（23）成语 borrow trouble 也是自找麻烦、自寻烦恼的意思。

例："Don't borrow trouble by worrying about next year. It's too far away." said Wu.

"别为明年的事情自寻烦恼，那毕竟太遥远了。"老吴说。

（24）成语 the joke is on someone 是说某人开别人玩笑结果开到自己身上，某人作弄别人反而作弄到自己头上，亦即自食其果,自作自受。

(25) 成语 bite a file 的字面意思是"咬锉刀",转喻"自寻烦恼""自讨苦吃"。这句成语出自《伊索寓言》中《蛇与锉刀》的故事:一条蛇悠来逛去,溜进一家铁匠铺。它在地上蜿蜒爬行,却被放在那里的锉刀划了一下,蛇勃然大怒,转过头露出毒牙猛地向锉刀咬去,却丝毫未能伤害这个沉重坚硬的铁家伙,不一会儿,它只好悻悻咽下怒气,自认倒霉。

例:He bit the file of English obstinacy, and broke his teeth.
英国人固执得似锉刀,他啃它结果把自己的牙齿也啃碎了。

(26) 成语 cut one's nails on Sunday 原意为"星期天修剪指甲"。此语源于中世纪的迷信说法:星期五悲伤事多,星期日诸事不吉,在星期日修剪指甲也会招致不幸。罗伯特·福比(Robert Forby)所编《美国东部的词汇》(1830)一书中有这样一句描述:

Cut them on Sunday, the devil will be with you all week.
星期日修指甲,倒霉一周。

这句成语后来就被人们用来表示"自寻烦恼""自讨苦吃"之义。

(27) He that mischief hatches, mischief catches. 是一句谚语,意思是作恶者必遭殃,喻害人终害己,自作自受。

(28) He has made a halter to hang himself. 是一句谚语,意为自做绞索套自己,喻自掘坟墓,作茧自缚。

(29) He that blows in the dust fills his own eyes. 是一句谚语，意为扬尘土的人迷了自己的眼睛，喻害人亦害己，自作自受。

(30) He who digs a pit for others falls into it himself. 是一句谚语，意为挖坑害别人，自己跌进去，喻害人反害己，自作自受。

(31) Self do, self have. 是一句谚语，意为自作自受。

(32) He has brought up a bird to pick out his own eyes. 是一句谚语，意为养的鸟啄瞎了自己的眼睛，喻自作自受。

(33) I have brought an ill comb to my own head. 是一句谚语，意为给自己的头带着一把坏梳子，喻自讨苦吃，自作自受。

(34) It is not good to wake a sleeping lion. 是一句谚语，意为唤醒正在睡着的狮子可不是什么好事，喻自讨苦吃，自作自受。

(35) Let his own wand ding him. 是一句谚语，意为以己之棒，击己之身，喻自作自受，近似于搬起石头砸自己的脚。

(36) Suffer the consequences of your deeds. 是一句谚语，意为你要承受你的行为的后果，喻自食其果。

(37) He who cooks a bad thing, eats of it. 是一句谚语，意为饭菜做得差，也得把它吃掉，喻自食其果。

(38) Bear patiently that which you suffer by your own fault. 是一句谚语，意为因自己错而闯下的祸，就得由自己来耐心忍受。喻自作自受。

(39) He who plays with fire gets burned. 是一句谚语，意思

是玩火者，火烧身，喻玩火者自焚。

（40）成语 lay up for oneself 的意思是自找麻烦，自讨苦吃。

例：He's laid up on end of trouble for himself.

他老是自讨苦吃没完没了。

（41）成语 put one's neck in the（或 a）noose 的意思是自套绞索，自入圈卷，喻自投罗网，自取灭亡。

例：For him to go there as a spy is simply putting his neck in a noose.

他去那里做间谍简直是自投罗网。

（42）成语 recoil on（或 upon）的意思是报应，自食其果。

例：His cruelty to others recoiled in the end upon himself.

他对别人的残暴最后报应在自己身上。

（43）成语 get into scrapes（或 a scrape）的意思是陷入困境，自找麻烦。

例：She got into a scrape with the police for parking her car in the middle of the road.

她因为把汽车停在路当中，给自己找了得同警局打交道的麻烦。

（44）成语 meet trouble halfway 的原意是在半路迎麻烦，转义为自寻烦恼。

（45）Never trouble trouble until trouble troubles you. 是句谚语，意为麻烦没有来找你，别去找麻烦。

（46）成语 wake a sleeping wolf 的原意是弄醒睡着的狼，转义为自找麻烦。

例:Chief-Justice: But since all is well, keep it so, wake not a sleeping wolf. Falstaff: to wake a wolf is as bad as to smell a fox.

大法官:可是现在既然一切无事,您也安分点儿吧;留心不要惊醒一只睡着的狼。福斯塔夫:惊醒一只睡狼跟闻到一条狐狸是同样糟糕的事。

(47)成语 what goes around comes around 之意为善恶到头终有报,自食其果。

例: Now they're driving us to the wall. What goes around comes around.

现在他们逼得我们无路可走。他们将来总有自食其果的一天。

(48)成语 lie in the bed one has made 的意思是躺在自己做的床上,指因自己的行为而承担后果,喻自作自受,自食其果。此成语尚有异体形式 make one's bed and have to lie in(或 on)it 及 As you made your bed, so you must lie on it.

例: She felt that she must no yield, she must go on leading her straitened, humdrum life. This was her punishment for having made a mistake, she had made her bed, and she must lie on it.

她觉得她不能放松自己,她必须继续过她那贫困而单调的生活。这是她犯错误得到的惩罚,她得自食其果。

(49)As you bake, so shall you eat. 是英语谚语,意思是自己烙饼自己吃,喻自食其果。

(50)He who throws stones on another gets them back on his

own bones. 是英语谚语，意思是投向他人之石，反落自己身上，喻自作自受。

（51）If you stir up the mire you must bear the smell. 是英语谚语，意思是搅动臭水坑，就得闻臭味，喻自作自受。

（52）He has made a balter to hang himself. 是英语谚语，意思是自己做绞索吊自己，喻自作自受。

（53）He is well worth sorrow that buys it with his silver. 是英语谚语，意思是用钱买来的痛苦是很值得的，讽喻自作自受。

（54）Make ado and have ado. 是英语谚语，意思是自找麻烦就会有麻烦，喻自作自受。

汉语成语例解：

（1）"作法自毙"亦作"为法自弊"，语出《史记·商君列传》："商君喟然叹曰：'嗟呼，为法之敝一至此哉！'"成语由此概括而来，意思是说自己制定的法规使自己受到困厄。

例：顷之，鼓又作，两蝶飞余冠。余笑云："作法自毙矣。"（清·蒲松龄，《聊斋志异·余德》）

（2）"飞蛾扑火"原作"飞蛾赴火"，语出《梁书·到溉传》，原意本为牺牲自己，照亮别人。今用其转义：自取灭亡或白白送死。

南北朝梁代有个姓到名溉字茂灌的人，颇有才学，当过梁武帝的散骑常侍、侍中、国子祭酒等官职，受到武帝赏识。他儿子到镜，死得较早，有个孙子叫到荩，文笔也很不错。据《梁书·到溉传》载：有一次，到溉和他的孙子跟从武帝游览京口（今江苏镇江），登上北固楼观赏风景的时候，武帝命到茞赋诗，茞顷刻而成。武帝看了诗，很高兴，指着诗句向到溉夸奖道："这孩子将来是个人才！你这辈子如比飞蛾赴火，心甘情愿地牺牲了一切，现在年纪已老，以后可让小茞帮你些忙，接你的班了。"说着，提笔写了几行字赠给到溉，其中有这样两句："如飞蛾之赴火，岂焚身之可吝；必耄年其已及，可假之于少茞。"

成语"飞蛾扑火"变异较多，除"飞蛾赴火"之外，还有"飞蛾投火""飞蛾投焰""飞蛾赴焰""飞蛾赴烛"等。

例：他走了，我一向寻他不着，他今日自来投到，岂不是飞蛾扑火，自讨死吃的。（元·杨显之，《潇湘雨》二折）

（3）"自投罗网"比喻自己进入对手预先设下的圈套。罗网是捕捉禽兽鱼类的工具。

这句成语最早见于《曹子建集·野田黄雀行》诗："高树多悲风，海水扬其波。利剑不在掌，结友何须多！不见篱间雀，见鹞自投罗。……"

例：譬如猎人，终日驱驰践蹂于草茅之中，搜收伏兔而搏之，不待其自投罗网而后取也。（宋·苏轼，《策别十七》）

（4）"自讨苦吃"的意思十分直白，即自己给自己找麻烦。

例：老夫原知传方是件好事，但一经通行。家中缺了养赡，岂非自讨苦吃么？（清·李汝珍，《镜花缘》二七回）

（5）"自取其咎"谓自己招取罪过、祸害。亦作"咎由自取"。

例：虽然城厢出了盗案是老兄们的责任，但这件事，据兄

弟看来，他们两家实在是咎由自取。(清·李伯元,《官场现形记》第五十一回)

(6)"自食其果"顾名思义是说自己吞食自己种出来的果实，多指做了坏事受到应有的惩罚，亦作"自食恶果"。

例：玩火者是会自食其果的。(郭沫若,《天地玄黄·玩火者必自焚》)

(7)"自掘坟墓"谓自己给自己挖坟墓，比喻做毁灭自己的事，自己走上绝路，自己断送自己。语出《三国志·蜀书·先主传裴注引葛洪神仙传》："仙人李意其，蜀人也，传世见之，云是汉文帝时人。先主欲伐吴，遣人迎意其。意其到，先主礼敬之，问以吉凶，意其不答而求纸笔，画作兵马器仗数十纸，便一一以手裂坏之，又画作一大人，自掘地而埋之，便径去。先主大不喜。而自出军征吴大败还，忿耻发病死，众人乃知其意。其画作大人而埋之者，即是言先主死意。"

例：帝国主义侵略者，如果一定要与世界人民为敌，敢于贸然发动侵略战争，最后必定是自掘坟墓。

(8)"作茧自缚"谓蚕吐丝作茧，把自己包在里面。比喻自己做事原希望对自己有利，结果却反使自己吃亏受累，自讨苦吃。语出唐代白居易《白氏长庆集·江州赴忠州至江陵已来舟中示舍弟五十韵》诗："烛蛾谁救活，蚕茧自缠萦。"

例：人生如春蚕，作茧自缚裹。(宋·陆游,《书叹》)

(9)"自作自受"谓自己做的事自己承受，自己受害，形容祸由自取。语出明代冯梦龙《醒世恒言》第十八卷："种瓜得瓜，种豆得豆。一切祸福，自作自受。"

例：自己坠下去的是自作自受，可恨者乃是还要带累超然似的局外人。（鲁迅，《"碰壁"之余》）

（10）成语"玩火自焚"谓玩火者反倒把自己烧死，比喻干冒险或害人的事，最终自食其果。语出《左传·隐公四年》："夫兵，犹火也，弗戢，将自焚也。"后演化为"玩火自焚"。

（11）成语"自作孽，不可活"谓自己作的罪孽，自己承受，没有办法挽救。语出《尚书·太甲》："天作孽，犹可违；自作孽，不可活。"（天降的灾害还可以防止和避免，自作的罪孽，那就逃也逃不了了。）

例：三嫂羞惭，还房自缢而死，此乃自作孽，不可活。（明·冯梦龙，《醒世恒言》第二卷）

40 "The mills of the God grind slowly, but they grind exceeding small." 与"善有善报,恶有恶报"

英语成语:

1. The mills of the God grind slowly, but they grind exceeding small.

2. Heaven's vengeance is slow but sure.

3. Punishment is lame, but it comes.

4. Justice has long arms.

5. The gallows will have its own at last.

6. Wickedness does not go altogether unrequited.

7. hand go, hand come

8. come home to roost

9. get what's coming to someone

10. Every sin brings its punishment with it.

11. Vice will have an evil recompense.

12. The punishment always fits the crime.

13. Good deeds return to the house of their author.

14. He that sows thistles shall reap thorns.

15. He that sows thistles, must not go barefoot.

16. Harm set, harm get.

17. It couldn´t happen to a nicer guy.

18. the farmer and the fox

19. sow the wind and reap the whirlwind

20. Every ill man has his ill day.

21. He that mischief hatches, mischief catches.

22. One good turn deserves another. One ill turn deserves another.

23. serve someone right

24. Evil be to him who evil thinks.

25. A bad life, a bad end.

26. The deed comes back upon the doer.

27. Sow virtue, and the harvest will be virtue, sow vice and the harvest will be vice.

28. What goes around comes around.

29. One´s own deed return to oneself.

30. The bad deed turns on its does.

31. Do well and have well.

32. Do not wait for a reward for good, the reward for ill will not miss you.

33. A wicked man is his own hell.

34. All wrong comes to wrack.

35. God hath leaden feet, but iron hands.

36. Kindness always begets kindness.

37. Who swims in sin shall sink in sorrow.

38. slow but sure

39. A good deed bears a blessing for its fruits.

40. A good life makes a good death.

41. Long threatening comes at last.

42. One ill turn deserves another.

汉语成语:

> 1. 天网恢恢,疏而不漏 2. 善有善报,恶有恶报

英语成语例解:

(1) The mills of the God grind slowly, but they grind exceeding small. 这句英语成语可追溯到罗马作家佩特罗尼乌斯(Petronius)"Dii pedes lanatos habent."(The gods are slow to act. 神的行动迟缓)的说法,后来希腊哲学家塞克斯都·恩披里克(Sextus Empiricus)有"The mills of the gods grind slowly, but they grind small."之句。1640 年英国神父兼诗人赫伯特(George Herbert, 1593—1633)曾将之收入他编的成语集(*Jacula Prudentum*)中。17 世纪时德国警句短诗作家罗高(Friedrich Von Logau, 1604—1655)写了一首短诗,美国诗人朗费罗(Henry Wadsworth Longfellow, 1807—1882)将之翻译成英文,并冠以《报应》(*Retribution*)的篇名:

40 "The mills of the God grind slowly, but they grind exceeding small." 与 "善有善报，恶有恶报"

> Though the mills of God grind slowly,
> Yet they grind exceeding small;
> Though with patience He stands waiting,
> With exactness grinds he all.
> 尽管上帝的磨转得不快，
> 却把谷粒磨得很细很细；
> 尽管他站着耐心等待，
> 他会精细地磨完一切。

这句成语用磨盘磨面粉来比喻上帝执法的方式，告诫人们上帝的磨盘虽然转得很慢，却碾磨精细，他有足够的耐心，把一切都准确无误地磨成碎末，无一遗漏，意指世间的公义迟早都会来临，罪恶最终会得到报应，天网恢恢，疏而不漏。

例：When I had narrated his lamentable death I ceased. For a minute or two we were all silent. Then Robert Strickland struck a match and lit a cigarette. "The mills of God grind slowly, but they grind exceeding small," he said, somewhat impressively. (William Somerset Maugham, *The Moon and Sixpence*)

在我谈完他惨死的情况以后我就没有再说下去了。有一两分钟大家都没有说话。后来罗伯特·思特里克兰德划了根火柴，点着了一支纸烟。"天网恢恢，疏而不漏啊。"罗伯特说，显然有点感动的样子。(威廉·萨默塞特·毛姆,《月亮和六便士》)

(2) 成语 Heaven's vengeance is slow but sure. 的意思是上天的报复虽然来得缓慢，却准确无疑，仍是天网恢恢，疏而不漏之意。

（3）成语 Punishment is lame, but it comes. 的意思是说惩罚虽步履蹒跚，但终会来到的，仍是天网恢恢，疏而不漏之意。

（4）成语 Justice has long arms. 的意思是说正义有两只长长的臂膀，隐喻天网恢恢，疏而不漏。

（5）成语 The gallows will have its own at last. 的意思是说绞刑架最后也要有它自己的归宿，意思天网恢恢，疏而不漏。

（6）成语 Wickedness does not go altogether unrequited. 是说邪恶是不可能不得到报应的，意即恶有恶报。

（7）成语 hand go, hand come 的字面意思是手去手来，亦有善有善报，恶有恶报之意。

（8）成语 come home to roost 是谚语 Curses, like chickens, come home to roost. 的缩略，表示回到原来的地方，报应到自己身上，亦即善有善报，恶有恶报之意。

例：Cervantes gives us a plain hint here that all our mistakes sooner or later surely come home to roost.

塞万提斯在这里明白地暗示我们，我们所犯的一切错误，早晚会报应到我们自己身上。

（9）成语 get what's coming to someone 的意思是得到应有的惩罚，意即恶有恶报。

例：He certainly got what was coming to him.

恶有恶报，他得到了应有的惩罚。

（10）Every sin brings its punishment with it. 是一则谚语，其意是"每个罪孽都携带着它的惩罚"，喻指恶有恶报。

(11) Vice will have an evil recompence. 是一则谚语，其意是"罪恶总有罪恶作为回报"，喻指恶有恶报。

(12) The punishment always fits the crime. 是一则谚语，其意是"惩罚对其罪恶有如量体裁衣"，喻指恶有恶报。

(13) Good deeds return to the house of their author. 是一句谚语，意为善举将返回行为者之家。喻善有善报。

(14) He that sows thistles shall reap thorns（或 prickles）. 是一则谚语，其意是"种蒺藜者得刺"，喻指恶有恶报。

(15) He that sows thistles, must not go barefoot. 是一则谚语，其意是"种蒺藜的人切不可光脚走路"，喻指恶有恶报。

(16) Harm set, harm get.（或 Harm watch, harm catch.）是意思相同的二则谚语，意即"制造伤害就会受到伤害"，喻指害人反害己，恶有恶报。

(17) 成语 It couldn't happen to a nicer guy. 的本义是"这种事情不可能发生在一个好一点的人身上"，喻指罪有应得，恶有恶报。

例：Joe got canned? It couldn't happen to a nicer guy!
乔被解雇了？真是罪有应得，恶有恶报！

(18) The farmer and the fox 一语出自《伊索寓言》，喻恶有恶报。故事是说：从前有一个农夫，他天生邪恶，而且好嫉妒。有一天，他发现邻居田里的庄稼长得十分旺盛，顿生妒意。于是，他捕捉了一只狐狸，在狐狸的尾巴上绑上一团麻絮，然后，他点燃麻絮，把狐狸扔进了邻居的田里。他心满意足地回到了家里。次日一早，他幸灾乐祸地跑去看邻居田里的热闹。然而，他却愣住了，简直不敢相信自己的眼睛，因为邻居田里完好无损，金黄的麦穗随风摇摆，而自己的庄稼则变成了一片焦土。后来，人们便引用 the farmer and the fox 作为成语，表示"恶有恶报"之意。

（19）成语 sow the wind and reap the whirlwind 的字面意思是"播下的是风，收获的却是暴风"。语出《圣经·旧约·何西阿书》。以色列人违背上帝为他们订立的"十诫"，弃善从恶，私造偶像。上帝大怒，降下各种灾难，使他们失去首领，流离失所，重过在埃及的苦难生活。结果他们播种的是风，收割的是暴风。(For they have sown the wind, and they shall reap the whirlwind.)

后人用这条成语表示"恶有恶报""因做坏事而遭到更严重的惩罚"，用 reap the whirlwind 表示"自作自受"。

例：If the IRA (Irish Republican Army) believe their cause is helped by massacres they are deluding themselves. They have plunged into a bloodbath of which they will reap the whirlwind. (*Daily Mirror*, 23 Nov. 1974)

如果爱尔兰共和军相信他们的事业是靠屠杀来促进的话，他们就是欺骗自己了。他们已经投身于血海，将最终成为其中的牺牲者。他们做了错事，将受到更严重的惩罚。(《每日镜报》，1974.11.23)

（20）Every ill man has his ill day. 是一句谚语，意思是每个恶人都有他的末日，喻恶有恶报。

（21）He that mischief hatches, mischief catches. 是一句谚语，意思是作恶者必遭殃，喻害人终害己，自作自受。

（22）One good turn deserves another. One ill turn deserves another. 是两句谚语，前者是善有善报；后者是恶有恶报。

（23）成语 serve someone right 之意为给某人应得的报应，某人活该，喻指恶有恶报。

例：And as the confiscation of wars profits, he was entirely in favour of it, for he had none, and "serve the beggars right!" (John Galsworthy, *To Let*)

至于没收靠战争发来的财，他是完全赞成的，因为他自己没有这种财，而且"那些家伙恶有恶报，理应如此"。（约翰·高尔斯华绥，《招租出让》）

（24）Evil be to him who evil thinks. 是一句谚语，意思是谁有邪念，灾难就会降落在谁的身上，喻恶有恶报。

（25）A bad life, a bad end. 是一句谚语，意思是作恶一生，不得善终，喻恶有恶报。

（26）The deed comes back upon the doer. 是一句谚语，意为所为者必有所报，喻善有善报，恶有恶报。

（27）Sow virtue, and the harvest will be virtue, sow vice and the harvest will be vice. 这是一句谚语，意为种善得善，种恶得恶，喻善有善报，恶有恶报。

（28）What goes around comes around. 这是 20 世纪末流行于美国的一句成语，意为恶有恶报。

（29）One's own deeds return to oneself. 是一句谚语，意为人自己的所作所为要返回到自己身上，喻善有善报，恶有恶报。

（30）The bad deed turns on its does. 是一句谚语，意为恶事

要返回到做恶事的人身上，喻恶有恶报。

（31） Do well and have well. 是一句谚语，意为做好事就会有好的结果，喻善有善报。

（32） Do not wait for a reward for good, the reward for ill will not miss you. 是一句谚语，意为做了好事你不必等待回报，但做了坏事，其回报是不会错过你的。意即善有善报，恶有恶报，不是不报，时辰未到，时辰一到，一切都报。

（33） A wicked man is his own hell. 是一句谚语，意思是恶人是自身的地狱，喻恶有恶报。

（34） All wrong comes to wrack. 是一句谚语，意思是一切错误都得走向毁灭，喻恶有恶报。

（35） God hath leaden feet, but iron hands. 是一句谚语，意思是上帝脚为铅灌，手为铁掌，喻善有善报，恶有恶报。

（36） Kindness always begets kindness. 是一句成语，意思就是善有善果，喻善有善报。语出索福克莱斯（Sophocles，约公元前496—前406）。

（37） Who swims in sin shall sink in sorrow. 是一句谚语，意思是在罪恶中漂游者，必在悲哀中沉没，喻恶有恶报。

（38） 成语 slow but sure 的意思是虽然慢但最后一定会实现。

例：Heaven's vengeance is slow but sure.

天网恢恢，疏而不漏。

（39） A good deed bears a blessing for its fruits. 是英语谚语，意思是善行能结出福果，喻善有善报。

（40）A good life makes a good death. 是英语谚语，意思是好生才有好死，是举行葬礼时牧师规劝人的话，喻善有善报。

（41）Long threatening comes at last. 是英语谚语，意思是早就该得到的报应总会来临，喻善有善报，恶有恶报。

（42）One ill turn deserves another. 是英语谚语，意思是一个恶行会转换成另一个该得的恶行，喻恶有恶报。

汉语成语例解：

（1）"天网恢恢，疏而不漏"原作"天网恢恢，疏而不失"。最早见于《老子》第七十三章。天网，指天道的网，比喻国法。"恢恢"为宽广之义。"疏"意为稀疏。天道的网又宽又大，看上去似乎稀疏，但决不会漏掉一个坏人，比喻作恶者逃脱不掉应得的惩罚。

例：陈某凶恶已极，罪通于天，虽经半载，犹必假之使自鸣其恶。天网恢恢，疏而不漏，信然。（清·淮阴百一居士，《壶天录》卷下）

（2）汉语俗语"善有善报，恶有恶报"或"善有善报，恶有恶报；不是不报，时辰未到"是用佛教"因果报应"之说来阐发"天网恢恢，疏而不漏"的道理的。

例：世人但知我满腹文章，是当代一个学者，却不知我秉性忠直，半点无私。从此奉上帝敕旨，屡屡判断阴府之事。果然善有善报，恶有恶报。如同影响，分毫不错，真可畏也。（无名氏，《误放来生债》杂剧楔子）

41 "give him an inch and he will take a yard" 与"得寸进尺"

英语成语：

1. give him an inch and he will take a yard
2. Show a dog a finger and he wants the whole hand.
3. Give a pig a chair, he'll want to get on the table.
4. Appetite comes with eating.
5. Avarice is never satisfied.
6. Much shall have more.
7. If you give a child your back it will ask to be carried in your arms.
8. If you give him your calf, he wants your thigh.
9. Little pigs eat great potatoes.

汉语成语：

1. 得寸进尺 2. 得陇望蜀

英语成语例解：

（1）英语成语 give him an inch and he will take a yard 的意思是给了他一寸，他还要拿一尺。这与汉语成语"得寸进尺"的意思完全相同，不仅比喻相同，思维方式也相同，这就更进一步说明了不同民族、不同语言在思想观念方面的相同。

这个成语还有 give him an inch and he will take an ell 和 give him an inch and he will take a mile 两个异体，其意思完全相同。ell 是英国旧时长度单位，等于 45 英寸；mile 是英里。

例①：If you give those people an inch, they might use our side path to reach their garden, now they have fenced in the path so that we cannot use it ourselves.

那些人真是得寸进尺，我们让他们用我们的便道去他们的花园，现在他们把便道围起来，我们自己反而不能用了。

例②：The counselor said to Jack, "No, I can't let you get a haircut until Saturday. It's against the rules, and if I give an inch, someone will take a mile."

学生辅导员对杰克说："不行，星期六以前我不能让你去理发。这违反规定，我给一寸，人家就会进一尺。"

（2）Show a dog a finger and he wants the whole hand. 是一句谚语，意为你若给狗一根手指头，它会想要你的整只手，喻得寸进尺，贪得无厌。

（3）Give a pig a chair, he'll want to get on the table. 是一句谚语，意思是如让猪上椅子，它就会想上桌子，喻人得寸进尺，欲壑难填。

（4）Appetite comes with eating. 是一句谚语，意思是胃口越吃越大，越有越想有，喻得陇望蜀。

（5）Avarice is never satisfied. 是一句谚语，意思是贪心永不足，喻欲壑难填。

（6）Much shall have more. 是一句谚语，意思是越是多，越想要，喻得陇望蜀。

（7）If you give a child your back it will ask to be carried in your arms. 是一句谚语，意思是你要背孩子，他却让你抱，喻得寸进尺。

（8）If you give him your calf, he wants your thigh. 是英语谚语，意思是如果你给他一只小腿，他就会想要一只大腿，喻人得寸进尺，贪心不足。

（9）Little pigs eat great potatoes. 是英语谚语，意思是小猪要吃大土豆，喻人心不足蛇吞象。

汉语成语例解：

（1）"得寸进尺"语出《战国策·秦策三》"王不如远交而近攻，得寸则王之寸，得尺亦王之尺也。"后来逐渐演变成"得寸进尺"，意为得到了一寸，又想得到一尺，喻贪心不足，要求越来越高。

例：加富尔既有成算，定步步为营得寸进尺之计，于是遂徇法请。（梁启超，《意大利建国三杰传》第十四节）

（2）"得陇望蜀"由《后汉书·岑彭列传》"人苦不知足，既平陇，复望蜀。每一发兵，头鬓为白"中"既平陇，复望蜀"演化而来,意即既得了陇,又想要得到蜀,形容贪心不足。陇是陇山,在陕甘交界处,后泛指这一带地方。

例①:宦资虽厚,然不入府县,别无调度,与东南士夫求田问舍、得陇望蜀者,未知孰贤?(明·何良俊,《四友斋丛说·卷十八·杂记》)

例②:湘云笑道:"得陇望蜀,人之常情。"(清·曹雪芹,《红楼梦》第七十六回)

42 "hit the ceiling" 与 "怒发冲冠"

英语成语：

1. hit the ceiling

2. out of his nostrils goeth smoke

3. fly off the handle

4. foam at the mouth

5. in high dudgeon

6. cross as two sticks

7. get the dead needle

8. go off the deep end

9. on the warpath

10. see red

11. throw a fit

12. up in arms

13. vent one´s spleen

14. blow a fuse

15. blow a gasket

16. blow one's top

17. blow up

18. get one's back up

19. get one's dander up

20. in a tiff

21. mad as a baited bull

22. mad as a tup

23. mad as a wet hen

24. at a white heat

25. get into a huff

26. get one's Indian up

27. get one's Irish up

28. have a mad on

29. hopping mad

30. get a miff

31. one's monkey is up

32. get it up one's nose

33. take pepper in the nose

34. lose one's rag

35. fly into a rage

36. on the rampage

37. in a bad skin

38. be in a wax

39. get into a wax

40. blow off steam

41. boil over

42. cut up rough

43. flip one's lid

44. get hot under the collar

45. go to market

46. have a hemorrhage

47. put one's hackles up

48. raise Cain

49. set one's teeth

50. take umbrage

汉语成语:

1. 勃然大怒 2. 怒气冲冲 3. 怒不可遏 4. 大发雷霆
5. 怒发冲冠

英语成语例解:

(1) 成语 hit the ceiling (或 roof) 是一个口头用语,原意为"碰到天花板(或屋顶)"。通常人的手是碰不着天花板或屋顶的。一个人只有当他暴跳如雷、拼命跳脚时才有可能碰到天花板或屋顶。因此,hit the ceiling (或 roof) 用来表示暴跳如雷、大发雷霆。这可以说是一个形象生动的夸张比喻。有时亦作 go through the roof,这又使我们想起汉语中"怒气冲天"的夸张说法。

例①：He hit the ceiling when she cancelled the appointment.

她取消约会使他怒不可遏。

例②：At the mere mention of her name, he used to hit the roof.

一提到她的名字，他就火冒三丈。

（2）成语 out of his nostrils goeth smoke 之意为"鼻孔冒烟"，典出《圣经·旧约·撒母耳记下》第 22 章大卫向耶和华所念的一首赞歌："我在急难之中求告耶和华，向我的上帝呼求。他从殿中听了我的声音，我的呼求入了他的耳中。那时因他发怒，地就摇撼战抖，天的根基也震动摇撼。从他鼻孔冒烟上腾，从他口中发火焚烧，连炭也着了。"后来，"鼻孔冒烟"一语被人们用来形容生气、发怒。

（3）成语 fly off the handle 源于美国。在美国拓荒时代，拓荒者所用斧子的斧柄多半是他们自己临时用木头削成的，比较粗糙。在伐木或砍柴时用力过猛，斧头往往会从斧柄上突然飞脱（fly off the handle），谁也无法控制，有时还可能伤到附近的人。使用铁锤也会发生类似的现象。后来人们在口语中就常用 fly off the handle 一语比喻"失去控制""大发雷霆"或"勃然大怒"，实际上是把它当作委婉语来使用的。这一成语最先是以 off the handle 的形式出现在美国作家尼尔（John Neal, 1793—1876）1825 年出版的小说《乔纳森大哥》（*Brother Jonathan*）中，1844 年才以 fly off the handle 的形式见于加拿大幽默作家哈利伯顿（Thomas Haliburton, 1796—1865）的作品里。

例①：You have to be very careful about what you say to him—he often just flies off the handle for no reason.

你跟他说话得十分小心——他常常莫名其妙地大发雷霆。

例②：She flies off the handle whenever anyone disagrees with her.

每当有谁跟她意见不同，她就要大发脾气。

(4) 成语 foam at the mouth 的本义为"口吐白沫"。疯狗口吐白沫，而人在盛怒时说话则唾沫四溅。据此，此成语常用来比喻"大怒""大发雷霆"。

例①：Michael was furious—foaming at the mouth. I've never seen anyone so angry.

迈克气得七窍生烟，唾沫四溅。我从未见过一个人像他那样发火。

例②：Bob raved, foaming at the mouth when he got a parking ticket.

鲍勃接到一张违章停车罚款通知单时，破口大骂，唾沫四溅。

(5) 成语 in high dudgeon 中的 dudgeon 一词有两个意思：一为"柄木"（用于短剑等的柄的木材）或"剑柄"；一为"愤怒"。这两者之间有无关系呢？中世纪，在 in high dudgeon 一语开始广为流行的时期，当一个出身高贵的人遭到侮辱或名声受损而极度愤怒之时，他往往会立即把手伸向剑柄，因此从"剑柄"到"愤怒"的词义演变是完全可能的。In high dudgeon

现仍表示"非常愤怒",多用于口语,其中 high 含有"极度的"或"强烈的"之义。

例①: The woman slammed the door and went off in high dudgeon.

那女人砰地把门关上,怒冲冲地离去。

例②: Eric stormed out of the meeting in high dudgeon.

埃里克气冲冲地退出会议。

(6) 成语 cross as two sticks 中的 cross 作形容词用时兼有"生气的"和"交叉的"两个意思。Cross as two sticks 一语的构成正是利用了 cross 一语双关的特点,意思是非常生气的。试想两个狂怒的人用棍棒对打,一根棍棒横架在另一根之上,就正好成了一个十字。因此,"气得跟两根棍棒似的"就是"气得不得了"。此成语多用于口语中。

例①: The old man was as cross as two sticks when the bus left without waiting for him.

公共汽车没等老人就开走了,所以老人气得不得了。

例②: For goodness' sake don't go near her, she's as cross as two sticks.

看在上帝的分上,别走近她,她在气头上。

(7) 成语 get the dead needle 为发火、恼怒之意。这个引喻来自做裁缝时给针刺了手指,但在第二次世界大战时被广泛地用来指空战时的激动情绪。

例①: He had got the dead needle to you because you have been talking about him.

他对你非常恼火，因为你在讲他的闲话。

例②：His refusal to admit his mistakes gives me the needle.

他拒不承认错误使我愤怒。

(8) 成语 go off the deep end 的原意是"在游泳池水最深的一端下水"。游泳者如果毫无思想准备，贸然从这一端下水，往往会手忙脚乱，无法控制自己。20世纪初以来，这一成语常用来描写感情的激烈爆发，尤其是大为震怒。

例①：John has gone off the deep end about owning a motorcycle.

约翰一时冲动想买一部摩托车。

例②：My father were off the deep end because I failed in all my examinations.

我各门考试都不及格，因此父亲大发脾气。

(9) 成语 on the warpath 在当今英语中的意思是大发雷霆、怒不可遏，其中 warpath 一词指美洲印第安人出征时所走的路线，即"征途"，on the warpath 的字面意思就是"在征途中"，可引申为"开赴战场"。但在语言实践中，它常被用于喻义，表示震怒。

例①：He scares me to death when he's on the warpath.

当他大发雷霆时我被吓得要死。

例②：Why are you always on the warpath? What's wrong?

你为什么总发火？是怎么了？

(10) 成语 see red 是怒不可遏、火冒三丈之义。此语可能源于斗牛。据说公牛见到红色的东西就要狂怒，所以斗牛士往往挥舞红旗或红披风来挑逗公牛。根据最近的研究报告,鲜艳的颜色虽然会使牛兴奋,但白布较之红布能更快地把公牛激怒。由于早先的错误看法已广为流传,人们很容易把"红色"同"愤怒"联系起来。See red 一语就是这样产生的。另有一种解释认为,此语源于如下看法:一个人在狂怒时会觉得眼前一片红色。

例①:When his son contradicted him, he really saw red.

他的儿子顶撞他,使他怒不可遏。

例②:When Reger realized that he had been duped, he started to see red.

当罗杰意识到受了骗,他立即火冒三丈。

(11) throw(或 have)a fit 的意思是大发脾气、勃然大怒。在一百多年前,它是一句美国俚语,意指歇斯底里地发狂,在第一次世界大战期间传入英国,成为口语。

例①:When I heard the noise I nearly threw a fit.

我听到那里的喧闹声时,几乎要发起脾气来。

例②:The child threw a fit after the mother had put him to bed.

母亲把孩子放到床上睡觉,那孩子大哭大闹起来。

(12) 成语 up in arms 除有"起来进行武装斗争"和"极力反对"之义外,还有发怒、恼火之义。人们常常为一些事情生气,在英语中使用 angry 来表达"生气的"非常普遍。Up in arms 的意思是"非常生气的"。人们生气一般是指心里不愉快,而使用 arms 是生气到了准备大打出手的地步,可见已经非常生气了。

例①：All us students are up in arms at the news that the school is raising our tuition ten percent.

当听到学校要提高10%的学费的消息时，所有学生都义愤填膺。

例②：There is no need to get up in arms over such a trifle.

用不着为了这么点小事动火。

（13）成语 vent one's spleen 的意思是发脾气、发火。Spleen 是人的脾脏。在中世纪时，西方人认为脾脏是一个人所有愤怒、忧愁、怨恨之源。成语中的 vent 是发泄之义。而"将脾脏发泄"所指的，便是将一个人身上所有不愉快的情绪都宣泄出来，也就是发火、发脾气。

例①：After a tiring day at the office, he vented his spleen on his wife.

他在办公室累了一天，回家后就对妻子发脾气。

例②：We should occasionally vent our spleen on issues in order to stay healthy mentally.

我们需要偶尔的情绪发泄，以维持心理健康。

（14）成语 blow a fuse 原意为"使保险丝熔断"，指电路超负荷导致保险丝熔断。同时，一个人的耐心是有限度的，超过这个限度，他就要发脾气。

例①：He blew a fuse when he heard that she had lost the money.

听说她丢了钱，他大发雷霆。

例②：When Mr. Mclarthy's son got married against his wish, he blow a fuse.

麦卡锡先生的儿子未照他的意思结婚，麦卡锡暴跳如雷。

（15）成语 blow a gasket 原意为"垫圈爆裂"。Gasket 是置于机器部件之间的垫圈。当压力增大到这个垫圈不能承受时，它就会破裂。同样，当人们遇到不顺心的事情时，心烦意乱，常常失去自我控制而大发脾气。

例①：When the Ambassador glanced at the list of who was sitting next to whom, he blew a gasket.

大使看了一眼那份排定谁坐在谁旁边的名单，立即大发雷霆。

例②：The Senator blew a gasket when he read the statement.

参议员一看到那份声明，不由得勃然大怒。

（16）成语 blew one's top 原意为"冲开头顶"。这句成语形象地将人的头顶与容器的盖子进行类比。当一容器内的压力过大时，就会把盖子冲开。同样，当一个人的内在情感过分强烈时，就会"冲开头顶"发泄出去。

例①：He blew his top and lost his job and came bellyaching to Loraine.

他发了一通脾气，为此丢掉了工作，于是带着满腹牢骚来找洛雷因。

例②：He got so upset over what she said that I thought he was going to blow his top.

她说的话使他狼狈不堪，我认为他要大发脾气了。

（17）成语 blow up 除有吹胀、夸大、加剧、责骂等义外，还表示大发脾气、暴怒之义。

例①：I'm sorry I blew up at you this morning.

对不起，今天上午我不该对你发脾气。

例②：I blew right up, saying that I disagreed completely with the conclusion of the report.

我立刻火冒三丈，说我完全不同意报告的结论。

（18）成语 get one's back up 的意思是发怒。猫在发怒时或受到威吓时就把背弓起，故有此语。变体有 put one's back up 或 set one's back up。

例①：His rude behavior really puts my back up.

他的粗暴行为使我大为发火。

例②：The mule got his back up and refused to move.

那只骡子发犟了，不肯动。

（19）成语 get one's dander up 的意思是发怒、恼火。此语产生于 17 世纪的美洲。最早见于书面是在 1831 年由芬（H. J. Finn）主编的《美国漫画年刊》（*American Comic Annual*）上。它的来源有几种说法：一种认为 dander 指"头皮屑"；另一种看法认为 dander 指西印度洋群岛上制糖蜜用的发酵剂，由发酵剂可引申指"激动"，由此产生了这一成语。这一成语有不少变体：put up one's dander, have one's dander up 以及 get somebody's dander up。

例①：You'll gain nothing by getting your dander up now—you should have complained when you were in the shop.

你现在发火毫无用处——早在商店里你就该提出意见了。

例②：Finally, she got her dander up and wrote direct to the president.

到了最后，她实在恼火了，就直接给校长写了信。

(20) 成语 in a tiff 的意思是生气、发火，自 18 世纪初使用至今，来源不详。它很可能是一个拟声词语，与蒸汽冒出来时发出的声响有关。

例：Abrupt Captain Anthony is in some tiff of his own.

粗鲁无礼的安东尼上尉正在气得呼哧呼哧地喘。

(21) 成语 mad as a baited bull 原意为"像遭犬袭击的公牛"，转义为恼怒、震怒。根据托马斯·福勒（Thomas Fuller）所著《英国名人录》（*The History of the Worthies of England*），这一用语源出 as mad as a baited bull of Stamford（疯得像斯坦福德地方受折磨的公牛）。根据福勒的记载，有一位华伦伯爵（Earl Warren）把一块草地赠给斯坦福德镇作为公园，但他提出一个附带条件，要求当地居民在每年圣诞节前献出一只公牛来，使它备受折磨以供人取乐六个星期。具体做法是用链条或绳子把公牛拴起来，或把它关起来，然后放狗去咬它。这种做法在 1835 年被法律所禁止。同义语有 mad as a baited bear 和 mad as a baited boar。

(22) 成语 mad as a tup 原意为"疯得像只公羊"。转义为恼怒、震怒。夏洛蒂·伯恩（Charlotte Burne）在《希罗普郡民间传说》（*Shropshire Folk-Lore*, 1883）一书中认为完整的成语是 mad as a tup in a halter（狂怒得像套上了笼头的公羊一样）。因为公羊一般总是自由自在地和母羊在一起，如果将它带上笼头缚起来，当然就要狂怒。

例：In Derbyshire…there is no commoner saying to express anger shown by anyone than to say that he or she was "as mad as a tup".

在德比郡，要形容一个人发怒，最常用的成语便是说他或她狂怒得像只公羊。

（23）成语 mad as a wet hen 原意为"像淋湿的母鸡一样"，常用来比喻狂怒。但养鸡户认为并无根据，因为全身淋湿的母鸡并不见得特别容易发怒。母鸡只是在遭到挑衅时才会发出愤怒的叫声。在汉语里，"落汤鸡"给人的印象则是一种可笑的狼狈相。

例①：The chicken farmers in Quebec…are mad as, well, a wet hen.

魁北克的养鸡户气愤得和淋湿的母鸡一样。

例②：Everybody that was not invited was as mad as a wet hen.

没有受到邀请的人个个都很生气。

（24）成语 at a white heat 的意思是在白热化的程度，喻盛怒、震怒。

例：He was at a white heat when I paid him a visit.

我去看他的时候，他正在大发雷霆。

（25）成语 get（或 go）into a huff 的意思是感到受到触犯，喻发怒。

例①：She got into a huff all of a sudden.

她突然大怒起来。

例②：She's gone into a huff because my brother didn't remember her name.

她因为我的兄弟忘了她的名字，就大生其气。

（26）Get one's Indian up 为美国俚语，意为发怒、失去克制力。

（27）成语 get one's Irish up 意为发怒、失去克制力。这种说法最早出现在美国政治家大卫·克洛科特（David Crockett, 1786—1836）的《叙事生活》"Narrative Life"一文中：Her Irish was up too high to do anything with her.（她火气太大，拿她毫无办法。）由于爱尔兰人多为红头发，因此给人的印象是脾气暴躁，而实际上并非如此。

例①：He got Irish in him. He got a lot.

他天生一副火爆脾气。他的火气大得很。

例②：Come! Come! Don't get your Irish up for nothing.

好了，好了！别无缘无故发火。

（28）成语 have a mad on 意为发怒、生气。

例①：She still had a mad on.

她余怒未息。

例②：When I want a personality course, friend, I'll go to someone who hasn't a mad on at the world.

如果我要上性格教育课，朋友，我要去找一个对世界没有愤怒情绪的人。

（29）成语 hopping mad 意为气得暴跳如雷、狂怒。

例：He was hopping mad when I told him such.

当我把这事告诉他时，他气得暴跳如雷。

（30）成语 get（或 have, take）a miff 的意思是生气、发脾气、愤怒。

例：If Mabel should get another miff, they'd never be able to appease her.

要是梅布尔再发脾气的话，他们就没有办法使她息怒。

（31）成语 one's monkey is up 的意思是发怒、生气。

例：Form matters very little when a man's monkey is up.

人一发脾气就不顾礼貌了。

（32）成语 get it up one's nose 的意思是生气、发怒。

例①：I have seldom seen a man who has got it so thoroughly up his nose.

我很少见过有人发这么大的脾气。

（33）成语 take pepper in the nose 的意思是发脾气、勃然大怒。

例：Why did he take pepper in the nose?

他为什么要大发脾气？

（34）成语 lose one's rag 的意思是发脾气、愤怒。

例：There are times when even the smallest mistake will make him lose his rag.

有时候甚至小小的错误也会使得他大发脾气。

（35）成语 fly（或 fall, get）into a rage 的意思是勃然大怒、

大发脾气。

例：To fly into a rage is futile. To bluff is also futile.

暴跳如雷是无用的。虚声恫吓也是无用的。

(36) 成语（be）on the（或 a）rampage（亦作 go on the rampage）的意思是极端愤怒、狂怒、暴跳如雷。

例："Here, out of the back door as fast as you can, Father's found his broken window and is on the rampage." said his brother.

"来，快从后门跑，爸爸已经发现窗户被打破了，正暴跳如雷呢。"他哥哥说。

(37) 成语 in a bad skin 的意思是发脾气、发怒。

例：Don't disturb him for he is in a bad skin.

别去打搅他，他在发脾气。

(38) 成语 be in a wax 之意为大发脾气、暴怒。

例：She's in a terrible wax, but she'll be all right by the time Billy comes back from his holidays.

她正在大发脾气，但是，等比利休假回来时，她的气就会消的。

(39) 成语 get into a wax 之意为发怒、生气。

例：Don't get into a wax because I said your hair is ginger——you know that it is.

不要因为我说你的头发是姜红色的就生气——你也知道你的头发就是这种颜色的。

(40) 成语 blow off steam 的字面意思是排放蒸汽，转义为发脾气。有时亦作 let off steam。

例：Don't go in yet, father's letting off steam about the razor you used to sharpen your pencil with.

不要进去，父亲正在发脾气，骂你用他的刮胡子刀片削铅笔呢。

（41）成语 boil over 的字面意思是沸溢，转义为发火、怒不可遏。

例①：When I said that, he just boiled over.

我一讲起那事，他就大发其火。

例②：John was boiling over and it was soon clear why: nobody had told him of our plans to move house.

约翰大发脾气，我们很快就清楚了他为什么生气：没人告诉过他我们要搬家的计划。

（42）成语 cut up rough 的意思是铁蹄踏过尘土飞扬，转义为发火、咆哮、大发雷霆。

例：The girl refused to marry Smollett, and old Smollett backed her up. Naturally, the parson and the village cut up rough.

那个姑娘不愿和史摩莱特结婚，史摩莱特老头儿居然支持她。自然，牧师和那个村子的人都气得暴跳如雷。

（43）成语 flip one's lid 的字面意思是"啪"的一声冲开盖儿，转义为发脾气。

例①：He nearly flipped his lid over the way they damaged his car.

他们把他的汽车损坏到这个样子，使他大发脾气。

例②: When that pushy salesman came back, mom really flipped her lid.

当那个缠人的推销员又回来时,妈妈真的发脾气了。

(44) 成语 get (grow) hot under the collar 的字面意思是领下发热,脸红脖子粗,转义为发火、生气。

例①: Mary gets hot under the collar if you joke about women drivers.

你若是拿女司机开玩笑,玛丽就会发火。

例②: Tom got hot under the collar when his teacher punished him.

汤姆受到老师处罚时,心里很生气。

(45) 成语 go to market (town) 的字面意思是去市场或进城,转义为生气、发火。

例: Peter came home drunk once every week, and made his poor wife milk the herd of twenty four cows by herself, and then about 8 p.m. he'd arise from the sofa and go to market because the poor woman hadn't cooked a hot tea for him.

彼得每星期都有一次喝得醉醺醺地回家,让他可怜的妻子一个人挤24头母牛的奶。然后在晚上大约8点时他会从沙发上站起来,因那可怜的女人还没有为他沏好热茶而大发雷霆。

(46) 成语 have a hemorrhage 的字面意思是大出血,转义为大怒、大发雷霆。

例: She has a hemorrhage every time I'm late.

我每次迟到她都要大发雷霆。

(47) 成语 put (get, have, raise) one's hackles up (show one's hackles) 的字面意思是竖起颈毛，转义为发脾气、愤怒。

例①：Don't get your hackles up about nothing.
别无缘无故地大发脾气。

例②：Drives to popularize drinks with low sugar content raise the hackles of sugar producers.
这一次次广泛宣传低糖饮料的活动使得生产食糖的厂商十分恼火。

(48) 成语 raise Cain 的字面意思是惹怒该隐，转义为发脾气。该隐是亚当夏娃之长子，他一怒之下杀死弟弟亚伯，因此该隐便成了"愤怒"的代名词。

例①：When John couldn't go on the basketball trip with the team he raised Cain.
当约翰不能随篮球队外出巡回比赛时，他大发脾气。

例②：If I am late again, the boss will raise Cain.
如果我再迟到，老板就要大发雷霆了。

(49) 成语 set one's teeth 的字面意思是咬牙切齿，转义为十分愤怒、怒不可遏。

例：She set her teeth when she thought of Arthur.
她一想到亚瑟就气得咬牙切齿。

(50) 成语 take (give) umbrage 的字面意思是阴沉下来，转义为生气、愤怒、恼火。

例①：He took umbrage at what I said.
他对我说的话很生气。

例②：Never take umbrage unless you can lick the guy.
除非你能打败那个家伙，否则千万别生气。

汉语成语例解：

（1）成语"勃然大怒"谓突然大发愤怒，用于人突然生气变脸色。语出汉代班固《汉书·谷永传》："是故皇天勃然发怒。"

例①：云长勃然大怒曰："吾虎女安肯嫁犬子乎！"（元·罗贯中，《三国演义》第七十三回）

例②：勃然大怒，放一把火烧光，算是保存自己的清白，则是昏蛋。（鲁迅，《拿来主义》）

（2）成语"怒气冲冲"形容十分愤怒，"冲冲"为感情激动的样子。亦作"怒气冲天"。

例①：先轸方在家用饭，闻晋侯已赦三帅，吐哺入见，怒气冲冲。（明·冯梦龙，《东周列国志》第四十五回）

例②：秦明怒气冲天，大驱兵马投西山边来。（元·施耐庵，《水浒传》）

（3）成语"怒不可遏"谓愤怒得抑制不住。

例①：顿时气愤填膺，怒不可遏。（清·李伯元，《官场现形记》第二十七回）

例②：慈禧后阅毕，怒不可遏，立碎其纸。（小横香室主人，《清朝野史大观》）

（4）成语"大发雷霆"形容大发脾气，高声斥责。语出《三国志·吴志·陆逊传》："今不忍小忿而发雷霆之怒吼。"

例①：陈秀才大发雷霆。(明·凌濛初，《初刻拍案惊奇》)

例②：胡统领此时大发雷霆，真按捺不住了，顺手取过一张椅子，从船窗洞里扔了出来。(清·李伯元，《官场现形记》一二回)

(5) 成语"怒发冲冠"的意思是愤怒得头发竖起来，顶着帽子，形容盛怒的样子。语出《史记·廉颇蔺相如列传》："王授璧，相如因持璧却立，倚柱，怒发上冲冠。"

例①：怒发冲冠，凭栏处、潇潇雨歇。(宋·岳飞，《满江红》)

例②：穷乡僻壤，有这样读书君子，却被守钱奴如此凌虐，足令人怒发冲冠！(清·吴敬梓，《儒林外史》第九回)

43 "all mops and brooms" 与 "酩酊大醉"

英语成语：

1. all mops and brooms

2. brick in one's hat

3. drunk as a fiddler

4. drunk as a lord

5. half seas over

6. have the sun in one's eyes

7. in one's cups

8. have the malt above the meal

9. have one over the eight

10. under the table

11. under the weather

12. be lit up like a Christmas tree

13. feel no pain

14. hang one on

15. get a bun on

16. have a buzz on

17. have a nose to light candles at

18. to go to bed in one's boots

19. in one's altitude

20. see double

21. the worse for liquor

22. three sheets to the wind

23. under the influence

24. stewed to the gills

25. have a bag on

26. in the bag

27. up the pole

28. well away

29. well oiled

30. be wiped out

31. shake a cloth in the wind

32. cannot see a hole in a forty-foot ladder

33. drunk as a fiddler's bitch

34. drunk as a skunk

35. drink like a fish

36. tight as a brick

37. lose one's legs

38. have a load on

39. drunk as a mouse

40. tie one on

41. get slopped

42. have snakes in one´s boots

43. have been in the sunshine

44. take too much

45. dead to the wide

46. done to the wide

47. in wine

48. blind to the world

49. zonk out

汉语成语：

1. 酩酊大醉　2. 烂醉如泥

英语成语例解：

（1）成语 all mops and brooms 意为喝酒喝醉了，至于醉到什么程度，各有各的理解。这句成语出现于19世纪初，但出处不详。有人推测，成语中的 mop 和 broom 与昔日英国有些地方一年一度雇用女仆的集市有关。那些来到集市选雇女仆的人，总是开怀畅饮，而待雇的妇女则手拿拖把和扫帚站在一旁，希望能被选中。

例①：There is not much doing now, being New year's Eve, and folks mops and brooms from what's in side them. Nobody took much notice. (Thomas Hardy, *Tess of the D'Urbervilles*)

因为是大年夜,没有多少事可做,大家喝得烂醉如泥,谁也没有多注意他们。(托马斯哈代,《德伯家的苔丝》)

例②:"Now Tom, you're drunk!"——"No Dame, not I, I'm only mops and brooms."

"汤姆,你醉了!"——"没有,姑娘,我没醉,我只不过有点醉意罢了。"

(2)成语 brick in one's hat 的原意为"在某人戴的帽子里面有一块砖头",这句成语来源不详,但有人解释说,由于砖头很重,人就难以保持身体平衡,致使走路晃晃摇摇,东倒西歪,像喝醉了酒一样。所以就用这句话形容人喝酒喝得醉醺醺。

例: Her husband had taken to the tavern, and often came home very late with a brick in his hat. (Henry Wadsworth Longfellow, *Kavanagh*)

她丈夫整天泡在小酒馆里,常常喝得醉醺醺的很晚才回家。(亨利·华兹华斯·朗费罗,《卡文那》)

(3)成语 drunk as a fiddler 的字面意思是"醉得像一个小提琴手那样",转义为酩酊大醉,烂醉如泥。在过去,作为演奏报酬,人们常请小提琴手喝酒。小提琴手常常开怀畅饮,喝得大醉,丑态百出。由此产生了这句成语。

例①: You should be ashamed of yourself, you were as drunk as a fiddler last night.

你真不害臊,昨天晚上你醉得像一摊泥似的。

例②: The man was as drunk as a fiddler.

那个人烂醉如泥。

（4）成语 drunk as a lord 的字面意思是"醉得像个贵族似的"。在 18 世纪至 19 世纪，英国社会不仅盛行一醉方休的习俗，人们还以自己酒量大而自豪，开怀畅饮成为表现绅士风度的一种体现。在筵席上，宾客们相互劝酒，觥筹交错，客人醉倒在桌子下面的情景屡见不鲜。

例①：On my birthday I got as drunk as a lord.

过生日那天，我喝得酩酊大醉。

例②：I couldn't understand what the man was saying; he was as drunk as a lord.

我听不懂那个男人在说什么，他喝得醉醺醺的。

（5）成语 half seas over 意为酩酊大醉，研究语言的权威人士一致认为这句成语源于航海用语，但对其含义有不同的解释。有人认为它的本义是航船渡海驶过航程的一半，转义为"距目的地还有一半路程"或"处于两种状态之间"，再转喻为"半醉"；另有人则认为这句成语表示"船已倾斜，即将覆没"。描述醉汉走路像快要颠覆的船一样，歪歪斜斜，随时都可能跌倒，因此用这句成语喻指"酩酊大醉"。

例①：Look at Frank—half seas over already, and the party's hardly begun. (*Oxford Dictionary of Current Idiomatic English*)

你看弗兰克，酒会还没有正式开始，他已经喝得醉醺醺的了。(《牛津当代英语成语辞典》)

例②：You had better take him home, he's half seas over.

你最好送他回家，他已经醉得不行了。

(6) 成语 have the sun in one's eyes 至少可以追溯到1770年。这句成语是对一个人喝醉以后走路东倒西歪的委婉描述，意思是说这样走路是"因为强烈的阳光照得他头昏目眩"的缘故。也有人认为这句成语可能是指由于过多的阳光照射正如过量饮酒那样使人的脸上发红或眼睛充血。这句成语有时亦作 have been in the sun。

例：He furthermore took occasion to apologize for any negligence that might be perceptible in his dress, on the ground that last night he had had "the sun very strong in his eyes"; by which expression he was understood to convey to his hearers, in the most delicate manner possible, the information that he had been extremely drunk. (Charles Dickens, *The Old Curiosity Shop*)

然后他又乘机替自己辩护说，他的衣着看来或许有些不整齐，原因是前一个晚上"太阳光在他的眼睛里太强烈了"，他是想借这种表达方式，尽可能巧妙地让听话的人明白，昨晚他喝醉了。(查尔斯·狄更斯，《老古玩店》)

(7) 成语 in one's cups 表示"在饮酒中"或"喝醉了"。Cup 一词常用来指酒杯或杯中的酒。这一成语从18世纪起使用至今，现在使用时常含有戏谑的意味。

例①：She used to come home in her cups and break the china. (John Arbuthnot, *The History of John Bull*)

她过去常常喝得酩酊大醉回家，把磁器打碎。(约翰·阿巴思诺特，《约翰牛的生平》)

例②：The banker was aged, violent and uncomely, habitually

in his cups, and abused his wife before the servants.

那个银行家已经上了年纪，又粗暴又难看，一天到晚喝得醉醺醺的，并且在佣人面前骂他的妻子。

（8）成语 have（或 with）the malt above the meal（或 wheat）始用于 16 世纪后期，malt（麦芽）本是酿酒原料，亦可指麦芽酿的酒，如啤酒等。如果一个人"把饮酒放在比吃饭更重要的地位"，那他就会经常酩酊大醉。这就是有人常说的"饭可以不吃，酒不能不喝"。

例：He marched home from the little public-house with "the malt above the meal".

他醉醺醺地从小酒店向家中走去。

（9）成语 have one over the eight 指一个人的正常酒量是 8 品脱，或 8 杯啤酒，如果超过这个量就会喝醉。因此就用这句成语表达喝醉酒了。

例①：He had one over the eight and fell down the steps as he was leaving the party. (*Longman Dictionary of English Idioms*)

他在宴会上喝多了，离开时从台阶上摔了下来。(《朗文英语成语辞典》)

例②：You'll ruin year health; last Saturday you had again one over the eight.

你会把身体搞垮的，上星期六你又喝得醉醺醺的。

（10）成语 under the table 的字面意思是"在桌子下面"。昔日英国社会曾把能否豪饮视作是否有绅士风度的重要标志。所以，王公贵族们为了显示自己的海量，总是在饮酒时逞能，每次饮酒不倒在桌下几个决不罢休。故而,这句成语成为描写酩酊大醉的最佳词语,常常被人使用。

例①: You pride yourselves on capacity, but he can drink you all under the table. (*Handbook of Commonly Used American Idioms*)

你们以海量自豪,但比起酒量来,他可能全叫你们甘拜下风,个个醉倒在地。(《美国常用成语手册》)

例②: We'll be under the table if we drink all that wine in one night.

要是我们一个晚上把这些酒全部喝光,我们会醉倒的。

(11) 成语 under the weather 有两种意思,一是指身体不适,二是指醉酒。人们相信天气状况与人的健康有着直接的关系。

例①: Many accidents are caused by drivers who are under the weather.

许多事故都是驾驶员喝醉了酒造成的。

例②: I didn't pay much attention to what he said, since he was obviously under the weather.

我没怎么在意他说的话,因为他显然是喝醉了。

(12) 成语 be lit up like a Christmas tree 的字面意思是"像圣诞树一般灯火通明",借喻酩酊大醉。

例①:"Fancy a decent chap like him being had up for attempted murder!"——"He must have been terribly lit up like a Christmas tree when he did it; that's the only possible explanation."

"想不到这么一个规规矩矩的小伙子会被控杀人未

遂!"——"他行凶时肯定是喝过了头,这是唯一可能的解释。"

例②:He is a quiet person usually, but he shouts wildly at everyone when he gets lit up like a Christmas tree.

他平时文文静静,可喝醉了酒就冲着人乱嚷乱叫。

(13) 成语 feel no pain 的本义是不觉得痛,因酒精有麻痹作用,转义为喝醉酒了。

例:After a few drinks, the man felt no pain and began to act foolishly.

这人几杯酒下肚就醉了,开始胡闹起来。

(14) 成语 hang one on 的本义是猛击一拳,转义为喝得大醉,这是 20 世纪美国英语中的俚语。

例①:After Smith lost his job, he went to a bar and hung one on.

史密斯丢了工作后,跑到一家酒吧喝得烂醉如泥。

例②:Every payday he hangs one on.

每次发薪那天他都喝得酩酊大醉。

(15) 成语 get a bun on 是醉酒的一种委婉的说法,始用于 1925 年,但其原由众说纷纭。

例①:He kept drinking till he got a bun on.

他喝个不停,直到喝醉。

例②:You've got another bun on.

你又喝醉了。

(16) 成语 have a buzz on 的字面意思是"有一种嗡嗡的感

觉",转义为醉酒,20 世纪 50 年代以来,这种说法颇为流行。

例①: I drank five more beers and finally got a buzz.

我又喝了 5 杯啤酒,终于有了一种飘然欲仙的感觉。

例②: After two Scotches he got a nice buzz.

两杯苏格兰威士忌下肚,他就酣醉了。

(17) 成语 have a nose to light candles at 的字面意思 "鼻子红得可以点燃蜡烛",转义为喝酒喝得酩酊大醉。这一形象的说法始用于 16 世纪,意思是酒徒的红鼻子仿佛是燃烧的微火,能将蜡烛点亮。

例: Their noses shall be able to light a candle.

他们的鼻子能将蜡烛点燃。

(18) 成语 to go to bed in one's boots 的意思是 "穿着靴子上床睡觉",可见醉到了何等程度,即酩酊大醉。

例: If old Simon drinks much more, he'll go to bed in his boots.

如果老西蒙再喝下去,他就要烂醉如泥了。

(19) 成语 in one's altitude 亦有喝醉了的用法,即口语中所谓的 "喝高了"。这是 17、18 世纪的一种委婉说法,一般多见于英语口语中。

例: He was in his altitude.

他喝醉了。

(20) 成语 see double 的字面意思是 "将一物看成两物",谓因饮酒而使视线模糊,转义为醉酒。这种以委婉的口吻形容醉酒的说法自 17 世纪以来从未间断。

例①：I don't think one glass of liquor will make him see double.

我不相信一杯酒就能使他醉眼蒙眬。

例②：He had a spat with his girl and is seeing double again.

他跟女朋友吵了一架，现在又喝成醉金刚了。

（21）成语 the worse for liquor 的字面意思是"因喝酒而搞糟的"，转义为醉酒。

例①：My conditions are these: that you do not come to me, but to my clerk, that you do not come here the worse for liquor. (Robert Louis Stevenson, *The Wrecker*)

我的条件是这样：你别来找我，去找我的秘书；你不能喝醉了酒来。（罗伯特·路易斯·斯蒂文森，《肇事者》）

例②：He found his partner to be very disagreeable, frequently he was the worse for liquor which made him surly. (Theodore Dreiser, *Sister Carrie*)

他发觉他的合伙人很不近人情，他经常喝得酩酊大醉，而且在喝酒的时候脾气变得很坏。（西奥多·德莱塞，《嘉丽妹妹》）

（22）成语 three sheets to（或 in）the wind 的本义是"迎风三帆缆"，转义为醉酒，酩酊大醉。Three sheets 原是航海用语，sheet 是指调节帆位角的绳索或铁链。如果一艘三帆船上的绳索全部松开的话，那么帆船在风中就会左右摇摆，船身就会偏离航道。该说法自 19 世纪起就被借来形容醉酒失态的模样。类似的说法还有：

both sheets in the wind 醉酒

two sheets to the wind 醉酒

a sheet in the wind 微醉

例①：The sailors came down the street, three sheets in the wind.

水手们喝得酩酊大醉，摇摇晃晃地沿街而去。

例②：Though Snow père might be a thought tipsy—a sheet or so in the wind, as folks say, he was not more tipsy than was customary with him. (Anthony Trollope, *Orley Farm*)

斯诺老人虽然有几分醉意——正如人们所说的，有一点飘飘欲仙，但并没有超过平日的程度。(安东尼·特里洛普，《奥利农场》)

(23) 成语 under the influence 的本义是"受其影响"，转义为"在酒力的支配之下"，即指醉酒。Under the influence 原本是 under the influence of alcohol 的截短说法，这样更显得模糊、委婉。

例：The police sergeant asked if I'd been drinking, I'd had a drink—and then he said I must go to the station with him, as he'd have to charge me with driving under the influence.

警官问我喝了酒没有。我喝了一点——于是他说我得跟他到警察局去，他要指控我醉酒驾车。

(24) 成语 stewed to the gills 的本义是"醉意已经上脸了"，转义为醉酒。

例①：He knew where the colonel lived from the time he'd taken him home stewed to the gills.

那位喝醉了的上校是他送回家的，打那时起，他就知道他的住址在哪里了。

例②：He came in stewed to the gills.

他醉醺醺地走了进来。

(25) 成语 have（或 get, tie）a bag on 之义为醉酒。

例：He had half a bag on and looked it.

他有些醉了，一眼便看得出来。

(26) 成语 in the bag 除有稳操胜券之义，还有醉酒之义。

例①：He was in the bag and staggering slightly.

他已经醉了，走起路来有点摇摇晃晃的。

例②：Steve was really in the bag last night.

昨晚斯蒂夫喝得酩酊大醉。

(27) 成语 up the pole 除有进退两难的意思外，还有酩酊大醉的意思。

例：He came home up the pole at 1∶00 a. m.

他半夜一点钟醉醺醺地回家。

(28) 成语 well away 除有事态进展迅速之义外，还有醉酒的意思。

例：By the time we arrived at the party, he was well away.

等我们到达晚会时，他已经喝醉了。

(29) 成语 well oiled 为醉酒之义，从 20 世纪初期开始流行。

例：He happened to be well oiled, as was usually the case.

当时他跟平常一样，也早已喝得醉醺醺的了。

（30）成语 be wiped out 除有筋疲力尽之义外，还有醉酒之义。

例①：Everybody had been too wiped out to watch.

大家都喝醉了，没法看电视了。

（31）成语 shake（或 have）a cloth in the wind 的本义是帆篷因顶风而发生颤动，转义为人喝酒喝多了时身体会摇摇晃晃，形容其醉态。

例：They all had got a cloth in the wind.

他们都有点醉了。

（32）成语 cannot see a hole in a forty-foot ladder 的本义是"在40英尺高的梯子上都看不见一个洞"，可见蒙眬的醉眼已模糊到了何等程度，极言醉酒之甚。

例：He has drunk too much, and can't see a hole in a forty-foot ladder.

他喝得酩酊大醉。

（33）成语 drunk as a fiddler's bitch 的字面意思是"醉得像一个二流子的母狗"，转义为酩酊大醉，此处的 fiddler 一词非为"小提琴师"，而是指那种吊儿郎当不务正业的人，或者"草包"，这一成语在英国从19世纪中期就广为使用。

例：It's all over, and nobody knows it but me, drunk as a fiddler's bitch, lasted too long.

有很长一段时间我经常喝得烂醉如泥，不过这是过去的事了,现在除我自己没人知道。

(34)成语 drunk as a skunk 的字面意思是"醉得像一只臭鼬",用以形容人喝得酩酊大醉。

例:They bring beer and cigarettes, are drunk as skunks.

他们带来了啤酒、香烟,大家喝得烂醉。

(35)成语 drink like a fish 的意思是像鱼在游动中张嘴饮水一样地饮酒,其结果只能是喝醉,由此形容人豪饮,喝得酩酊大醉。这个直喻的成语出自17世纪中叶英国剧作家詹姆斯·雪利(James Shirley, 1596—1666)的剧本《美人的胜利》(*The Triumph of Beauty*)。其实,鱼在游动时,虽然大张着嘴,给人一种饮水的感觉,但并不将水吞下。

例:Mr. Ball will kill himself before long, he drinks like a fish.

鲍尔先生将不久于人世,因为他总是喝得醉醺醺的。

(36)Tight as a brick 与 tight as a boiled owl 二成语皆为大醉、烂醉如泥之义。

例:He drank to his heart's content, and was as tight as a brick.

他尽情地喝酒,结果喝得酩酊大醉。

(37)成语 lose one's legs 意为喝得东倒西歪、酩酊大醉。

例:He is said to have lost his legs.

听说他喝醉了。

(38)成语 have a load on 意为喝醉,是美国俚语。

(39)成语 drunk as a mouse 的意思是大醉、烂醉。

例：You came home as drunk as a mouse.

你喝得烂醉如泥才回家。

(40) 成语 tie one on 意为喝得大醉。

例：John sure tied one on last night.

昨天晚上约翰确实喝得酩酊大醉。

(41) 成语 get slopped 的意思是喝醉。

例：It's the only place where a man could get slopped and not be arrested.

这是男人可以喝醉而不至于被拘禁的唯一一个地方。

(42) 成语 have snakes in one's boots 的意思是靴内有蛇，转义为喝醉酒。

(43) 成语 have been in the sunshine 之意为醉酒。

例：He was in that condition which his groom indicated with poetic ambiguity by saying that "master had been in the sunshine."

他的情况可以从他仆从那句含糊而有诗意的话看出来。他说："眼际迸金星，主人已酩酊。"

(44) 成语 take too much 的意思是喝得过量，转义为喝醉。

例：Though Bill often visits the public-house, he never takes too much.

比尔虽然经常上酒店，但从不喝醉。

(45) 成语 dead to the wide 之意为酩酊大醉。

(46) 成语 done to the wide 之意为大醉，烂醉如泥。

(47) 成语 in wine 之意为喝醉，此成语来自法语 dans le vin。

例：He was brought home in wine.

他喝得醉醺醺地被送回家。

(48) 成语 blind to the world 意为醉得不省人事、烂醉如泥。

(49) 成语 zonk out 除表示入睡外，还表示酩酊大醉。

例：You won't get a coherent word out of Joe, he was zonked out.

乔说话语无伦次，他已酩酊大醉了。

汉语成语例解：

(1) 成语"酩酊大醉"谓喝酒喝得大醉，酩酊形容醉醺醺的样子。

例①：不两个时辰，把李逵灌得酩酊大醉，立脚不住。(元·施耐庵，《水浒传》第四十三回)

例②：月夕花朝，无不酩酊大醉。(明·张岱，《五异人传》)

(2) 成语"烂醉如泥"形容饮酒过量，醉得昏昏沉沉，东倒西歪。语出《后汉书·周泽传》："时人为之语曰：'生世不谐，作太常妻，一岁三百六十日，三百五十九日斋，一日不斋醉如泥。'"

例①：王庆一日吃得烂醉如泥，在本府正排军张斌面前露出马脚。(元·施耐庵，《水浒传》第一百〇一回)

例②：曾烂醉如泥，沉睡座间。(清·蒲松龄，《聊斋志异·黄英》)

44 "go west" 与 "与世长辞"

英语成语：

1. go west

2. turn up one's toes

3. give up the ghost

4. go the way of all flesh

5. lie with one's fathers

6. pale horse

7. join the (great) majority

8. kick the bucket

9. debt to nature

10. go to kingdom come

11. go to pot

12. be sent to one's account

13. buy the farm

14. buy the box

15. cash in

16. cash in one's chips

17. cross the Great Divide

18. cross the River Styx

19. cross over the River Jordan

20. cross over

21. go belly up

22. the golden bowl is broken

23. gone for a Burton

24. leap in the dark

25. push up daisies

26. shuffle off this mortal coil

27. sleep with one's fathers

28. step off

29. the wages of sin

30. abiit ad plures

31. answer the final summons

32. be asleep in the Arms of God

33. be asleep in the valley

34. be at rest

35. be at peace

36. be brought to one's last home

37. be called

38. be called home

39. be called to the beyond

40. be cast into outer darkness

41. be gathered to one's fathers

42. be home and free

43. be in Abraham's bosom

44. be promoted to glory

45. be removed to the divine bosom

46. be rocked to sleep

47. be salted away

48. be taken to paradise

49. be translated into higher sphere

50. call of God

51. depart (from) this life

52. depart to God

53. depart to the world of shadows

54. drop off the hooks

55. final departure

56. final sleep

57. go home

58. go the way of all flesh

59. go to one's glory

60. go to heaven

61. go to meet one's maker

62. go to one's grass

63. go to one's long home

64. go to one's own place

65. go to one's reward

66. go to the land of heart's desire

67. God rest his soul

68. Great Unknown

69. have fallen asleep (in the Lord)

70. have found rest

71. be called to one's eternal rest

72. go to one's (long) rest

73. one's last rest

74. take rest

75. have (be) gone to a better place

76. have (be) gone to the happy hunting grounds

77. have one's name inscribed in the book of life

78. in heaven

79. join one's ancestors

80. join the angelic choirs

81. join the angels

82. join the feathered choir

83. yield up the ghost

84. join the immortals

85. leave this world

86. depart out of this world

87. go out of this world

88. go to a better world

89. pass over the Jordan

90. pay Charon

91. pay one's fee

92. pay the debt of nature

93. pay Saint Peter a visit

94. play one's harp

95. push the clouds around

96. rest in peace

97. return to dust

98. in the dust

99. say hello to Charon

100. to sleep the big sleep

101. to sleep one's last sleep

102. to sleep the sleep that knows no waking

103. sup with Pluto

104. take one's departure

105. undiscovered country

106. answer the last roll call

107. be blown across (over) the creek

108. be present at the last roll call

109. be written off

110. bite the dust

111. do one's bit

112. fire one's last shot

113. grounded for good

114. it's taps

115. lay down one's life

116. make the ultimate sacrifice

117. be no longer with us

118. be out of pain

119. breathe one's last

120. check out

121. draw one's last breath

122. go out

123. have gone under

124. He (She) is not coming home.

125. negative patient care outcome

126. be gone to Davy Jone's locker

127. coil up one's ropes

128. cut adrift

129. hit the rock

130. last voyage

131. launch into eternity

132. safe anchorage at last

133. slip one's ropes (cable)

134. be cut off

135. cancel one's account

136. close up one's account

137. go to one's long account

138. hand in one's account

139. pay one's last debt

140. settle all scores

141. settle one's account

142. black out

143. bow off

144. bow out

145. curtain call
146. drop the curtain
147. fade away
148. fade out
149. final curtain
150. fold up
151. last bow
152. last call
153. make one's (final) exit
154. pass out of the picture
155. out of the picture
156. quit the scene
157. switch out the lights
158. be cleaned out of the deck
159. be down for good
160. be knocked out
161. be out of the game
162. be thrown for a loss
163. call all bets off
164. drop the cue
165. end of the ball game
166. kick off
167. final kick off
168. go to the races
169. jump the last hurdle
170. lose the decision

171. peg out

172. run one's race

173. strike out

174. take the long count

175. take a count

176. throw in the sponge

177. toss in one's alley (marble)

178. throw up the cards

179. throw sixes

180. go to the last roundup

181. hang up one's harness

182. hang up one's hat

183. hang up one's tackle

184. lay down one's pen

185. take the big jump

186. write the last chapter

187. go off the hooks

188. lose one's life

189. lie low

190. make away with

191. meet one's maker

192. lose the number of one's mess

193. pass on

194. pass out

195. at peace

196. hop the perch

197. go to one's own place

198. pop off

199. cross the river

200. quit the scene

201. go down to the shades

202. fatal shears

203. die in one's shoes

204. drop short

205. slam off

206. big sleep

207. fall on sleep

208. long sleep

209. never-ending sleep

210. sleep the sleep that knows no waking

211. give up the spirit

212. hop the twig

213. pass beyond the veil

214. go the way of all the earth

215. the way of all flesh

216. slip one's wind

217. go out of this world

218. go to a better world

汉语成语：

1. 寿终正寝 2. 呜呼哀哉 3. 与世长辞 4. 一瞑不视

英语成语例解：

（1）英语成语 go west 有戏剧的意味，指人的时候表示"死亡"；指事物的时候表示"毁灭"。至于这个成语的来源，则有多种不同的解释。

日落西方表示一天的结束，人们常用西方象征死亡，所以 go west 与太阳西沉有关。其他许多民族都有类似的说法，听说泰国人睡觉时头要朝向东方，只有尸体的头部才能朝西停放。因此 go west 也就意味着死亡。

另外，古埃及神话中有一位叫奥塞利斯的人，他死了以后成为冥神，统治着尼罗河以西的土地。因此，西方民族一直沿用"去西方"来表示死亡。这种用法与汉语中的"上西天""归西"不谋而合。

还有人说，美国西部尚未开发时，那里一片荒凉，野兽出没频繁，去西部的人多半不能活着回来，因此 go west 就代表了"死亡"或"不要指望"了。1832 年，纳撒尼尔·韦恩曾经作了两次西部"日落地区"的探险，结果均告失败，铩羽而归。

例：I shall once again be in the company of dear old friends now "gone west".

我将要和那些已经归西的老朋友们重新结伙了。

（2）成语 turn up one's toes 本是一句戏谑之语，是说尸体仰面躺着，足趾自然朝上，转义为死亡。

例：So then old Ropner has turned up his toes at last. How old was he?

就这样老罗普纳终于死了。他多大年纪了？

（3）成语 give up the ghost 典出《圣经·新约·约翰福音》第19章耶稣基督被钉十字架临终时的情景："站在耶稣十字架旁边的，有他母亲和他母亲的姐妹，并革罗罢的妻子马利亚和抹大拉的马利亚。耶稣见母亲和他所爱的那门徒站在旁边，就对他母亲说：'母亲，看你的儿子！'又对那门徒说：'看你的母亲！'从此那门徒就接她到自己家里去了。这事以后，耶稣知道各样的事已经成了，为要使经上的话应验，就说：'我渴了。'有一个器皿盛满了醋，放在那里，他们就拿海绒蘸满了醋，绑在牛膝草上，送到他口。耶稣尝了那醋，就说：'成了！'便低下了头，将灵魂交付上帝了。"后人便用"将灵魂交付上帝"一语表示离开人世或死亡。

例：There was nothing that a beetle could have lunched upon. The pinched and meager aspect of the place would have killed a chameleon; he would have known, at the first mouthful, that the air was not eatable, and must have given up the ghost in despair. (Charles Dickens, *The Old Curiosity Shop*)

连甲虫也摸不到东西吃。这地方的那种寒酸贫苦的样子足以杀死一条蜥蜴，它只要尝一尝便会感到连空气也会不能入口，

只好绝望地断气。(查尔斯·狄更斯,《老古玩店》)

(4) 成语 go the way of all flesh 是由《圣经》中的两节改写而成的,一是《约书亚纪》第 23 章第 14 节:"我现在要走世人必走之路"(This day I'm going the way of all the earth);二是《列王纪上》第 2 章第 2 节:"我走世人必走的路"(I go the way of all the earth)。

"The earth"在这儿的含义是"生活在地球上的人",而古英语中"flesh"的含义就是世人、人类。故此成语的含义是死去、逝世。

例: The greatest artist of the first half of this century, Picasso, has at long last gone the way of all flesh.

20 世纪上半叶最伟大的艺术家毕加索,最终也作古了。

(5) 成语 lie with one's fathers 的意思是随先人长眠于九泉之下,即指死亡。典出《圣经·旧约·创世记》第 47 章:迦南地闹饥荒时,以色列人的第三代祖先雅各打发自己的儿子去埃及籴粮,只把最小的儿子雅悯留在身边。雅各的儿子们风尘仆仆来到埃及,遇到被他们出卖了的兄弟约瑟,而约瑟已成为埃及主管粮食的宰相。约瑟不计怨恨,将兄弟们领到埃及法老面前,法老重重地赏赐了他们,并要他们回迦南把父亲雅各接到埃及。雅各率领全家迁居埃及,来到歌珊地。约瑟在歌珊地与父亲相会,悲喜交集,热泪横流。经法老同意,雅各全家从此定居埃及的歌珊地。他们仍以牧羊为业,并置办产业,生儿育女,过着无忧无虑的游牧生活。雅各在埃及住了 17 年,临终时把约瑟叫到床前,嘱咐道:"我若在你眼前蒙恩,请你把手放在我大腿底下，用慈爱和诚实待我，请你不要将我葬在埃及。我与先辈同眠的时候，你要将我带出埃及，葬在他们所葬的地方。"为儿孙们祝福后，雅各就与世长辞了，终年147岁。法老派臣仆和长老们随同约瑟及其弟兄们为雅各举哀，经过长途跋涉，将他的遗体运回迦南，葬在比麦拉洞内。

（6）Pale horse 在《圣经》中是死亡的象征，语出《圣经·新约·启示录》第6章："When he opened the fourth seal, I heard the voice of the fourth living creature saying, 'Come!' And I looked, and behold, a pale horse! And its rider's name was Death, and Hades followed him. And they were given authority over a quarter of the earth, to kill with sword and with famine and with pestilence and by wild beasts of the earth."（"揭开第四印的时候，我听见第四个活物说：'你来！'我就观看，见有一匹灰色马，骑在马上的名字叫作死。阴府也随着他。有权柄赐给他们，可以用刀剑、饥荒、瘟疫、瘤疫、野兽杀害地上四分之一的人。"）Pale horse 一语，后人引用时仍喻指死亡。

（7）成语 join the (great) majority 的意思是"死亡"。英语中有不少表示"死亡"的委婉语，join the (great) majority 就是其中之一，按字面意思是"加入大多数的行列"。亘古至今死亡的人总数总比活着的人多。故用 majority（大多数）一词表示死人。但该成语如今已不多用。亦作 go over to the majority。

例：Mr. Jackson has gone to join the great majority.
杰克逊先生已经去世了。

（8）成语 kick the bucket 本义是"翘辫子"，也是英语中表示"死亡"的一种委婉说法。此语属俚语，常含有诙谐意味。

旧时，人在悬梁自尽时常常先站在一个倒置的水桶（bucket）上，然后把系好的绳子往脖子上一套，再把脚下的水桶踢开，就这样一命呜呼了，所以 kick the bucket 常被用以喻指"死"。

例：Scarcely anyone was sorry when the old tyrant finally kicked the bucket.

当那个年老的暴君最后翘辫子时，几乎没有人为他伤心。

(9) 成语 debt to nature 比喻人生是一笔债，不管付息与否，必须用死来偿还。这成语通常和动词 pay 连用，pay one's debt to nature 即表示"死亡"。这句成语从中世纪起就开始流行，常作为死亡的委婉用语被刻在墓碑上，尤其在 20 世纪初最为盛行。

例：He had paid his great Debt to Nature, without taking notice of the small one due to me.

他死了，偿清了欠自然的大债，但没有顾及欠我的小债。

(10) 成语 go to kingdom come 出自《圣经·马太福音》第 6 章，耶稣在谈论祷告时，曾教导信徒们不要学习那些爱站在教堂里或十字路口的伪君子，故意让别人知道他在祷告；也不要在祷告时喋喋不休，并念了一段祷告文，其中一句是这样说的：

Our Father, who art in heaven...Thy kingdom come...
我们在天上的父亲啊！……愿您的国度来临……

成语中的 kingdom 指的是天国。"天国的来临"便是表示死亡。这句成语属非正式用法。

例：Lora's grandfather was blown to kingdom come in the war when he stepped on a land mine.

罗拉的祖父在战时因误踩地雷而过世了。

（11）成语 go to pot 表示死去、消亡、完蛋等义。据说有一位裁缝，每当镇上有人去世时，出葬的队伍若是行经他的门前到墓地，他便会放一颗石子到一个罐子中，后来他死，也同样葬在同一块墓地中，人们便说他也到罐子里去了（go to pot）。

例：The company Jasmine works for is going to pot because of poor management and Jasmine has to look for a new job.

贾丝敏的公司因为经营不善而即将破产，贾丝敏也得开始找新工作了。

（12）成语 be sent to one's account 表示死亡，或被上帝召去。典出莎士比亚悲剧《哈姆莱特》第一幕第五场：心狠手辣、野心勃勃的克劳狄斯（Claudius）趁哥哥（丹麦国王）在花园午睡之机，将毒药灌入哥哥耳中，把他害死。克劳狄斯登上了王位，娶兄嫂为妻。老王的鬼魂向王子哈姆莱特详细叙述了事情的经过，告诉他："于是我在睡梦中就这样被我亲兄弟的手一把抓去了我的性命，我的王冕，我的王后；我罪孽深重的一生，没行餐礼，没行忏悔，没有涂油，就算是断绝了。"（No reckoning made, but sent to my account. With all my imperfections on my dead.）现在此成语常用 gone to one's account 表示。

例：He has gone to his account, God forgive him!

他去见上帝了，愿上帝宽恕他！

（13）成语 buy the farm 原意为"买农场"。人们认为这句成语出自英国空军飞行员之口。他们常喜欢说："等到战争结束后，我将定居下来买一个农场。"但许多飞行员在作战中丧生，他们的梦想永远不能实现。因此，buy the farm 便成了死亡的一种委婉说法。

例：Sir, the only thing I can tell you is that two of my people have bought the farm, and if I don't get it (a medical evacuation helicopter), two more will.

长官，我只能向您报告，我的部下已有两名死了，如果我不要求派医用直升飞机前来撤离伤员的话，还有两个人要死亡。

（14）成语 buy the box 的字面意思是"买棺材"，这种说法亦喻指死亡。

（15）Cash in 原本是表示"兑现""兑付"的说法，后成为表示"死亡"的一种委婉说法。

例：He was shot through the body and knew he was going to cash in.

子弹穿透了他的身体，他明白自己快要死了。

（16）成语 cash in one's chips 原本为扑克牌戏结束时玩牌人"将筹码换成现金"，后转喻为死亡。这种用法从19世纪70年代开始使用至今。在此之前还有一些类似的委婉说法，例如：to cash in one's checks；to pass in one's checks

例：When the outlaw cashed in his chips, he was buried with his boots on.

那个匪徒死后，立即就把他埋掉了。

（17）成语 cross the Great Divide 的意思是死亡、上西天。这是一句美国口头用语，Great Divide 本指北美大陆分水岭，即落基山脉。北美开发初期，人们把落基山以西的大西部视作一个可怕神秘的地方，越过落基山去大西部，即预示着走向死亡。Great Divide 转义为假想中的生死分界线，cross the Great Divide 便成了"死亡"的委婉用语。

例：I'm still residing in Portland, Oregon, …where I hope to remain until I cross the Great Divide.

我还住在俄勒冈州波特兰市……我希望在那儿一直住到死。

（18）成语 cross the River Styx 本义是"渡过第克斯河"，转喻"死亡"，也是一种表示死亡的委婉说法。The River Styx 是古代希腊神话中的冥河。死者的灵魂经此河被渡河神卡戎（Charon）载往冥府。在《圣经》中，the Styx 是将荒原和迦南（上帝赐予亚伯拉罕之地）分开的界河。

（19）成语 cross over the River Jordan（渡过约旦河）亦是表示死亡、归西的一种委婉说法。

（20）Cross over 本义为"由此方到彼方""渡过"，现也常用来表示死亡。

例：He has crossed over.

他死了。

（21）成语 go belly up 的意思是"肚子朝天"，是美国俚语，原指鱼死后肚子朝天浮在水面，喻指人已死去。

（22）成语 the golden bowl is broken 的意思是一生结束、

死。出自《圣经·旧约·传道书》第 12 章：传道人劝导人们年轻时就要记住造物主，不要等到太阳、月亮、星星变为黑暗，……银链折断，金罐破裂，瓶子在泉旁损坏，水轮在井口破烂（the silver cord be loosed, or the golden bowl be broken, or the pitcher be broken at the fountain, or the wheel broken at the cistern）时才敬奉上帝，那时一切都晚了。

例：And thus the slaves go on from year to year, until the golden bowl is broken.

就这样，奴隶们一年又一年地干下去，一直到死为止。

（23）成语 gone for a Burton 原意为"去喝伯顿啤酒了"，喻指"死亡""完蛋了"。这是一句产生于英国本土的成语，始用于 1939 年，为英国皇家空军创造。伯顿（Burton）是英国中部一个城市，以酿酒业闻名。在第二次世界大战期间，英国空军人员把在与德军空战中牺牲的战友委婉地说成"去喝伯顿啤酒了"，以避免使用"他已阵亡"之类的不祥用语。这句成语在英国现仍经常使用，但已没有以前那种凶险的含义。

例：Our plans to build a new school have gone for a Burton because the government can't give us any money.

我们建造一所新学校的计划由于政府不能给我们钱而告吹。

（24）成语 leap in the dark 的字面意思是"跳进黑暗中"，喻指冒险行为，有时也指死亡。英国哲学家、翻译家霍布斯（Thomas Hobbes, 1588—1679）临终时曾使用此语来表达死的概念。他说："Now am I about to take my last voyage—a great leap in the dark."（现在我将开始我的最后航程——死亡。）

例：I make decisions on the spur of the moment. But you'd never take a leap in the dark. (Thomas Stearns Eliot, *The Confident Clerk*)

我不假思索临时作出决定，但你决不可轻举妄动。(托马斯·斯特尔那斯·艾略特,《信心十足的办事员》)

(25) 成语 push up daisies 的意思是"死亡"，语中的 daisy 指人们常在新坟顶上种的雏菊。因此，push up daisies 的字面意思是"托起雏菊"，喻指死亡、入土，是一种委婉的说法，从 19 世纪中期便开始普遍使用。其变体有 turn one's toes up to the daisies。

例：In ten years' time I think I should be pushing up daisies.

我想再过 10 年，我就长眠地下了。

(26) 成语 shuffle off this mortal coil 原意为"脱去腐朽的皮囊"，喻指摆脱人生的羁绊、大解脱、死亡。语出莎士比亚悲剧《哈姆莱特》第三幕第一场：哈姆莱特王子决心要负起重整乾坤的责任，可是却由于找不到正确途径而陷入迷惘、忧郁和苦恼的精神危机之中，他感到自己力量微薄，越发顾虑重重，"生存还是毁灭"，他反复自问。

> Hamlet：…to die—to sleep—
> To sleep！Perchance to dream：—ay, there's the rub；
> For in that sleep of death what dreams may come,
> When we have shuffled off this mortal coil,
> Must give us pause.

哈姆莱特：……死，就是睡眠；

睡眠，也许要做梦，这就麻烦了！

我们一旦摆脱了尘世的牵缠，

在死的睡眠中究竟要做些什么梦，

一想到就不能不踌躇。

例：One other week and this mortal coil would be shuffled off.
再过一个星期他就要离开尘世了。

（27）成语 sleep with one's fathers 原意为"随祖先长眠"，出自《圣经·旧约·申命记》：摩西带领以色列人于120岁时到达了摩押（Moab），上帝对他说："你的死期临近了，……你必须和你列祖同睡。（thy days approach that thou must die...thou shalt sleep with thy fathers.）"上帝吩咐摩西登上西巴琳山的尼波山（Mount Nebo），在摩押地与耶利哥（Jericho）相对处观看上帝赐给以色列人的迦南地（Canaan）。"你必死在所登的山上，归你列祖去，像你哥哥亚伦死在何珥山上，归他的列祖一样。"（And die in the mount whither thou goest up, and be gathered unto thy people; as Aaron thy brother died in mount Hor, and was gathered unto his people.）正如上帝所说，摩西死于摩押。此成语亦作 be gathered to one's fathers; to be put to one's fathers.

例：He suffered from an incurable disease and was gathered to his fathers at last.

他得了不治之症，最后去世了。

（28）成语 step off 原意为"走完"，它通常有两种用法。

其一，当作"结婚"时是 step off the carpet 的缩略形式。指新娘新郎走完教堂内铺着地毯的通道，来到主持婚礼的牧师面前。其二，当作"死亡"时指走完了人生道路的最后一步。

例：The old man and I are both due to step off if we're caught.

我和那老头如果被抓住，就都活不成了。

（29）成语 the wages of sin 原意为"罪恶的代价"。出自《圣经·新约·罗马书》：耶酥基督的使徒保罗（Paul）规劝信徒不能心存私欲，萌生罪恶之念，也不能将自己的肢体用作犯罪的器具；而应像死里复活的耶稣一样将自己献给上帝，多做善事、义事，这样就能在上帝的恩典下得以永生。因为"罪的代价是死亡"（For the wages of sin is death），但是上帝所赐给我们的恩典是跟主基督耶稣合而为一，得到永恒的生命。成语 the wages of sin 除用于表示"报应"之外，多用于表示"死亡"。

例：She had enough faith in spiritual values to feel that they would be the better for it, the wages of sin did no one any good.

她对精神价值有足够的信念，因此感到做一次祷告对他们会更好一些，得到罪恶的报应对任何人都没有好处。

（30）成语 abiit ad plures（或 abiit ad majores）的意思是随群、随大溜，为拉丁文，是表示"死亡"的一种委婉说法，意思与 join the majority 同。

（31）成语 answer the final summons 的意思是"最后一次应召""去见上帝"，也是表示死亡的一种委婉说法。其变体为 answer the final call，两者均多见于 19 世纪末的英语中。

（32）成语 be asleep in the Arms of God 的意思是"安睡在上帝的怀抱中"，是表示死亡的一种委婉说法，多见于19世纪和20世纪的美国英语中，其变体有 be asleep in Jesus 和 be asleep in the arms of Jesus。

（33）成语 be asleep in the valley 的意思是"安睡在谷地中"，是死亡的一种委婉说法，语中的 valley 系指 the valley of shadow of death（死荫的幽谷），源出《圣经·诗篇》：Yea, though I walk through the valley of shadow of death…（我虽然行过死荫的幽谷……）

（34）成语 be at rest 的意思是"在休息"，转义为死亡、安息，也是表示死亡之义的一种委婉说法。

例：Long ere they were within sight of land, Lucy Passmore was gone to her rest beneath the Atlantic waves.

露丝·帕斯莫尔葬身于大西洋海底之后很久，他们才看到陆地。

（35）成语 be at peace 的意思是"处于平静状态"，也是"死亡"的一种委婉表达方式。这一说法源自 the Mass for the Dead。祭奠死者话语中的 RIP（拉丁文 Requiescat in pace 的缩略），相当于英语的 May he, she or they rest in peace! 愿彼安息！

（36）成语 be brought to one's last（或 long）home 的意思是"被送回老家去"，也是"死亡"的一种委婉表达法。

例：A fever, which, in a few days, brought Sir Everhard to his long home…

一次发烧，只有几天时间，就把爱弗哈德先生送回老家去了……

（37）成语 be called 的意思是"被召唤到上帝那里去"，亦是"死亡"的一种委婉表达方式。

例：All the doctors in Christendom…can't save him, he is called.

在所有信奉基督教的国度里，没有医生能够挽救他的生命，他是应召去见上帝的。

（38）成语 be called home 的意思是被召唤回家，也是一种常用的表示死亡的委婉说法。

（39）成语 be called to the beyond（或 the Great Beyond）的意思是被召往遥远的地方，被召往彼岸，也是表示"死亡"的一种委婉说法。其中 the Great Beyond（不可知的彼岸）是表示"来世"的委婉语。

（40）成语 be cast into outer darkness 的意思是被抛入冥冥之中，用以委婉地表示死亡。但 to be cast into outer darkness 往往用以表示坏人的死亡，当表示好人死亡时，则用 to slip into outer darkness（潜入冥府）。

（41）成语 be gathered to one's fathers 的意思是"被聚集在先人身边""去见老祖宗"，是表示死亡的一种委婉而又比较正式的说法。

例：He was ninety when he died and was gathered to his fathers.

他90岁那年死了，随祖先去了。

(42) 成语 be home and free 的意思是"到家自由了",常被委婉地表达人已死去的概念,相当于汉语的"入土为安"。

(43) 成语 be in Abraham's bosom 的意思是"在亚伯拉罕的怀抱中",意即"与祖先一道安息",也是死亡的委婉说法,这一委婉说法来源于《圣经·路加福音》第16章第12节:And it came to pass that the beggar (Lazarus) died and was carried by the angels into Abraham's bosom. [后来那讨饭的(拉撒路)死了,被天使带去放在亚伯拉罕的怀抱里。]亚伯拉罕是犹太人的始祖,即所谓的"万民之父"。在实际使用中,动词 be 还可换成 live、sleep、lie 和 rest 等。

例:Two or three old Ladies, who are languishing to be in Abraham's bosom, as the only man's bosom to whom they can hope for admittance.

有两三位老太太,她们苦苦地希望着投入亚伯拉罕的怀抱,那是她们唯一可以指望被接纳的男人的怀报。

(44) 成语 be promoted to glory 的意思是"升入天国",是一种源于宗教的死亡的委婉说法。这是基督教救世军常用的委婉语,其中 glory 的原意是"天国的荣耀"。

(45) 成语 be removed to the divine bosom 的意思是"被移放在天父怀里",常译为"升天"或"去见上帝",也是一种源于宗教的死亡的委婉说法。其来源及用法可参见 be in Abraham's bosom 一条。

(46) 成语 be rocked to sleep 的意思是"被摇晃入睡",也是一种表达死亡的委婉语。

(47）成语 be salted away（或 down）的意思是"被腌制起来"，有不朽之意，转喻死去，也是表达死亡的一种委婉说法。这一说法是借用厨房用语来替代较为夸饰的 to join in the immortals（加入不朽者之列，即死去）。腌制的食物颇像不朽的灵魂，不会腐烂变质，可以永存。这一委婉说法多见于 19 世纪、20 世纪的美国口语中。

（48）成语 be taken to paradise 的意思是被带进天国，也是一种源自宗教的表达死亡的委婉说法。

（49）成语 be translated into higher sphere 的意思是被送入上界，意即升天，也是表达死亡的一种委婉语。这是一种最新的说法，实际上，它还可以使用其他一些及物动词，如 to be called（launched）into higher sphere 或不及物动词，如 somebody has joined（gone, slipped）into higher sphere。

（50）成语 call of God 的意思是上帝的召唤、去见上帝，是死亡的一种委婉表达法。

（51）成语 depart（from）this life 的意思是离开今世、撒手人寰，是死亡的委婉表达法，其变体为 to depart from this world（for ever）。

（52）成语 depart to God 的意思是出发去了上帝处、去见上帝，为死亡的委婉表达法。

（53）成语 depart to the world of shadows 的意思是出发去幽冥世界、一命赴黄泉，为死亡的一种委婉表达方式。

（54）成语 drop（go, pop, slip）off the hooks 的意思是自钩上解下、脱钩。这是英国 19 世纪常用的委婉语，它很可能是暗指被钉死在十字架上的耶稣后来被放下一事。但也有人认为它是源于航海术语。

例：Brown dropped off the hooks years ago; we've had three different secretaries since his day.

布朗多年前就去世了，从那以后我们已经换了三个秘书。

（55）成语 final departure 的意思是最后离去，为死亡的委婉说法之一。

（56）成语 final sleep 的意思是最后一觉，死亡的这一委婉说法一般多见于 19 世纪、20 世纪的美国口语中。

（57）成语 go home 的本义是回家，但这里的 home 非指通常所说的"家庭"或"住宅"，而是委婉地指"坟墓"，即是那个"永久的家"。因此，go home 可委婉地形容死亡。这句成语有时也可以说成 to go to one's last（long）home（回到最后的家中，回到永久之家）。

例：O' Henry's last words, spoken with a smile, were, "I don't want to go home in the dark."

欧·亨利临终时的最后一句话是面带笑容地说："我不想在黑暗中死去。"

（58）成语 go the way of all flesh 的意思是走众生之路，为死亡的一种委婉说法。《圣经·列王记》第 2 章第 2 节有"I go the way of all flesh"（我要走众生之路）之说，但这一说法之所以能广泛流传至今，还要归功于作家塞缪尔·巴特勒，是他的小说取名 *The Way of All Flesh*（《众生之路》），才使得这一说法流行起来，并多见于口语之中。

例：He pardoned us off-hand, and allowed us something to live on till he went the way of all flesh.

他马上宽恕了我们，并且答应一直供养我们，直到他逝世为止。

（59）成语 go to (one's) glory 的意思是荣升天国，语中的 glory 之义为"天国的荣耀"。这是一句源出宗教的表达死亡的委婉语。

例：Had we got caught in this, we should have … gone to glory.

要是让我们碰上这样的事，我们全得完蛋。

（60）成语 go to heaven 的意思是进入天堂、升入天国，也是表达死亡的一种委婉语。

（61）成语 go to meet one's maker 的意思是去见创世主、去见造物主、去见上帝。这一表达死亡的委婉语通常以过去时的形式出现，即 went to meet one's maker，一般多见于19世纪中叶以来的美国英语。

例：The old man has gone to meet his maker.

那个老人已经去世了。

（62）成语 go to one's grass 的意思是去草莽、被青草埋没，为死亡的一种委婉说法。To go to grass 是 to go to grass with one's teeth upwards 的简略说法，一般多见于19世纪及20世纪初期的英语。

（63）成语 go to one's long home 的意思是回到永久之家，乃死亡的一种委婉表达法，来源于英王詹姆士一世钦定《圣经》

英译本译文,是布道时常用的一句套话。

例:…man go to his long home, and the mourners go about the streets.

……人回了老家,吊丧者沿街踟蹰。

(64)成语 go to one's own place 的意思是回老家,也是一种表达死亡的委婉说法。

(65)成语 go to one's reward 的意思是得到报偿、得到报应。这是美国近现代口语中常见的一种表达死亡的委婉说法,有时还可以插入形容词加以强调,如 go to one's last (final) reward(得到最后的报应)、go to one's just reward(得到应有的报偿)和 to be called to one's reward(应召去得到报偿)。

(66)成语 go to the land of heart's desire(或 the mansions of rest, Jordan's banks, Kingdom come)的意思是去心中向往的地方(或去休息大厦,去约旦河岸,去未来王国)。总之,都是表达死亡的委婉说法。

(67)成语 God rest his soul 的意思是上帝保佑他的灵魂安息吧,这是说"他死了"的委婉表达法。

(68)成语 Great Unknown 的意思是"伟大的未知地",这种表达死亡的说法一般多见于19世纪、20世纪的美国口语中。

(69)成语 have fallen asleep (in the Lord) 的意思是"(在上帝的怀抱中)入睡了",也是表达死亡或长眠的一种委婉说法。

例:Fallen Asleep, Not Dead but Sleeping, Asleep in Jesus. (a common child's epitaph in the 19th century)

已入睡了,不是死去,只是睡着而已,是安睡在耶稣的怀抱里。(19世纪常见的夭折儿童的墓志铭)

(70)成语 have found rest 的意思是"得到安息",是表示死亡的一种委婉表达说法。

(71)成语 be called to one's eternal rest 的意思是"被召唤到最后的栖息处",是表示死亡的一种委婉表达说法。

(72)成语 go to one's (long) rest 的意思是"去自己长眠之处",是死亡的另一种委婉表达方式。

例:One more old Forsyte going to his long rest…Wonderful how he had held on! (John Galsworthy, *In Chancery*)

又一个老福尔赛要永远安息了……他能支撑这样久,真是了不起!(约翰·高尔斯华绥,《骑虎》)

(73)成语 one's last rest 的意思是"最后的安息",也是表达死亡的一种委婉说法。

例:A few words, a sprinkle of earth, the thrusting of the coffin home, and Aunt Ann had passed to her last rest. (John Galsworthy, *The Man of Property*)

几句祷词,一撮黄土,棺柩安放下去,安姑太便得到她最后的安息。(约翰·高尔斯华绥,《有产业的人》)

(74)成语 take rest (或 take one's rest) 的意思是休息、安眠,也已成为表达死亡的一种委婉说法。

例:The old man lay taking his rest after a life of bitter hardship.

这老人含辛茹苦一辈子,现在长眠于地下了。

(75) 成语 have (be) gone to a better place (land, world, life) 的意思是"到一个更美好的地方去了"("去过一种更美好的生活""到极乐世界去了"),为表达死亡的一种委婉语,该委婉语还可以简化为 to be gone (走了)。

例:Gone are my friends from the cotton fields away, gone from the earth to a better land I know.

我的朋友都从棉田离去,离开人间,进入天国。

(76) 成语 have (be) gone to the happy hunting grounds 的意思是"去了那片欢乐的狩猎场",婉义指死亡、升天,或上了天堂。语中 the happy hunting grounds 原是印第安人传说中的"天堂",那里满是飞禽走兽。他们可以打猎、欢宴、为所欲为,该委婉语一般多见于 19 世纪、20 世纪的美国英语中。

例:I have read of old Indian warriors taking their horses and dogs with them to the happy hunting grounds. (John Galsworthy, *Caravan*)

我曾在书上读到年老的印第安武士带着他们的战马和猎狗登上了那片乐土。(约翰·高尔斯华绥,《商队》)

(77) 成语 have one's name inscribed in the book of life 的意思是留名于永生簿上,这是来源于宗教用语的表达死亡的委婉语。在犹太人的宗教葬礼上,悼词一般总是说"for those whose names are inscribed in the Book of Life"(为那些留名于永生簿上的人祈祷吧)。

(78) 成语 in heaven 的意思是在天堂,即指人已升天,为死亡的委婉表达法。

（79）成语 join one's ancestors 的意思是加入先人的行列、随先人于地下，亦是死亡的一种委婉的表达方式。

（80）成语 join the angelic choirs 的意思是加入天使们的唱诗班，是源自宗教的一种表达死亡的委婉说法。

（81）成语 join the angels 的意思是加入天使的行列、跻身于天使之中，也是表达死亡的一种委婉说法。

例：Do not ask me after my dear John Thomas—he has joined the angels.

不必问候我那亲爱的约翰·托马斯了，他已升天了。

（82）成语 join the feathered（heavenly, invisible）choir 的意思是"加入带翼天使（天堂，隐形）的唱诗班"，皆为死亡的委婉说法。

（83）成语 yield up the ghost（soul, spirit, breath）的意思是灵魂出窍、魂出躯壳，不论选用括号中的哪个词，其意思都是表示人已气绝，是表达死亡的一种委婉说法。

例：And when Jacob had made an end of commanding his sons, he gathered up his feet into the bed, and yielded up the ghost, and was gathered unto his people.

雅各嘱咐众子已毕，就把脚收在床上，气绝而死，归他列祖那里去了。

（84）成语 join（be among）the immortals 的意思是加入不朽者之列、跻身于仙人之中，谓人已成仙，亦是一种表达死亡的委婉说法。这一说法源于古代的希腊和罗马。那时 immortal 一词是用来指"神"，后来也兼指神化了的凡人——仙人、圣人。

例：She thought she saw her husband in a place of Bliss among many Immortals.

她认为自己看见丈夫在极乐世界里与诸神同在。

（85）成语 leave this world 的意思是离开这个世界，也是表达死亡的一种委婉说法。

（86）成语 depart out of this world 的意思是告别今世，即逝世、去世，也是表达死亡的一种委婉说法。

（87）成语 go out of this world（go out of the world）的意思是离开人世，也是表达死亡的一种委婉说法。

例：My grandfather has gone out of this world.

我祖父已经去世了。

（88）成语 go to a better world 的意思是到一个更美好的世界去、到极乐世界去，亦是表达死亡的一种委婉说法。

（89）成语 pass over the Jordan 的意思是"渡过约旦河"，基本意思与 cross over the River Jordon 相同，都是表达死亡的委婉说法。

（90）成语 pay Charon 的意思是"付款给卡戎""付黄泉路资""下阴曹地府"。卡戎（Charon）是希腊神话中在冥河上摆渡亡灵去冥府的船夫。

（91）成语 pay one's fee 的意思是付费，有时也作为表示死亡的一种委婉说法。

（92）成语 pay the debt of nature 的意思是偿还拖欠大自然的债务，有时亦作 pay one's debt to nature，皆为表达死亡的委婉语。

例：The old man paid his debt to nature four years ago.
那位老人四年前就去世了。

（93）成语 pay Saint Peter a visit 的意思是拜见圣彼得，这是美国20世纪才出现的表达死亡的委婉说法。圣彼得是基督教传说中掌管天国大门钥匙的守护神。该委婉语不仅没有严肃的气氛，反倒带有戏谑意味。

（94）成语 play one's harp 的意思是弹奏竖琴，也用来委婉地表达死亡之义。

（95）成语 push the clouds around 的意思是拨开重重云雾，言下之意是"进入天国"，常用以委婉地表达死亡。

（96）成语 rest in peace 与 to be at peace 之义相同。

（97）成语 return to dust（earth）的意思是归于尘土（泥土），为死亡之委婉义。按照《圣经·创世记》中的说法，人类始祖亚当是上帝按照自己的形象用尘土塑造的，然后将生气吹入其鼻孔使其成为"有灵的活人"。亚当的原始意思是"出自泥土"，所以，死亡自然就是"归于泥土化作尘"。

（98）成语 in the dust 的意思是"在泥土之中"，也是委婉表达死亡的一种说法。

例：He is in the dust now.
他现在已经死了。

（99）成语 say hello to Charon 的意思是"向卡戎问好"。转义为死亡，亦是一种表达死亡的委婉说法，可参见 to pay Charon 一条。

（100）成语 to sleep the big sleep 的意思是睡大觉、长眠。Sleep 是英语中最常用的表示死亡的委婉词，其历史源远流长，早在两千多年前，亚历山大时期的著名学者和诗人卡利马科斯（Callimachus，公元前 310—前 240）就曾以"睡觉"来婉指"死亡"。

例：What did it matter where you lay once you were dead? In a dirty sump or in a marble tower on top of a high hill? You were dead, you were sleeping the big sleep, you were not bothered by things like that.

一旦你死了，葬身何处又有什么关系？管他是在污水坑里还是在高山之巅的石塔之中。你已经死了，长眠不醒了，不再为这些事情烦恼了。

（101）成语 to sleep one's last sleep 的意思是最后一次入睡，即此次入睡再也不会醒来了，喻指死亡，也是经常被用到的一种委婉表达死亡的说法。

例：The spirit of the old woman lying in her last sleep had called them to this demonstration. (John Galsworthy, *The Man of Property*)

这位老妇人的亡灵号召他们举行这次示威。（约翰·高尔斯华绥，《有产业的人》）

（102）成语 to sleep the sleep that knows no waking 的意思是睡起了不知醒来的觉，喻指长眠不醒，也成了一种表达死亡的委婉说法。

（103）成语 sup with Pluto 的意思是与阎王共进晚餐，这是表达死亡的一种委婉说法。Pluto 是希腊神话中的冥王。

（104）成语 take one's departure 的意思是离去，除真正表达字面意思"离开"之外，还用以委婉地表达死亡之义。

（105）成语 undiscovered country 的意思是尚未发现的国度，这是莎士比亚创造的一句表达死亡的委婉语。他在《哈姆莱特》一剧中写道："…death, The undiscovered country from whose bourn No traveller returns…"（"……死亡，这一未知的国度，前去者从无一人返回……"）

（106）成语 answer the last roll call（或 answer the last muster）的意思是回应最后一次点名（回应最后一次集合），为表达死亡的委婉说法。

（107）成语 be blown across (over) the creek 的意思是被抛到小溪对岸，为死于非命的一种委婉说法。这一说法通常用来指横祸致死，它始用于 19 世纪。当时美国的军火工厂——特别是杜邦火药厂——大多位于宾夕法尼亚州和特拉华州的小河边，经常发生意外爆炸。遇难工人有时真的被炸飞到小河对岸，故有此说。该委婉语今天仍在使用，其变体为 to be gone across (over) the river（到河对岸去了）。

（108）成语 be present at the last roll call (the last muster) 的意思是出席最后一次点名（出席最后一次集合），两种说法都是表达死亡的委婉语。

（109）成语 be written off 的意思是被勾销、被注销，后被转义用来喻指死亡，成为表示死亡的又一委婉说法。

（110）成语 bite the dust 的意思是（落马）嘴啃泥土，这是表示"倒下死去"或"阵亡""战死"的一种委婉说法。这一说法听上去颇像"老话",原因也很简单,因为它很多世纪以来一直被反复使用,尤其自19世纪末以来,它在美国英语中更是频繁使用。至于其渊源,也有人持异议,认为它不是来自战争而是来自马术、拳击或摔跤等体育运动比赛。它还有几种变体。如:to bite the ground, to bite the sand, to kiss the dust。

例: Squire and Gray fired again…Two had bit the dust, one had fled…(Robert Louis Stevenson, *Treasure Island*)

乡绅与格雷又来火了……两个被打死,一个逃走了……(罗伯特·路易斯·斯蒂文森,《金银岛》)

(111) 成语 do one's bit 的意思是恪尽职守、尽本分。在第一次世界大战期间,这一说法是指参军上前线或在后方努力工作报效祖国,后来被引申用以委婉地表达阵亡、为国捐躯之义。

(112) 成语 fire one's last shot 的意思是射出了最后一发子弹,但常被用来表示"死"或"牺牲"。

(113) 成语 grounded for good 的意思是被永久停飞,这是空军中最近出现的一种表达"死亡"的委婉说法。

(114) 成语 it's taps 的意思是熄灯鼓(或息灯号)响了、丧葬号(或鼓)响了,后来用以委婉地表达人死了。在来自军营的表达死亡的委婉语中,这一条最为常用。它首见于1824年的《国会报告》(Congressional Report)中,原指美国陆、海军中熄灯或丧葬时敲击的鼓声。但英国诗人 Willian and Mary Morris 夫妇却认为它是来自16世纪英国英语中的"tatoo"(归营号声)一词。

（115）成语 lay down one's life 的意思是放下自己的生命，转义为献身、为国捐躯、牺牲等，成为文学作品中表现死亡的最为常用的成语。

例：He was willing to lay down his life rather than survive in disgrace.

他宁愿死去而不愿忍辱偷生。

（116）成语 make the ultimate sacrifice 的意思是作出最后的牺牲，转义为死亡或牺牲，成为一种表达死亡的委婉说法。

（117）成语 be no longer with us 的意思是不再与我们在一起了、永远离开我们了、与我们永别了，这也是通常表达死亡的一种委婉说法。

（118）成语 be out of pain 的意思是摆脱了疼痛、不再痛苦了，转义为死亡，也成为表达死亡的一种委婉说法。

（119）成语 breathe one's last 的意思是作了最后一次呼吸，转义为死亡、断气、咽气，成为在医院表达死亡的一种常用的委婉语。

（120）成语 check out 的本义是住院后出院结账，却成为医院里最常听到的一种表示死亡的委婉语，指人已死亡，了了一生的账。

（121）成语 draw one's last breath 的意思是吸了最后一口气，也是表达死亡的一种委婉说法。

（122）成语 go out 的意思很多，用法也较为繁杂，但其中有"失去知觉"一义，后被转义为死亡，成为医院常用的一种表达死亡的委婉语。该委婉语始用于第一次世界大战期间，现已普遍使用，尤为医护人员所常用。

例：He said, knowing there was no hope of recovery for him, "It's the one thing that will make me go out with an easy mind, Sarah, the knowledge that you and Terry and Pauline will not suffer financially."

明白自己已没有康复的希望了，他说："莎拉，现在唯一能使我安心离去的事，就是知道你和泰利及波利在经济上不再有困难了。"

（123）成语 have gone under 的本义是失去知觉、量不出血压。这是医护人员常用的表达死亡的委婉语。海员也常用此语，其本义为"沉没"。殡葬人员使用此语是婉指"下葬"。

（124）成语 He (She) is not coming home. 的意思是"他（她）不回家了。"这是委婉地说："他（她）死了。"这是一句医院用语，也作 He (She) won't be coming home. [他（她）不会回家了。] 两者皆指病人不治身亡。

（125）成语 negative patient care outcome 的本义是病人没有疗效、治疗无效，婉指死亡。这一说法最早出现在 1981 年 11 月份《纽约时报》的一篇署名文章中。该文作者指出，在里根政府的领导下，人民生活没有安定感，唯一确定不变的是：死亡与增税（negative patient care outcome and income enhancement）。

（126）be gone to Davy Jone's locker 的意思是到海神的宫殿去、到龙宫去，婉指"葬身海底""葬身鱼腹"。这是一句源于水手的成语，带有诙谐意味。Davy Jones 是水手对海神的戏称。Davy Jone's locker（海神的库房）是"海底"或"水手之墓"

的别称。其变体还有 to go to Davy Jone's locker 和 be in Davy Jone's locker。

例:"What port are you to sail to?" "For the port of Davy Jone's Locker, my son," replied the captain. (Robert Louis Stevenson, *The Wrecker*)

"你准备驶向哪个港口?""驶到海底琼楼去,孩子。"船长答道。(罗伯特·路易斯·斯蒂文森,《打捞船》)

(127) 成语 coil up one's ropes 的本义是卷起缆绳,婉指死亡。

(128) 成语 cut adrift 的本义是砍断缆绳任船漂流,转义为死亡。

(129) 成语 hit the rock 的意思是触礁,在海员中间也用来委婉地表示死亡。

(130) 成语 last voyage 的意思是最后一次航行。在航海界也用以委婉地表示死亡。

(131) 成语 launch into eternity 的本义是启航驶向永恒。现在也成为表示"一命归天"或"死亡"的委婉语。

(132) 成语 safe anchorage at last 的意思是终于安全抛锚了,谓终于安息了。是死亡的委婉义。这是英、美海员墓碑上常见的一句铭文。

(133) 成语 slip one's ropes (cable) 的本义是解缆,亦是死亡的委婉表达方式。这一说法源于航海术语,自 18 世纪一直使用至今。其中,在第一次世界大战之前还有 to slip one's wind 和 to slip one's breath 两种变体。

例：He was dreadfully frightened at the prospect of slipping his cable in a foreign land.

他想到未来客死异乡的情景，非常害怕。

（134）成语 be cut off 的意思是（电话或电报）被切断，转指人被夺去生命，是死亡的一种委婉说法。

例：He was suddenly cut off by a heart attack.

他因心脏病发作突然死亡。

（135）成语 cancel one's account 的意思是销账，但有时用来婉指死亡。

（136）成语 close up one's account 的意思是结账，后来被用以婉指死亡。

（137）成语 go（或 be called, be sent）to one's long account 的字面意思是去（或被召去，被派去）清账，为死亡的一种委婉说法。

例："We have come too late," he said sternly, "whether to save or punish. Hyde is gone to his account and it only remains for us to find the body of your master."

"无论是拯救他还是惩罚他，我们都来得太迟了，"他严厉地说道，"海德已经死了。我们现在剩下来要做的，只是找你主人的尸体了。"

（138）成语 hand in one's account 的本义是交出账本，后成为表示死亡的委婉说法。基督教认为，在最后审判日那天，人人都得交出自己的功过簿，供上帝裁判。

例：The hotel remains today pretty much the same as when

Jonathan Bayley handed in his account in 1840.

旅馆如今还是那个老样子，与乔纳森·贝利1840年死的时候差不多。

（139）成语 pay one's last debt 的意思是付清最后一笔债，常用以婉指死亡，这也是当前比较流行的一种委婉说法。

（140）成语 settle all scores 的意思是彻底清账、偿清债务，后被转义婉指死亡。

（141）成语 settle one's account 的意思是结账，也常用来婉指死亡。

（142）成语 black out 的本义是（剧间或剧终时）熄灭舞台灯光，有时被用以婉指死亡。

（143）成语 bow off 的本义是最后一次露面、谢幕，有时也用以委婉地表达人的死去。

（144）成语 bow out 的本义是最后一次露面、谢幕、退下，其委婉义亦是死亡。

（145）成语 curtain call 的意思是（终场）谢幕、落幕，也常被用来婉指死亡。

（146）成语 drop the curtain 的本义是落幕、闭幕，常被用来婉指死亡。

（147）成语 fade away 的意思是逐渐消失、褪色，转义为死亡的委婉语。

（148）成语 fade out 的本义是"渐隐""淡出"，转义为"死亡"的委婉语。

（149）成语 final curtain 的本义为（剧终）闭幕，转义为死亡的委婉语。

（150）成语 fold up 的本义是折叠起来、垮掉，转义为死亡的委婉语。据说，fold up 婉指死亡，可能是由剧院的折叠椅联想而来。它于 1941 年首用于英国口语中。

（151）成语 last bow 的本义是最后鞠躬谢幕、告别，转义为死亡的委婉语。

（152）成语 last call 的本义是（终场）谢幕，转义为死亡的委婉语。

（153）成语 make one's (final) exit 的本义是（最后一次）退场，转义为死亡或退出人生舞台的委婉语。这是一句源于戏剧术语的委婉说法，所以常被用来表示名伶之死。

例：Poor Bill Bones! He was drunk last night as usual and made his exit by falling under a lorry.

可怜的比尔·博尼斯！他昨晚像往常一样又喝醉了，结果倒在一辆卡车下面被压死了。

（154）成语 pass out of the picture 的本义是走出画面、从画面上消失，转义为死亡的委婉语。这是一句源于电影艺术的委婉语，一般多见于 20 世纪的口语中。

（155）成语 out of the picture 的本义是走出画面、从画面上消失，转义为死亡的委婉语。这种比喻的说法首见于 1930 年的《每日邮报》，它来自 to pass out of the picture 一语。

（156）成语 quit the scene 的本义是退场、离场，转义为死亡、离开人间的委婉语。

（157）成语 switch out the lights 的本义是关掉灯光，转义为

死亡的委婉语。

（158）成语 be cleaned out of the deck 的本义是（打牌）被清除牌局，后被转义婉指死亡。Deck 在语中是指一副纸牌。

（159）成语 be down for good 的本义是被永远击倒，后转义婉指死亡，这是一个来自拳击比赛的委婉语。

（160）成语 be knocked out 的本义是被击倒判败，后转义婉指死亡。这是一句源自拳击比赛的委婉语，原指被击倒后在规定的 10 秒钟内尚未立起而判败，引申后婉指死亡。

（161）成语 be out of the game 的本义是（比赛）没有取胜的希望，转义婉指死亡。

（162）成语 be thrown for a loss 的本义是被擒抱摔倒而不得动弹，转义婉指死亡。这一委婉语是来自摔跤或橄榄球比赛的术语，原指被对方擒抱摔倒在地。

（163）成语 call all bets off 的本义是宣布停赌、取消一切赌注，转义为婉指死亡。

（164）成语 drop the cue 的本义是（打台球）扔下球杆，转义为婉指死亡。

（165）成语 end of the ball game 的本义是球赛结束，转义为婉指死亡。英美人常把人生视作一场比赛，而死亡则是比赛的结束。

例：When you are out there 200000 miles from earth, if something goes wrong, you know that's the end of the ball game.

当你到了离地球 20 万英里的太空中，一旦出了什么差错，那就意味着你要完蛋了。

(166) 成语 kick off 的本义是开球,转义为婉指死亡。这是一句来自足球比赛的委婉语。

例:Mr. Jones was almost ninty when he kicked off.

琼斯先生死时快 90 岁了。

(167) 成语 final kick off 的本义是(足球)最后一次开球,转义为婉指死亡,与 kick off 同义。

(168) 成语 go to the races 的本义是去看赛马,转义为婉指死亡。

(169) 成语 jump the last hurdle 的本义是跳过最后一道障碍,转义为婉指死亡,这是一句来源于障碍赛马的委婉语。

(170) 成语 lose the decision 的本义是被判定失败,转义为婉指死亡,语中 decision 是指拳击比赛中按得分或各裁判员的意见而作出的判定。

(171) 成语 peg out 的本义是赢得满分,在一种牌戏中,每人发 6 张牌,先凑足 121 分或 61 分为赢牌,转义为婉指死亡。

例:"Not a blessed thing. Still, I've got to find something, or peg out."(John Galsworthy, *The Silver Spoon*)

"一点也不知道。可是我得去找点什么,不然就没命了。"(约翰·高尔斯华绥,《银匙》)

(172) 成语 run one's race 的本义是跑完了自己的赛程,转义为婉指死亡。这也是源自赛跑的一句委婉语,其变体为 to run the good race(跑完了自己的赛程;寿终)。

例:His race is nearly run.

他的生命快要结束了。

（173）成语 strike out 的本义是（在棒球比赛中）三击不中退场、使（击手）三振出局，转义为婉指死亡。这是一句来自棒球运动的委婉语，从 20 世纪 30 年代一直沿用至今。20 世纪 50 年代有位医学教授曾对他的学生这样说道："Sometimes, no matter what you do, the Great Umpire up above will call 'strike three'."（有时不管你如何竭尽全力挽救病人，那至高无上的裁判总会喊道：'三振出局'。）

（174）成语 take the long count 的本义是数 10、被判失败，转义为婉指死亡。这是一句源于拳击比赛的委婉语。运动员在被对方击倒后，裁判便开始计数，数到 10 秒时尚未起立就被判失败。后来，"数 10" 就被引申来婉指 "死亡"。

（175）成语 take a (the) count 为 take the long (last, final) count 的缩略形式，亦是喻指死亡。

（176）成语 throw in the sponge 的本义为扔掉海绵，转义为婉指死亡。这也是一句源于拳击比赛的委婉语，原指扔掉擦身用的海绵表示认输，引申后可婉指死亡。

（177）成语 toss in one's alley (marble) 的本义是 "交进大弹石（弹子）"，转义为婉指死亡。

（178）成语 throw up the cards 的本义为丢牌、退出牌局，转义为婉指死亡。

（179）成语 throw sixes 的本义为（掷骰子游戏）掷了六点，转义为婉指死亡。

（180）成语 go to the last roundup 的本义是最后一次去赶拢牛群，转义为婉指死亡。据《西方语言》(*Western Words*) 一书的说法，last roundup 是最典型的表示"死亡"的牛仔语，一般多见于20世纪的美国西部口语中，但由于频繁使用，现在带有陈词滥调之感。

（181）成语 hang up one's harness 的本义是挂起自己的马具，转义为婉指死亡。

（182）成语 hang up one's hat 的本义是挂起某人的帽子，转义婉指死亡。

（183）成语 hang up one's tackle 的本义是挂起自己的马具，转义为婉指死亡。

（184）成语 lay down one's pen 的本义是放下笔、搁笔，转义为婉指死亡。这是 to lay down one's life 的变体，常用来表示作家之死。

（185）成语 take the big jump 的本义是纵马大跳，转义为婉指死亡。这是个源于牛仔语汇的委婉语。

（186）成语 write the last chapter 的本义是写完最后一章，转义为婉指死亡，这一说法常用来婉指作家之死。

（187）成语 go off the hooks 的意思是死亡。

例：The heart attack was so sharp that he instantly went off the hooks.

他心脏病突然发作，立即死亡。

（188）成语 lose one's life 意为丧命。

例：The sailboat was capsized by a squall, and one person lost his life.

帆船被暴风刮翻，死了一人。

（189）成语 lie low 原意为平卧，转义为死亡。

（190）成语 make away with 除有"拿走"之意外，尚有"杀死"之意。

例：He made away with himself.

他自杀了。

（191）成语 meet one's maker 之意为见上帝，喻死亡。

（192）成语 lose the number of one's mess 之意为死亡、阵亡。

例：I have an idea that some of us will lose the number of our mess.

我有一种感觉，我们中间会有几个送命。

（193）成语 pass on 的原意是过去，转义为死亡、逝世。

例：He passed on quietly at his home last night.

他昨夜在家里不声不响地死去。

（194）成语 pass out 之意为死亡、逝世。

例：Mr. John passed out last night.

约翰先生昨晚逝世。

（195）成语 at peace 本义为处于平静状态，转义为长眠、死亡。

（196）成语 hop（或 tip over）the perch 的意思是败落，转义为死亡。

（197）成语 go to one's own place 的意思是回到自己的地方去，喻死去。

（198）成语 pop off 除表示匆匆离开之外，还表示突然死掉之意。

例：Now you can all stop talking about my money: I've no intention of popping off yet.

好了，你们大家不用再谈我钱的事了，我现在还不打算死呢！

（199）成语 cross the river 本义是渡河，转义为死亡。

例：He at last crossed the river.

他终于死了。

（200）成语 quit the scene 原意为退场、离场，转义为死亡、离开人世。

（201）成语 go down to the shades 原意为走到阴暗处，转义为到阴间去，死亡。

（202）成语 fatal shears 之意为死亡，源于希腊神话，有三个命运女神，一个拿着生命的纺线杆，一个纺织生命线，另一个在死去时把生命线剪断。

（203）成语 die in one's shoes（或 boots）（亦作 die with one's shoes on）意为死亡、不得善终。

例：The badman of the Old West usually died in their boots.

旧日美国西部的不法之徒常常都是不得好死的。

（204）成语 drop short 之意为死。

例：One of these days he must drop short.

他几天内一定会死。

（205）成语 slam off 的意思是离开，转义为死去。

例：He slammed off with a cold.

他患感冒死了。

（206）成语 big sleep 的意思是长眠，转义为死亡。

（207）成语 fall on sleep 的意思是入睡，转义为死亡。

（208）成语 long sleep 的意思是长眠，转义为死亡。

（209）成语 never-ending sleep 的意思是永无结束的睡眠，转义为死亡。

（210）成语 sleep the sleep that knows no waking 的意思是睡不知道醒来的觉，转义为死亡。

（211）成语 give（或 yield）up the spirit 之意为死亡。

例：After he had cried three times with a loud voice, he gave up the spirit.

他大叫了三声之后，就死了。

（212）成语 hop the twig（或 stick）除有突然离开之意外，还有死亡之意。

例："I hear that that old rascal Giles has hopped the twig at last. Good riddance, too!"

"我听说贾尔斯那个老恶棍终于死了，死得好！"

（213）成语 pass（或 go）beyond the veil 的意思是死去、逝世。

例：He has passed beyond the veil, and we shall hear his voice no more.

他已与世长辞，我们再也听不见他的声音了。

（214）成语 go the way of all the earth（或 of all flesh of nature）之意为死去、逝世。

例：He pardoned us off-hand, and allowed us something to live on till he went the way of all flesh.

他马上宽恕了我们,并且直到他逝世为止,一直供给我们的生活费。

(215) 成语 the way of all flesh 之意为众生之道,人生必然的归宿、死亡。

例：He's gone the way of all flesh: died last week.

他已走向人生必然的归宿,上星期死了。

(216) 成语 slip one's wind（或 breath）之意为断气、死亡。

例：As soon as the doctor quitted the room, Captain Kearney opened his eyes and beckoned me to him. "He's a confounded fool, Peter," said he, "he thinks I am slipping my wind now—but I know better…"

医生一走出房间,克尔尼船长就睁开他的双眼,招手叫我到他身边,告诉我说,"他是一个大傻瓜,彼得,他以为我快断气了——但是我知道并不是如此……"

(217) 成语 go out of this world 意为离开人世、死去。

例：My grandfather has gone out of this world.

我祖父已经去世了。

(218) 成语 go to a better world 原意为走到一个更好的世界,喻死去、归天。

汉语成语例解：

(1) 成语"寿终正寝"指的老时安然死于家中,也泛指人死去,有时比喻事物的消亡。寿终,年纪很大才死;正寝,旧式住宅的正房。

例:这样看来,邮递这条路是要断绝了,刊物也就不免寿终正寝了!(邹韬奋,《患难余生记·流亡》)

(2)成语"呜呼哀哉"原为表示哀痛的感叹语,在旧时的祭文中经常使用。现借指死去或完结。呜呼,叹词,相当于唉。哉,语气助词。哀哉,太让人伤心了。语出《诗经·大雅·召旻》:"於呼哀哉,维今之人,不尚有旧。"

例:死如有知,相见蒿里,呜呼哀哉!(魏晋·陶潜,《祭程氏妹文》)

(3)成语"与世长辞"谓同人世永远告别,指脱离尘世或逝世。

例:曹冷元那斑白的头发茬和胡须都烧焦了,脸上起着一片红泡,眼睛含着浑泪,与世长辞了!(冯德英,《迎春花》第十九章)

(4)成语"一瞑不视"谓一闭上眼睛,就再不睁开,指人死亡。语出《战国策·楚策一》:"有断脰失腹,一瞑而万世不视,不知所益,以忧社稷者。"

例:果其如是,则二人者,天上人间,会当相见,定非一瞑不视者矣。(清·纪昀,《阅微草堂笔记·姑妄听之》)